THE PURPOSE OF DESTINY

THE PURPOSE OF DESTINY

CHET NORTH & MELISSA KROPF MORRIS

C&M United

PREFACE

Is everything in this world connected? As we go about our daily lives, our paths will cross with certain people and not with others. Today, when you go out into the world, I challenge you to take in the experience with a new and enlightened spirit. Open the front door and take in a deep breath, and with it the essence of the day God has set forth especially for you. Embrace every event, good and bad, that will make you a stronger and wiser individual. Be aware of all those you come in contact with and what could possibly transpire.

Your life is like a pebble, dropped into a quiet pool of water, causing ripples to move outward. As they come in contact with other ripples, created by other people's dropped pebbles, yours and theirs will be altered, reflected and rebounded. Where your ripples end up, whose they touch or whose they affect is up to fate. Our lives will invariably come in contact with others, and this is the incredible mystery of our destiny and the endless possibilities set before us. Today as you drop your pebble into the pool of water, you will change other people's lives, and surely they will change yours as well. Open the door each day and breathe in life and exhale love. Take that first step and make waves that will powerfully move outward into the world and have a unique impact on others. It only takes a brief moment or simple gesture to influence another's life. Then be prepared to experience the incredible journey that your pebble has created and set forth for you. Be prepared to experience God's love, as he sets in motion the fact that everything that happens in life has a purpose, that if we embrace God's love and love others through him, we will always find our true destiny in life.

Romans 8:28 "And we know that everything works together for the good of those who love God and are called according to his purpose for them."

CHAPTER 1

In 1969, being a young American male in his late teens brought with it a ticket tohell on Earth. Unlike today's military, made up mostly of enlisted soldiers and reservists, you were registered for the draft and required to serve the glory of the red, white and blue. Robert Nance had been one of these draftees and, at this moment, he lay face down in a three-quarter-square-mile swampy rice field in Vietnam, feeling the relentless rain pelting his back and hearing the hiss of shrapnel flying over his head. The enemy had patiently waited for the unit to advance halfway across the lush green and yellow clearing before opening fire from the dense trees and underbrush. This war was being fought against an invisible and cunning foe that used tactics over technology to wage battle. They knew the terrain of the land, built tunnels and hid in trees, ruthlessly waiting for their prey to wander into their fatal trap. And now, Robert and his unit had done just that, and were being ambushed from what seemed like all sides. His mind was full of thoughts. Had everything come down to this? Was this going to be where his life would come to an end? Was his end going to be here in muddy, foreigns oil, over 10,000 miles from his home in sunny northern California, by an enemy who was unwilling to show it's face?

He felt a thud against his upper back as he dove to the earth and into the sparse protection of the foot-high rice stocks immersed in water. He thought he might have been hit, but lifting his arm to check would give the Vietcong a clear target to aim at. He decided to keep his head low, forced to taste the murky fluid saturating the ground surrounding his face. He felt drops flowing down the center of his back and pooling at the base of his spine. He had no way to discern whether it was simply the rain or his own blood oozing from a gaping wound. It is odd how the body works when stricken by fear; how the sensation of warm blood and cool water can feel exactly the same. Whether it was the body's protective mechanism or the overwhelming presence of adrenaline, his senses were being teased. He moved his toes and twisted his torso as a quick self-evaluation. He didn't feel any unnatural pain, and everything seemed to be functioning properly, so he assumed he was ok for the moment. This could not be said for many of his fallen comrades whose carnage was visible all around him. He looked to his left and saw a boy, who was from New Mexico, covered in blood lying on his back and screaming towards the gray clouds above. To his right was another young man, who he recalled was from Arizona, named Graham. He would probably not make it, as he was in the fetal position using both hands to try to stop the blood flowing freely from his abdomen. Robert shook his head slowly and buried his face back into the muddy earth.

He had witnessed death before. In fact he had killed for the cause many times since coming to this God-forsaken country. This made the inhumanity and destruction more striking, already causing him to lose his initial reasoning and direction. Now it was a matter of the United States saving face in a war that had spun entirely out of control, embarrassing a nation politically as well as psychologically. This war had already taken the lives of over forty thousand American men, and wounded over a quarter-of-a-million young American soldiers like Robert. These young men were miles from their homes and families, and a world away from any form of sanity. In the last three weeks he and his unit had been in ambush after ambush. Dealing with death had become as normal as getting up in the morning, getting dressed and having a meal, assuming one had the stomach to eat. It simply became routine, in a morbid sort of way. Some days one's shoulders would ache and cramp up from carrying stretchers of dead andwounded men back to the make shift medical stations. Other days one's shoulders would ache merely from the mental load created from guilt and hardship.

What wasn't normal was hearing that his two best friends from back home, Mark and Carl, had been shot in a serious attack near the Cambodian border. The three had bonded as kids through make-believe war games. They had crafted machine guns from tree branches and used a pocket full of pinecones to serve as grenades. Their play battlestook place around their homes, only to end with the first sign of hunger pangs, or when a misguided pinecone came in contact with someone's face.

Mark was the clown of the group. He was one you envied because of his quick wit and fearlessness, although one may not envy how he had become that way in his life. His character undoubtedly had much to do with the fact that he grew up from the age of four without a father. His father had simply vanished from the face of the earth; lost at sea along the California coast in a fishing boat accident during an early fall storm. For whatever reason, Mark was always seeking attention with constant talking and endless pranks, and often cheating harm. On one occasion, it was broadcast on the news that a lion a tthe local zoo could not be found in its large and spacious safari-replicated cage. Within hours, it was rumored to have escaped and was roaming through the neighborhood. This was too good of a story for Mark to let pass by so his mischievous mind formulated a plan. His plan was at the expense of their dog, a collie and golden retriever mix. With shears in hand, he shaved the mutt down practically to its skin, leaving a flowing main on the animal's head and a tuft of fur at the end of its tail. Humiliated, the dog fled for cover under the porch of the house in the back yard. Mark was able to coax the dog out, pulled it to the street, and proceeded to yell and tackle the "ferocious beast". The neighbors up and down the street heard and saw all the commotion, curiously running to see what all the noise was about. Once they saw the horrific scene, some ran back into their homes for safety. Others went to call the police, while a few rendered heroic assistance to the poor, defenseless child being devoured by the powerful "lion". Once he had exhausted himself and the excitement of the stunt wore off, Mark let the terrified dog go. With its tail between its legs the dog ran straight back under the porch again, not to be seen for over a week. As for Mark, he was grounded for a month. But, needless to say, after the weeks passed, Mark was back playing in the group again and up to his old tricks. Jumping off of rooftops with only an old bed sheet in hand, yelling "incoming paratroopers" was one of his favorites. The dog, on the other hand, finally grew its hair back but was never the same again.

Carl was Mark's polar opposite. He was smart, calculated and conservative. His makeshift machine gun for back yard battles was fashioned from wood and nails from his dad's meticulously organized garage. His mom had made him a pouch that he flung over his shoulder, along with his gun, which looked, at first glance, like a US Army issue. The pouch supplied him with pinecone grenades, a six-inch rubber knife, a canteen and often a peanut butter sandwich. Robert loved how Carl would show up to the neighborhood battles with a calculated game plan and detailed map he would have worked on the night before.

Carl and Mark were true friends that made Robert's childhood complete. The news he received from his commander that both were going back to the states was devastating. Mark would be going home in a box draped with an American flag. Carl would return to California, probably never to know who or where he was again. This news had come only a few days prior to laying here in this rice field and had been one of the most horrific moments Robert had ever experienced.

It was earlier that very same month that Robert and his unit had been crossing a narrow part of a river entering enemy territory, and all hell broke out. Water was up to their chests. As the first group of soldiers stood to exit the river and enter the jungle, the Vietcong opened fire. They were literally sitting ducks. Bullets, grenades and smoke filled the air. The noise was deafening and the carnage brutal. Bodies floated past him in blood red water. Only Robert and a few of his comrades were able to survive. Sadly, their only chance at survival was to use the lifeless bodies floating by as shields from the incoming barrage of bullets. As suddenly as it had begun, the shooting simply ceased, asthe enemy quickly retreated and vanished back into their camouflaged world of dense foliage within the jungle. Twenty-seven comrades perished that fateful day int he river next to him. This number in the big picture would seem deceptively insignificant. But twenty-seven dead of the thirty-eight who entered the river put it into a much clearer perspective.

Death had been everywhere, and day after day Robert's life had been spared, but only at the expense of his soul. He had wondered several times why the Lord had so often let him live while others around him died horrible deaths. Rationalizing God's will never seemed honorable nor fair here. But then again, Robert had also wondered whether God could be anywhere near this place at all.

Robert kept his head just below the top of the rice stock, occasionally peering over them. Shrapnel hitting the ground around him caused muddy water to fly up into the air. He watched the bullets impact the ground in front of him . . . forty feet, thirty feet, twenty feet, ten feet, only to stop just before it would have surely ripped apart his body. He could see the other men in his unit scattered about; men who had no names to go with their faces. It had become much easier to cope with death if they had no identity connected to them. They were just American soldiers like him. Some were shooting into the trees at nothing in particular, others making quick sprints through the sludge before diving back to the ground, and then there were those unfortunate ones who were struck by a lethal blow from the phantoms in the forest. Robert could see some men lying motionless, eyes wide open, surveying their bleak situation, while others looked straight ahead with a blank expression; for it was here they had met their maker.

A part of him was envious of those who had been killed. Finally they were at peace. No more pain, no more fear; only a spirit that would leave the battered body and ascend to be with God instead of being in this incomprehensible dilemma. As he looked around in horror, he had the fleeting thought to end it right here and now. If God weren't going to take him, then he would take matters into his own hands. A pistol in the mouth, a quick pull of the trigger, and it would be over. The ambush had been going on for about ten minutes now. He looked at his mud splattered Timex watch on hiswrist. It was just after twelve noon. He made a quick calculation in his mind.

"Abby," he whispered to himself. "Oh, Abby, you are sleeping so soundly right now. How I wish I were with you. I love you, Baby. "

Abby, Robert's beautiful wife of one year, was back in Palo Alto. He pulled the photo, safely placed in a small plastic bag, from his chest pocket. It was the strip taken in the photo booth on their first date down on the boardwalk at Santa Cruz. He put the photo to his lips and kissed it. She was his purpose for surviving; not the cause he was sent here for, dictated by men in Washington in their fancy pressed suits. It was Abby, and the promise that he made to her that he would be back with her soon, that they would start a family and grow old together. He would stay alive for Abby; for she was his destiny.

CHAPTER 2

Abby Bowers was raised in what one might call the perfect family. She was one of three children. She had an older brother, Theodore, and a younger sister, Susan. Abby's father worked as a theology professor at a local college, making an above average income, while her mom stayed home tending to the housework and diligently having dinner on the table precisely at 5:30 each evening. They would have a family prayer led by her father, a brief time for sharing each other's day, followed by open conversation filled with laughter and good humored teasing. This was a family that truly loved each other and sincerely enjoyed each other's company. Nothing with their family was pretentious, but instead they had a natural way of expressing themselves.

Each year before school would begin again in the fall, Abby's family would fill up the wood paneled station wagon and take a family vacation. They would venture toplaces like the Grand Canyon and Yellowstone National Park. Their favorite time together was spent moving from one campsite to the next, up the California and Oregon coast. They would pitch their tents, roast marshmallows and hotdogs over the smoldering fire, and talk under the stars during the late summer night.

It wasn't as though the Bowers were without normal family issues and squabbles. And it wasn't that Abby's parents' marriage was without disagreements, differences of opinions, and genuine arguments. It was simply that they respected each other and had created a healthy atmosphere of unconditional love and security. They were committed to one another and that was their vow. Not only was the vow to stay together through sickness and health, but also even more importantly, to love one another until death do they part. They were one of those rare couples that actually learned to love each other more with each passing day of their lives. They lived this premise, and its example was instilled in the children as well. The children of the family felt the security that comes with faith, and a sense that the world will be very similar tomorrow to what it was today. Their lives had structure and a foundation in which to believe in and feel safe. It was a world that any family could have and every family should strive for, but for Abby's family, it simply came naturally and with ease.

Robert and Abby had been in the same schools throughout their lives; however the fact that Robert was a year older than Abby had created a social boundary keeping them from really getting to know each other. They simply had their own group of friends in their individual class level. Also, during middle school, Abby was very plain and looked quite young for her age. She was cute, average height, very thin, and wore braces. Her smile and genuine kindness made her easy to like, but although Robert knew who she was, he was never interested in getting to know her any more deeply, until his senior year of high school when she began to change before his eyes.

The fall of 1966 was a time of transition and, for Abby, this held true. Over the summer months she had blossomed from a simple girl into a young woman. It surely began before this, but the slow process was difficult to perceive, for those who saw her daily. Upon reintroduction to the student body in the fall, however, evidence of her transformation was mind-boggling. The Lord had blessed her with a natural, womanly beauty that she simply took in stride with humbleness and a sweet demeanor. For Robert this meant an awakening. As an adolescent man laden with testosterone, witnessing a skinny little girl become a woman, it was a phenomenon that bewildered the mind and tantalized the body. It was something he could not ignore.

When Robert first saw Abby in early September, on the first day of school, she was wearing a dark blue skirt with a thin white blouse clinging to her petite, toned body. He was entranced by her shapely legs, slender hips and perfectly round breasts, yet what made him smitten with her most was her face and her demeanor. Abby's sandy brunette hair rested on her shoulders, framing her soft, lightly tanned skin, bronzed from the summer sun. Her nose was flawless, nestled between two deep brown eyes with long natural lashes. Her small but gentle lips curved upwards as she smiled with innocence and not the slightest sign of pretentiousness. Abby's teeth, that had once been hidden by braces, were now bright white and illuminated any room with her ever-present happy expression and radiant smile. This plain duckling had become a glorious swan over the last few months and Robert wasn't exactly sure how he was to deal with his new attraction towards her. This was a nice girl who now had the power over adolescent boys that she was unaware she even possessed. And this part of her naïve character made her even that much more desirable.

Through the fall months, Robert and Abby got to see each other more and more. They didn't date - or even spend time together - at first but Robert saw her often. She had become quite popular around the high school, and even became a cheerleader for the football team. This made seeing her easy for Robert, since he just so happened to be the football team's star quarterback. He would see her practicing her cheer routines with the other girls on the squad or quietly painting inspirational posters for the weekend warriors alone on the gymnasium floor after everyone else had left. Still he was uncertain regarding his feelings for Abby, which made it easier to focus on football; and that is exactly what he did.

Robert's sense of responsibility made him the perfect leader. He was the general that the other players looked to for instruction and confidence on the playing field. Week after week, through his leadership, they dominated their opponents. He had broken every school record for a quarterback, and had surpassed even the rushing record that had always previously been held by running backs. Robert was a natural leader, as proven when Mountainview High posted an 11-0 record at the end of the season. Any domination in the state playoffs, however, would prove to be a daunting task to say the least. Mountainview was forced to stage an incredible comeback in order to defeat Crescent City High in the quarterfinals, yet in the end, what many felt were the two best teams rose to the top, and Mountainview was to meet Dorsey for the state championship.

Dorsey, too, was unbeaten and they were the defending champions. They were also big, fast and agile. They were a complete team, and what was even more impressive was that they believed that they were the best. The game was a battle from the opening whistle. It wasn't a savage battle where players would cheap shot one another. Quite the contrary, both teams shared a deep respect for each other's success throughout the season. Each team knew that they wanted to play each other to prove their superiority. Dorsey had been in this championship game several times in the last fifteen years, whereas Mountainview was a new-comer to the spotlight based on the leadership of their star quarterback. Robert Nance had made an average team into a championship caliber team in just a few short years. Everyone in the state knew it, and so did numerous college scouts who were attending the game.

By halftime, as Robert sat bruised and battered in the locker room, they were looking at a 9-23 deficit. It was at this point, while watching the coach diagram plays on the rickety old chalkboard, that some form of an epiphany came over Robert. In one brief moment, while he looked around the room at his teammates taking in every word being spoken by the coach, he simply realized a great fact. He realized that this was just a game. Where or how this concept had snuck into his mind, he wasn't exactly sure. What he did know was that he had a strange feeling that he was about to embark on a new beginning. He knew he was to go out in the second half and give it everything he had. He knew he was to leave it all on the field of battle, but now there was a new peace about the entire concept regarding the game.

Robert stared across the room, slowly scanning all the other warriors in their football armor. It seemed so quiet, even though he knew the coach was still talking loudly. It seemed that everything had slowed down. It felt as if God had put him into a slide show that was barely moving. The team let out a group yell, which brought him back to reality and to his normal senses. Everyone came to the middle of the room with dirt and grass stained hands raised high in the air, clasping at one pinnacle in the center of the crowd.

As the coach ended his instructions, Robert let out a yell above the rest. "Hey," he hollered.

He paused for a moment until the room fell silent. "Hey guys, I just wanted to say a little something to you all." Robert looked around at all the sweating faces focused totally on him. "I know you expect a big pep talk from me right now, but that isn't what is on my heart. I just wanted to say thank you."

Many of Robert's teammates looked at him a little puzzled, but still very intent on hearing their leader's comments. He began again. "I want to thank you for being my teammates for the last four years, but more than that I want to thank you for being my friends." Some of the heads in the room began to shake up and down in agreement and respect.

"I want to thank you for making me look so good this season for all those scouts out there," Robert continued, "I couldn't have done it without you all. I will never forget you guys. Every one of you should be very proud of yourself. I sure am. We took a program that hadn't made the playoffs in over twenty years and now we are in the championship game for the state of California. What is really on my heart though is this . . . we have already proven to our school, to our community and to the other schools in this state that we belong; that we deserve their respect. Guys, I want to win this game but that is all it really is, a game. A game that, on the scoreboard, will determine the winner of the game but not the winners in life. You guys already did that. You won the respect of everyone you know. In life that is all that matters. No one can take from us what we did this season. We accomplished something very special and we did it together. We were all put together at this place and time to fulfill something. Maybe we win this game. Maybe we lose this game. But this is a moment that we live out and then let go. It will always be apart of us but only a chapter in the long book of life. After tonight, and after this school year, our paths may or may not cross again. But I know one thing for sure. Every one of you had an impact on my life. An impact that will alter how I live mine in the future. I just hope when you look back and think of me, that I had an impact on your lives too."

The room was quiet and then there was one single clap, then another, and another until the room was vibrating with the noise of sixty-four pairs of hands beating as one. They all gathered around Robert hitting his helmet.

Then the coach let out a holler. "Let's go kick some Dorsey butt!"

Next, the mass of humanity headed for the door in unison. Robert let them leave, so he would be the last one to exit. When everyone was gone, and the noise subsided, he slowly turned and looked back at the locker room. It was empty and quiet. A sly smirk came across Robert's face. He turned to the door, and as he walked out, he hit the lightswitch leaving the room dark. He then ran into the bright sun and a beautiful California afternoon.

The battle cry worked as the Mountainview defense stymied their opponents. Then, early in the third quarter, Robert was able to establish a drive that culminated into a touchdown pass to Carl, who had run a perfect slant-and-go route. Mark followed by kicking the extra point directly through the uprights, leaving the Dorsey lead at seven points for what seemed like an eternity. The battle ensued for a quarter and a half and was rendered by no one. The center of the field was worn down by the cleats tearing at the surface. Back and forth . . . four downs and punt . . . a rare firstdown. An injured player removed, only to shortly return to join his fellow warriors. The battle raged on! Each team fought with all they had, and then found a little bit more from some deep, hidden store of energy. It was as if the rest of the game would be a stalemate, until unexpectedly a moment of fate changed the course of the contest.

With eleven seconds left in the game, Dorsey was on its own 19-yard line with the ball when the quarterback and center exchange was muffed. The ball sat motionless on the ground like a chunk of gold waiting to be claimed. And it was. It was claimed by a Mountainview linebacker who swooped up the leather treasure and raced for the end zone as time expired. The stadium exploded in pandemonium. Fans, coaches and players jumped, yelled and ran in utter hysteria. Robert, on the other hand, understood the situation. He slowly and methodically put on his helmet and walked onto the field towards the end zone. He turned around, walking backwards, so he could look at the coach on the sidelines. Their eyes met and Robert raised his hand in the air with two fingers extended, signaling to the coach that they would run a play for two points to win, rather than kick the extra point and settle for a tie and overtime. The coach calmly nodded in agreement and watched his young general turn and jog towards his teammates, who were waiting for their trusted leader to instruct them once again to victory. He entered the huddle and all fell silent. All eyes were focused on Robert.

"OK, guys, I think the coach messed his pants back there." The entire huddlebusted into laughter.

"Sorry, guys, you all seemed too tense," continued Robert, "I had to throw in a little humor at Coach O'Grady's expense to get you to relax a bit. Well, it comes down to this. We have to move the ball 2 yards to become champions. Who would have thought that? You, Carl, what about you? After all those days in the backyard tossing the ball and dreaming of a moment like this?"

Robert gave his life long friend a playful shove then redirected himself back to the group, "Can't ask for much more than this. I am proud of you guys and whether we make these extra points or not I will still be proud of you. You gave it your all, and that is all anyone can ask of you. Now, are we ready?"

After only a soft mutter in reply, Robert repeated, "I asked . . . are we ready?"

"Yah!" Came a loud team reply.

"I thought so," yelled Robert, "Now let's see what fate has in store for us. Twenty-four dive, eighteen option, sweep right on two. Break!"

The team all clapped at once and broke the huddle, turning towards the line of scrimmage. Robert slowly followed his team while looking left and right scanning the opponents shifting defense. He rested his hands under the center and continued checking the defense as they adjusted to the play Mountainview had called.

At that moment everything seemed to slip into slow motion for the second time that day. There was no noise from the fans, the coaches, the band, or even the opponents who were barking out commands for defensive shifts. Robert looked into the enemy's face. Their eyes were transfixed on him. They were sweaty, dirty and exhausted just like him. They had put out a valiant effort today for the right to be called the best. He found himself feeling a great respect for the Dorsey team; a feeling which had grown over the last few hours. He unconsciously winked at their middle linebacker who returned a quick nod of understanding. This was it. One last play for Robert in a Mountainview jersey and one last play for Dorsey to determine who would be called champions.

"Hut one!" he shouted to his team.

In Robert's mind, the words quietly echoed. He thought to himself that there would be no losers today; only dedicated warriors on both sides who had come to fight a fair battle.

"Hut two!" he shouted a bit louder.

The ball was driven hard into his hands by the center, and the mass of humanity churned in front of him with grunts and groans. Moving to his right down the line, he faked the hand off to the fullback, plunging through the four hole, taking two or three would be tacklers with him. Robert continued down the line until he saw his opening. He gave a quick, exaggerated fake toss back to his halfback who was five yards off his right shoulder. He then tucked the ball under his right elbow, planting his right foot hard into the turf, and lowered his head towards the goal line. In an instant the turmoil of all the gladiators reached a crescendo before it fell silent once again. Whistles blew loud and deliberate, and the voice of the referee instructed everyone not to move as he reached down to spot the ball.

****

As Robert sat in the end zone leaning against the goal post, he watched Dorsey High celebrate their triumph some fifty yards away, near their bench, and jubilant Dorsey fans dancing in the stands. The state championship trophy was hoisted high in the air above them as each player attempted to touch it in order to validate his moment in history. Robert's teammates stood, sat and laid scattered about the football field. They were exhausted and quiet in stunned disbelief. Soon Dorsey moved their celebration into the locker room. The Mountainview players began to face the reality of the game's outcome and to meander to wherever their own personal sanctuary could be found. Robert, though, just sat there against the goal post and took it all in.

"Robert, are you ok?" came a female voice from behind him.

Startled but still composed, he turned his head around slowly to his right and saw Abby walking towards him. She was wearing her blue and white cheerleading uniform and blue tennis shoes. Her hair was in a ponytail behind her head, exposing all the wonderful beauty that her innocent face possessed.

"Excuse me?" Robert politely responded.

"I just wanted to make sure you were ok. You were all alone over here and I wanted to make sure you were alright," replied Abby. She knelt down on her knees a few feet in front of him.

Robert simply looked at her with a smile while saying nothing.

"What?" Abby asked.

"Nothing, Abby, just looking at you. I just wanted to sit here and let everyone leave so I could think."

"May I ask what you wanted to be alone to think about?" asked Abby.

"Life, Abby. Just life."

"Are you sure you are OK, Robert?"

He laughed and gave her a wink. "Yes, I am fine. Better now that you are here."

Abby began to blush. "Really?"

"Yeah. Let me ask you something. Do you believe things happen for a reason?"

"Of course I do. That is Biblical. Romans 8:28."

"Tell me what that verse says, Abby."

"It says that God causes everything to work together for the good of those who love God and are called according to his purpose for them."

"So you are standing here right now because God wants you to be, right?"

"I suppose that's what the verse would mean."

"And we didn't win the game because it wasn't God's purpose for us to, right?"

"Yeah. It wasn't God's will if that is what you are asking."

"You know what, Abby. I agree with that. I believe we were not to win the game and you were to be placed in front of me right here and right now."

"Why do you feel that way, Robert?"

"Abby, I have never felt a peace like I do right now. It's as if God is doing something in me. I can't exactly put my finger on it but I know I am where I am supposed to be. I am not upset with the outcome of the game. In fact, I would have to say that it was one of the most incredible games I have ever been a part of. We just didn't win, and that is OK. But there is something else, Abby."

"What is that?" asked Abby.

"You. You, Abby. You were supposed to come talk to me. You were put here by God. Abby, may I be very open and honest?"

"Of course you can, Robert. I always want you to be."

"Abby, I have had a crush on you since the beginning of the school year and now that football is over, it is as if God put you square in front of my face. It's as if He is telling me that it's time to get to know you more."

Abby was blushing behind her smile. Her heart was racing, and emotions churned within her. Robert smiled back at her through his sweaty and dirt covered face.

"What are you doing tonight, Abby?"

"Just going home. No real plans, I guess."

Robert heaved himself off the ground and stood up, towering over her. She toostood up but was still a foot shorter than his six foot, two inch frame; a frame that appeared twice the size with the shoulder pads he was wearing.

"Well I guess I had better get cleaned up. I'm sure I don't smell or look my best right now," said Robert with a chuckle.

Abby smiled. "Yes, you do look a bit messy."

"I really appreciate you coming and checking on me. That was very nice of you." With that Robert tucked the helmet under his arm, smiled, turned and headed towards the locker room.

Abby smiled back a little perplexed, then turned back towards the bleachers where her friends had been waiting for her.

"Abby?" hollered Robert from a distance.

She turned to see Robert facing her about fifteen yards away. "Yes?" she responded.

"I will be done here in about half an hour. Would you be interested in going out later tonight?"

A smile beamed across Abby's face. "Sure, that would be wonderful."

"How about I pick you up at seven o'clock?"

"Ok."

"It's a date then. See you at seven." With that he gave her a wink, turned and headed across the field.

Abby began to walk towards her friends until she could not hold it in anymore. She broke out into a joyful skip, then a joyful run.

"My first date with Robert Nance," she whispered to herself.

CHAPTER 3

Robert pulled up to Abby's home just before seven. He was on time more out of anticipation than respect. After turning off the car, he pulled a small, black comb out of the inside pocket of his letterman's jacket. Looking into the rear view mirror in front of him, he parted his thick, brown hair on the left and pulled it over to the right. He then placed the comb back in his pocket and checked his watch. At seven, he opened the door and walked around the front of the car, heading up the brick walkway that lead to the front door. As he walked slowly towards the house, he noticed the perfectly manicured yard and flower bed that lined the front of the home. He stepped up the three cement stairs to the large wooden door with a brass knocker located under a smallrectangular window. Robert straightened out his jacket, checked himself over, and rang the doorbell. He could hear the bell going off inside and a man's voice. The door opened and there stood Mr. Bowers in the doorway.

"Robert, so nice to see you. Come on in. Abby will be down in a moment," he said.

"Thanks, Mr. Bowers. This sure is a nice house."

"We like it. Been here almost twenty years now. Since just before Theo was born. Have a seat, Robert. Can I get you a soda or something?"

"Yes. That would be great."

Mr. Bowers left the room for a moment. Robert sat down on the couch with his hands together. While he waited, he noticed there were a National Geographic and a Time magazine on the coffee table in front of him, accompanied by some coasters to protect the shiny varnish on the tabletop. Robert then looked around the room and noticed how it was decorated. What struck him most were the photos. On each wall and across the hearth of the fireplace were photos of the family. Near the entrance to the kitchen was a wall that had each of the children at chronological stages of their lives. Robert stood up and approached the photos of Abby from her day of birth to this fall's picture in her cheerleading uniform. Robert looked closely at each stage of her life sequentially displayed in the five photos in front of him. He was astonished as to howmuch she had changed.

"They grow up fast." Mr. Bowers said entering the living room again with two glasses of soda. He handed one to Robert and began drinking the other. "It seems like just yesterday I was carrying Abby around in my arms and now she is a grown woman. Where do all the years go?"

"Can't answer that one, Sir, but time sure does fly."

Right then Mrs. Bowers walked through the kitchen doorway with an apron on. "Hi, Robert. I would shake your hand but I am covered with flour from the apple pies I just put in the oven. How are you doing?"

"Good, Ma'am. A little sore from the game but that is normal," replied Robert.

"Robert, I am sorry about the game today." Mr. Bowers interjected, "so close to the championship."

"No worries, Sir. I am proud of what we accomplished. It's odd, but I feel very much at peace about it all."

"So, where are you and Abby going to go tonight?"

"Out to the boardwalk at Santa Cruz. It is such a nice night," replied Robert.

A door closed upstairs, and a moment later Abby appeared at the top of the stairs. Robert looked up at her. She looked radiant. She was wearing a dark blue skirt and a pressed white blouse. Around her neck was a light blue sweater. Her hair loosely framed her face and a hint of makeup emphasized her eyes. Though she was dressed very casually, Robert's breath was taken away by her very presence.

"So, what are you men talking about?" Abby asked with a smile.

"Hey, Honey," Mr. Bowers replied, "Just being a good host."

"Hi, Robert. Is he drilling you with questions?"

"Nah. Not really. Actually he is being very hospitable. I can take it. You look nice."

"Thanks," she replied and began to walk down the stairs holding onto the handrail. She stopped at the bottom near the front door, and then continued, "Are you ready?"

Robert drank half of the glass of soda and placed it on a coaster on the coffee table. "Yah, I'm ready. Thanks for the soda, Mr. Bowers. I will take good care of Abby. I promise." He walked towards the front door with a smile on his face.

"Home by eleven, Abby." said her father.

"Yes, Daddy," Abby replied.

"I will get her home on time, Sir." Robert added.

Robert winked at Abby and opened the door for her. He looked back at her father before exiting. Mr.Bowers was smiling at him.

Robert and Abby slowly moved down the walkway next to each other. Robert looked down at her. Abby looked back up at him out of the corner of her eye, squinting as she smiled back at him. She swung her shoulders teasingly, yet with a slight shyness. Neither of them said a word. They just slowly walked towards the car looking at each other and savoring the initial moments of their first date. Robert opened the door for Abby. She hopped in, and as she looked back at him, their eyes remained locked as he closed the passenger door. Robert then walked around the front of the car keeping his eyes fixed on Abby's gaze through the windshield. She smiled, causing him to grin and shake his head. Breaking their stare, he opened the door, hopped in the car, and then inserted the key into the ignition. As the car engine started, he again glanced over at Abby and her cute, flirtatious smile. Once again he grinned.

"So, Mr. Nance, where are you taking this young lady?" she asked.

"Well, I was thinking of Tahiti or Fiji, but maybe for our first date we should settle for Santa Cruz. Your dad did give you a curfew," Robert replied.

"I see. So you are trying to win my heart by winning over my dad's respect. That is very transparent, Mr. Nance, but also very honorable. Might just have to give you bonus points for that. Yet, I have to admit Tahiti sounds quite intriguing."

"Well I don't want to offend him and lose my chance of a second date."

"Oh, so you are already sure I would choose to go out with you again? Very presumptuous, Mr. Nance. I like that kind of confidence in a man. More bonus points for you."

"So what do I get to do with all my bonus points, Miss Bowers?"

"We'll see. Depends on how many points you end up with."

"That's fair. I can live with that."

They were both quiet for a few minutes as they headed west towards the ocean, until Abby broke the silence.

"Robert, may I ask you something?" said Abby.

"Of course," replied Robert.

"Why did you ask me out tonight?"

"Well, that's easy. I have been interested in you since the beginning of the school year but just never got around to it I guess."

"You were interested in me?"

"Of course I was."

"I didn't know that. You never really showed me any signs of that."

"I know. I guess I just didn't know how to initiate my feelings towards you."

"What feelings, Robert?" Abby asked.

"Abby, I am going to be totally honest with you. You changed a lot this last year. I mean, you look incredible - not to say you were not attractive last year - but, Abby, you became a stunning woman over the summer. Do you realize how much you changed?"

Abby smiled with a hint of a blush warming her face.

"Abby, do you?" Robert pushed.

"Yes. I know I have changed. It even surprised me, and I am the one living it. In like six months I went through three different bra sizes and grew about four inches. It's hard not to notice. But, Robert, I am still the same person inside. It tends to keep me incheck when your father is a theology professor and we are in church twice a week. Believe me, my dad has let me know that I have become a woman too. He has warned me about all you guys. I may act a bit sheltered, but part of that is due to how I want to present myself. However, Robert I am far from naïve."

Robert smiled at her. As he looked back at the freeway he felt her hand grasp his.

"Do you mind if I sit next to you, Robert?" she asked.

He turned his head towards her, and responded, "I would like that."

Abby moved across the seat. Her thigh pressed warmly against his, as she rested herhead on his shoulder. The trip through the winding roads of the mountainsleading to the ocean was silent, but their communication continued non-verbally, as their bodies radiated a warmth and attraction that neither of them could ignore.

Once in Santa Cruz, the two walked the shoreline hand in hand. The sun was still just above the horizon, and small waves lapped on the beach with the rhythmic tone of a never-ending symphony. Music, talking and laughter could be heard from the many residents and tourists visiting the gift shops, restaurants and carnival rides that lined the boardwalk. Abby was holding her shoes in her free hand, letting the cool water occasionally brush over her feet. Robert squeezed her hand and looked at her. She quickly responded by looking back at him.

"Are you hungry?" he asked.

"A little."

"How about we get a few slices of pizza and eat at an outside table up on the boardwalk?"

"Sounds great to me,"she responded.

The two ordered their meal and found a table near the railing overlooking the water. Soon the sun began to settle just above the ocean.

"Abby, I will be right back," said Robert.

"Ok. Is everything alright?"asked Abby.

"Definitely. Be right back."

Robert headed back towards the area where they had gotten their pizza - he had seen something in a store window that he needed to buy

- and within a few minutes he was back with Abby at the table holding a small white bag. He sat down and reached over towards her, handing her the bag.

"This would be for you," he said.

"Really? So what is it, Mr. Nance?"

"Just something I thought you had to have. Go ahead. Open it."

Abby took the bag and looked inside. "Oh. It's adorable. I love it!"

She pulled out a small brown teddy bear and hugged it tightly against herself. The smile on her face then became more serious. "Robert, I love it. Thank you so much."

She walked around the table and wrapped her arms around Robert's neck. Then she quietly whispered in his ear. "If you are not careful, Mr. Nance, this woman may just fall for you."

Abby moved her face back just a little so she could see his face. He was smiling. "I would like that, Abby. Very much."

Robert moved his face towards hers. She responded instinctively. As their lips met, the world around them evaporated. They kissed as the sun disappeared below the horizon and the warm pizza cooled in the light breeze.

Though the day and the food may have cooled, these two hearts had been warmed by a moment destined by God. After they ate, they frolicked around the carnival and their souls continued to intertwine. They rode the large Ferris wheel looking out over the ocean, then the Scrambler, and then took photos in the small photo booth for twenty-five cents. The pictures showed themselves to be a beautiful couple. Each photo displayed the couple with various expressions holding the little brown teddy bear, and in each photo, the teddy bear displayed a continuous, approving smile.

On the drive home, Abby rested her head against Robert while he draped his arm around her. The night was peaceful with a full moon hovering over the mountains in the east. Soft music played on the AM radio. Neither Robert nor Abby wanted the evening to end, yet they both knew it was really just the beginning. Robert pulled the car up to the curb at just after eleven. He walked her to the door and gave her a kiss. By the time Abby entered the house and turned off the front porch light it was after eleven-thirty. Let it be known, however, that Mr. Bowers never once in the future brought up their tardiness.

CHAPTER 4

With football over and various universities desiring his athletic talent, Robert began to formulate his goals and his plans to attain them. The thought that the likes of Notre Dame, Texas or Penn State even knew who he was astonished him. He had never been out of the state of California, and why would he, for California was a world within itself. It had the ocean, mountains, sunshine almost every day and, of course, Disneyland. Though humbled by all the major universities in the country that were recruiting him, Robert had already made his choice. Robert's mind had been on one school for as long as he could remember - the school that had sent scouts to every one of his games for the last two and a half years - Stanford University in Palo Alto. Stanford was only minutes from Mountainview, and he had absolutely no desire to go anywhere else or wear anything but the school's red and white. He had worn these colors since he was ten years old playing football in the back yard with Mark, Carl and several other local kids. He dreamed of playing at Stanford, fantasized about playing at Stanford, and now Stanford was his choice. It was an easy choice at that.

Stanford also boasted an outstanding mechanical engineering program, and while Robert realized that football was his ticket to college, he was also aware that it was not a career one could count on. He was too responsible to bank his future on a game that could be taken away in one unfortunate instant. Robert desired a family and he knew getting an education could help him better provide for one. He also enjoyed the thought of creating things, and with the country's rapid advances in technology, he just might be able to play a vital role in America's future.

Maybe he would create the next big break-through for all of mankind. NASA was well on its way to outer space with the Gemini program. Maybe NASA would be in his future. Regardless, as Robert saw it, there were so many opportunities on the horizon, and committing to his academic future would bring him almost anything his mind could conceive. For this was America. Land of opportunity. He just had to do the work to establish the foundation for his future, and doing the work would be the exciting part of this journey.

Then there was Abby. Abby had become the greatest reason that solidified his ultimate decision to attend Stanford. Though he already knew his choice of school, he also realized that life without Abby in it was not a life at all. He had to be near her, for everythought he had about his future had her as part of it. Over the last several months they were practically inseparable. It wasn't as if they could not live independent lives as two strong and mature individuals, they just simply wanted to be together. Abby would take her books and coursework to the library and study for the hour after school that Robert spent lifting weights as part of the conditioning program Stanford had given him. Then he would join her with his homework and together they would study for another hour or more at the corner table next to the window. Shortly after 5:00 p.m. they would collect their belongings, walk to Robert's car, and head to Abby's for dinner which was always served on time. It was a dinner prepared with love and purpose. A place where a blossoming relationship found comfort and nourishment. Nourishmentnot only provided from the food, but also the company and the spiritual presence that went far beyond the prayer before each meal.

Robert was becoming more and more a part of this special family gathering. He enjoyed being at the Bowers home. It wasn't that he didn't like his home. He loved his parents and admired his dad's success in business. What he liked about the Bowers household, though, was that their faith was so important above being successful. You could sense their faith in the essence of the home and it felt natural for him to be there. It even felt natural for he and Abby to be growing closer as a part of the family together. By spring, Robert had begun to attend the same church as the Bowers. He had felt that this was a vital part of he and Abby's journey before making their final commitment. It was something he had shared with her father and something her father supported wholeheartedly. For in Robert, Mr. Bowers saw a mature young man, sensitive to Abby's happiness, but he also saw Robert's sensitivity to the role a father desires to have in his cherished daughter's life when it comes to marriage.

At the end of the school year, Robert and Abby knew that they had each found their soul mate; the other half of themselves that made them both better. They were more complete individuals, because they were inspired from within by the love the Lord had blessed them with for each other. This is a love we all dream of and know exists but few find. Robert and Abby had found it and they nurtured it daily with fun, romance, and their faith. It seemed that life was all falling into place.

CHAPTER 5

June was a whirlwind to say the least. Robert graduated on the sixth, registered for the draft on the tenth, which was his eighteenth birthday, then proposed to Abby on the twenty-eighth. July was spent planning for an early August wedding just beforeRobert was to leave for Stanford's two-a-day scheduled football practices. The plan was that he would stay at the university dorm the first year as Abby finished her final year of high school at Mountainview. Then, after her graduation, they would get a small house near the university with the financial help of her father. Their dream of being together, raising a family, and growing old together was becoming clearer and clearer with each passing day, but on July 31st, 1967, their world would change in ways they could never have imagined.

On that particular day Robert's dad met him at the front door with a solemn demeanor and a United States government issued envelope in his hand. It was the late sixties. A time when America was at war in a small country with a funny name, Vietnam. But nothing was funny about it for Robert, as he received his invitation to this strange land in the form of a draft notice. In an instant everything in his life changed. The excitement of the wedding, going to Stanford, playing football, raising a family, and starting a career seemed to rush over his senses like wind whistling past his ears. He felt the burden of the world come upon him. His dreams and plans were no longer his to choose. Those choices would be made by the military, for Robert was a soldier now. This news was bad but the worst was yet to come. He had to break it to Abby. And that was not going to be easy.

Telling Abby was the hardest moment of his eighteen years of life so far. He could barely get the words out, for it felt like his throat was swollen shut. There was no perfect place or perfect time to tell her, so he just did the best he could do. He didn't know someone, anyone, could cry so much. The look of sorrow and confusion on Abby's face would forever be imprinted on his mind. It mystified him, almost paralyzed him, to have to tell her something that would cause her so much pain. But he did. He had to. And after hours of tears, before acceptance could even creep in, they were at least grateful that the wedding was only a few days away. The days that followed, though somber, were kept busy with wedding plans.

The wedding went off as planned with the sun shining and only a slight breeze keeping it comfortable. The bridesmaids wore peach colored dresses and the men looked dashing in their dark tuxedos. Robert and Abby shared their vows through precious words and smiles, yet each felt the anxiety over what the time ahead would bring. Marriage was supposed to be a time to ponder the special days ahead that you would have together. In their case, however, Robert and Abby were well aware that in about eight weeks he would be gone to the war on the other side of the world. And that only the picture album from this wedding day and the rose from his tuxedo pressed in her Bible would be there to satisfy her until he returned. Though both knew this was the scenario for many other young couples starting their lives as husband and wife during this time period, the knowing did not take away the sting of their own relationship's upcoming separation and their intense sadness over how their plans had been so radically changed.

Since all the plans with college had been altered, Robert and Abby stayed in a room at Abby's parent's house until he left for boot camp, where Abby would stay after his departure as well.

Arriving back home to visit in late September after boot camp, Abby met Robert at the door. She wrapped her arms around him, squeezing him tight, not wanting to let him go. She then whispered into his ear that she was pregnant.

****

The summer of 1967 was truly a season of activity, events and change. Robert remembered that. But now it was 1969 and Robert's reality was Vietnam. He lay here in a rain soaked rice field thousands of miles from home and in despair for his life. At that very moment his reality was made even more evident by the intense sound of jets screaming very low and very fast from behind him.

Once, while looking overhead, he saw the bombs dropped from the belly of three aircrafts which instantaneously nosed straight up, disappearing into the dense haze of clouds above him. Within seconds, napalm engulfed the forest around them, squeezing the life out of the North Vietnamese who once inhabited it. The enemy had all but been incinerated before his eyes. Everything grew eerily silent except for the crackling of the fire still dancing in the jungle. Robert looked to his right and saw a soldier about thirty feet away cautiously raising his head to peer over the rice plants and take in what had just happened. It was Graham, the young man from Arizona with the abdominal wound. He had survived. The soldier then looked back over at him and nodded his head. Robert nodded back and gave him an exhausted wink. Once again he had survived the brutality of war. Well, at least his body had.

CHAPTER 6

The war officially ended in March of 1973. The final toll was almost 58,000 Americans dead, over 1000 missing, and some 150,000 seriously injured. There were thousands more injuries unseen to the naked eye, as they were psychological in nature. Now, a new infusion of patients entered the already beleaguered American Veterans Administration hospital system. For some, the Vietnam War may have ended once they returned home to the United States, but for many others the battle from the war had only just begun.

****

Once back in the states after the war the young men found themselves faced by another cruel enemy, the American public. Northern California in 1971 was a cultural phenomenon, with the San Francisco area as its epicenter. Robert, like many of his fellow comrades, struggled daily with returning to the real world back home. They had done everything the leaders of the nation told them to do as soldiers in a far away foreign country. Yet it was here, in their own country, that they continued to be demoralized. The students at the University of California Berkley were relentless with their message. They were outraged with the way the war was being handled by the government and the soldiers were easy targets. Their freedom of speech and protest only seemed to nurture the paranoia, guilt and shame that the soldiers returning home had to live with. The students could be seen nightly on the evening news marching, calling the soldiers baby killers and burning the American flag. This was the same flag the soldiers fought so hard for and draped over the caskets of the G.I.s who had lost their lives. Robert often thought it ironic that they fought for these students' right to protest them. He pondered over the fact that he and other young men fought and died for the virtue of democracy, yet the students freely mocked them within the safe confines of the American border they so valiantly protected. It was truly a time of confusion, hypocrisy and anger in the United States. This was a time in our country's history that would not settle for a long while.

Robert's football hopes had been demolished by a sniper's bullet that sliced through his thigh and shattered his kneecap. Focusing on the family was the only real option Robert felt he had. This was a much different perspective compared to life's abundant options that he felt prior to being drafted for the war. He and Abby bought a small house with the help of both their parents in the suburbs of Palo Alto. It was in a quaint neighborhood, with each house having similar white picket fences and rose bushes scattered about the front yard. It was a peaceful and safe area perfect for raising their three-year-old son, Stephen Anthony Nance. It was also near enough to the bay area that Robert could drive the hour-long trek north on I-5, referred to as the 5 by locals, to work with little trouble. He had taken a job as a machinist repairing diesel engines on ships near the East Bay Bridge. This was a far cry from one of his dreams of creating the next great break-through in engines for American automobiles. And it was even further from his past thoughts about the Space Program. Though it wasn't the life he had planned for himself four years prior, it could have been a good life to live.

The problem was Robert couldn't seem to adjust to being back in the states. He simply did not know how to live in this world he was plunged back into. He felt as if his emotions were detached from his heart or simply wired wrong. His feelings were sometimes in a state of numbness, while other times they were heightened to the point where he feared everything around him. It was unbelievable how something as simple as an insect flying by could stir up feelings he felt in Vietnam and send him into a tailspin. His rational mind knew better, but the traumas from Vietnam would take ahold of him and squelch out any rationality. It was as if he were living a constant nightmare that he seemed to have little control over. One moment he would feel somewhat at peace and, within an instant, the curtains would rise for another scene of past horror from the war. Nighttime would be the worst, when the greatest dilemma was his need for sleep and the knowing that the dream world brought with it vivid views in which he did not want to revisit. He dreaded the night. It was for all accounts a living hell. Waking up covered with sweat, his eyes wide open to unrelenting fear, and a heart pounding so hard it hurt was as common to him as the need for sleep itself. Too much had happened - and too fast - for him and many other men during the war in Vietnam. There had been no time to process the events as they happened, only a need to power through and trudge on. The aftermath of this lead to a horrific response in many veterans that would later, in the 1980's, be labeled Post Traumatic Stress Disorder (PTSD). For Robert, even though it was not yet labeled, PTSD was very real. He felt trapped with no way to escape and no way to ask for help. After all, who would understand everything he had seen, gone through, and, unfortunately, done?

Things at home had not been going well at all. Abby, having grown up in a very supportive and loving family, was feeling extremely abandoned. Not only did she physically feel this way when Robert would retreat to find some personal space and isolation, but she also felt this way emotionally. She felt the distance that her husband created to protect his wounded and hardened heart. She also felt powerless in finding a way to reconnect with him. Robert was an entirely different man than she had met, fallen in love with and married. He was an entirely different person than the Robert Nance she was with on their wedding night. She had even told him how alone and unloved she felt. She pointed out that he was often void of emotions and how it tore her up inside. She expressed that she not only hurt for herself but also for their son. This only seemed to cause Robert to move further away, as it fueled his deep-rooted feelings of guilt. At these times Robert would walk away, distancing himself from the issue even more. What could he say? He had no defense. She was entirely correct. He would stare out the window and ponder what Abby had said, what it made her feel like, and what it was doing to their marriage. But he could do nothing. He wanted so desperately to feel; to reconnect with her, his son, and the world around him, but it was as if someone had simply cut the wires that gave him the capacity to do so.

It wasn't that Robert didn't remember what love was. He had once experienced it. He knew how it worked and why it was necessary; especially for a woman in a marriage. It was simply that there was something within him not willing to engage in that aspect of life anymore. On rare occasions he would even bring Abby some flowers he had picked up on his way home from work. Yet Robert knew in his heart that he was only going through the motions.

One day, he was cleaning the garage and unpacking some of the boxes from the move, when he came across the small gift he had given Abby on their first date to Santa Cruz. The little teddy bear, with its constant smile, stared back at him. A tear rolled down Robert's cheek as he remembered that special time. He remembered the photos of him, Abby and the teddy bear they had taken on the boardwalk. It was this photo from the photo booth that he had looked at so many times in Vietnam to keep him going. He remembered so vividly the kiss that Abby had given him that day. For a brief moment, as he looked at the little stuffed animal, he found himself smiling back at it. Robert rose from the stool he had been sitting on and walked over to his workbench. When his project was complete, he had made a small replica of his dog tags except he had engraved the initials SN on them for his son. He placed them around the bear's neck and headed into the house. Stephen was in the middle of one of his fits because he was tired and Abby was trying to calm him with a cup of juice. Robert gently reached out and handed the teddy bear to Abby.

"You remember this little guy?" he asked.

"Of course I do. Where did you find him?"

"Just in a box from the move. I made a set of dog tags for him. I thought little Stephen might take a liking to him."

She placed the bear in front of Stephen. He became quiet as he reached out for the toy. "My bear," he whispered as he hugged it tightly.

Abby looked at Robert. " I think he likes it."

Days and then weeks passed, and still Robert was putting off the one visit he knew he would have to make and dreaded the most. Today was not yet that day. It was a cool yet sunny California morning. Robert sat near the kitchen window having just finished the eggs, toast and hash browns that Abby had prepared for him an hour earlier. His coffee cup warmed his hands as he stared out the window that had become a stage for the water drops provided by a rare early morning rain shower. Robert focused on the tiny drops of water slowly coming together until the weight of their union caused them to quickly dash down towards the bottom of the window. He had become oblivious to the actions of the kids playing in the street and their scurrying to the sidewalk each time a car passed by. This was the way Robert's mind had begun to function. He had become very introverted and unaware of the world around him. Sometimes it was actually crippling.

Pondering the water droplets a few feet in front of him and how they bonded together to become one made Robert think of Abby and how they had become one. His mind slowly drifted back to the day he asked her to be his wife . . . . .

18-year-old Robert may have been the most popular guy at Mountain View High School but he didn't let that go to his head. His six-foot-two-inch frame was chiseled with tight, lean and defined muscles. His muscles almost made him intimidating, yet his engaging smile and blue eyes tended to put people at ease and draw others to him. What had made Robert so very different though was his character. He was a very confident person who knew he could become anything he desired; yet he had a demeanor of appreciation, excitement and peace about life. It was a character that Mr. and Mrs. Bowers had come to admire and respect while he dated their daughter. Robert would never have come out and asked Abby to marry him without her dad's blessing, especially when she was only seventeen years old. When the time neared, he took her father out for a nice steak dinner. There he asked for his daughter's hand in marriage. He explained the love he had for her, his plans for their immediate future, and the plans to have two or three children when the time was right. Her father gave his approval, openly sharing he and his wife's adoration for Robert. With this blessing, Robert made special plans for his proposal to Abby, hoping to make it the most memorable and special day possible.

The moment came on a beautiful March afternoon. It was a warm California spring day and the Bower family had plans to enjoy it. As had become the routine over the last few months, the entire family, including Robert, attended morning services together. Afterwards a wonderful meal was prepared by Mrs. Bowers to be served around two o'clock. This had become an incredible time for the family to truly get to know Robert and vice versa. Robert loved the smell of the house on those afternoons. He would take in the tantalizing aroma of the roast and freshly baked bread as it was placed on the counter top and cut into slices. There would almost always be a cherry pie cooling on a rack and accompanied by a coffee pot brewing the deep, black powder that distinctly laid its claim to one's senses. What he enjoyed the most though was the talking, joking and laughter that filled the kitchen, dining room, and spread throughout the house as the table was being covered with a vast array of colorful and appetizing foods. Robert always felt like a king awaiting the feast of roast beef, mashed potatoes, gravy, glazed carrots, spinach salad, bread, fresh strawberries and, of course, the pies. Abby, her sister and her mom would cater to his, her brother's and Mr. Bower's every whim as the guys would sit in the adjacent living room talking, watching basketball or the Giants game, and observing the food circus run its course until Sunday's supper was complete. When everything was set, the men would be told that it was time and they would take their places. Mr. Bowers sat at the head of the table while Abby and Robert sat on one side and her brother and sister sat on the other. Mrs. Bowers sat at the opposite end from her husband after taking off her apron and placing it on the back of her chair.

"Ok, honey." She would instruct her husband. "Time for you to say grace and thank the Lord for another blessed day together."

This was his signal to welcome their Lord to this meal. Mr. Bowers had a keen way of letting God know he appreciated all the blessings he had been given through his family and loved ones. It had become a little bit of a joke between Robert and Abby that her dad's prayers would practically last as long as the morning services had. Robert would squeeze her hand and look over at her and wink. She did her best to keep from giggling. An "Amen" finally came and the dishes were passed around until everyone had what they desired. The conversation would continue throughout the meal. There were endless stories of the family's past experiences and undoubtedly the key ones to embarrass Abby in front of Robert. Robert would share his stories about life too. It truly had become a special time for family bonding throughout the months and now it naturally included Robert.

On this particular spring Sunday, at two forty-five, on cue, the doorbell rang. No one moved for a moment until Mrs. Bowers spoke up, " Abby, why don't you get the door and I will go get the dessert from the kitchen."

"Ok, Mom," She replied as she got up and disappeared into the living room on her way to the front door.

Abby opened the front door to see a deliveryman standing on the porch. "Hello ma'am. I am with Special Moments Gifts and Flowers."

"Yes. Can I help you?" Abby answered inquisitively.

"Yes you can ma'am. I have a delivery for a Miss Abby Bowers. Is she at this address?"

Abby looked over the man's shoulder and saw the white van with the store name written elegantly in red letters. "That's me."

"You are Abby Bowers ma'am?"

"Yes, yes I am."

"Then ma'am this is for you. Can you sign this for me?"He handed her a form that she in turn signed. Then he handed her a white box about three feet long with a large red ribbon tied on it near the top.

"Thank you very much ma'am. Enjoy." He then turned around and headed back to his vehicle.

Abby stood perplexed for a moment. There didn't seem to be a card or note on the outside of the box. She pulled the ribbon off the top of the box and opened it up, exposing a dozen long stem red roses.

Abby closed the door and slowly turned, heading back towards the dining room. She admired the flowers filling the long slender gift box. As she rounded the corner to the room she surprisingly noticed that everyone was gone. That was everyone except for her father, who was now off to the side of the table with his eye pressed against the viewing lens of a large movie camera.

"Daddy what is going on? Where did everyone go?"asked Abby.

"They went out to the back deck to enjoy the spring sunshine, Honey," he answered.

"Why are you taking pictures, Daddy?"

"Abby, can't a proud father take pictures of his beautiful daughter on such a wonderful Sunday afternoon when the flowers in the yard are in full bloom and his family is all present? These are special days and I want to remember them long after you all leave this house. Why don't you join the rest in the back?"

"I will right after I put these roses in a vase with water," Abby answered.

"Honey, your mom will do that later. Take your roses out of the box and show everyone what you got. I am sure they would love to see them."

She laid the box on the dining room table and carefully removed the flowers. She put them to her face and took in the fragrance. This brought a smile to her face. "They are beautiful aren't they, Daddy?"

"Simply beautiful. Just like you." He replied with a smile. "Darling, go ahead and join everyone out back."

Abby walked down the hall leading to the family room and the door to the back porch. As she did, she was strangely compelled to glance at the numerous photos hanging on the wall from all the family's past vacations. The pictures were from every stage of their lives and taken all over the west coast. There were pictures of them camping in the mountains, including the one of her and her brother holding up the half dozen small trout they had caught when they were seven and eight years old. There was the one of her and her brother and sister on their knees making sand castles on an Oregon beach. And there was the one that was her favorite of the whole family having a picnic near a Washington State lighthouse located on a hill with the vast Pacific Ocean in the background. Abby smiled. Life had been good to her and she thanked God under her breath for that. As she approached the door to the backyard she felt a sense of warmth, satisfaction and contentment. She felt God's presence penetrate her soul. She simply felt that this moment in time had significance.

With the roses held in her left hand, Abby opened the back door and stepped out into the beauty of the back yard and the scent of all the flowers her father had worked so hard to grow. The trees along the white fence were in full bloom, with their white and pink tuffs looking like cotton balls filling their branches. A various array of colorful flowers scattered the entire area. This backyard had become her father's own botanical garden. However, it wasn't the spectacle of foliage or the hint of spring freshness in the air that stopped Abby in her tracks. It was something far more surprising than seasonal plant life. It was the fifty to sixty close friends and relatives lined up against the far side of the fence that began to clap in unison upon her entrance to the backyard. She could only stand speechless as she took in the essence of the moment. The porch was not large, but what also caught her attention was the three-foot wide red carpet that met her at the door, ran down the two small stairs, and out about twenty feet into the plush green manicured yard. Everyone had surrounded the carpet now, yet leaving the carpet itself vacant. Abby smiled and looked for Robert but could not see him. Her father had inched his way past her and was now taking her picture from off to the side of the deck.

"Daddy, where is Robert?" Abby asked. Her father pulled his face away from the viewing lens and smiled at her. He then turned the camera toward the crowd and specifically the end of the red carpet in the yard.

Abby looked out into the crowd of people when all of a sudden Robert stepped into sight wearing a stunning black tuxedo and white shirt. He slowly made his way to the far end of the carpet and then knelt down on one knee. He looked directly into Abby's eyes and winked, bringing a smile to both of their faces. The realization of what was happening came over Abby, causing a vast array of emotions to swell up within her. A tear slowly formed, then drifted down her cheek.

The group fell silent while birds sang in the background. "Honey," her dad said as he lowered the camera, placing it carefully on the railing. "That is a special man kneeling at the end of the carpet. He is a man of dignity, faith and purpose and a man I truly respect and admire. He has asked me for permission to take your hand in marriage. I cannot answer for you, Angel, but I do know that your mother and I would be honored to have him as a part of this family."

Tears rolled down both of Abby's cheeks as she rushed to her father and embraced him. "I love you, Daddy. I love you so much. Thank you so much for everything you have done for me."

Her mom then walked up the stairs and joined in her daughter and husband's embrace. Abby openly cried in her parents' arms as they beamed with happiness.

After a minute or so her father pulled away slowly still holding her shoulders. He looked into her eyes, admiring the beautiful creation the Lord had entrusted to him for the last seventeen years and smiled. "Honey, it is time for a new beginning. It is time to live the most wonderful chapters of your life. Go now. You and Robert have all our love and blessings."

With that statement, Abby instantaneously turned in Robert's direction to see he was still smiling at her at the end of the carpet. She began to walk slowly down the stairs, with flowers in hand, never taking her eyes from Robert's. The crowd began to applaud again as she neared him, then fell silent once more as she took a knee and placed her hand in his. The only sound heard was the singing of the birds combined with an occasional sniffle from Abby. Robert squeezed her hand in one of his and wiped a tear from her cheek with his other.

Looking deep into her eyes he began. "Abby, my one and only love, I have never seen a more beautiful woman. You have everything in a woman that I dreamed of. Everything I ever prayed for. I truly thought I would never find you, yet the Lord found favor with me and sent me such a blessing. You are a gift that I will honor and cherish every day on this earth and in Heaven for eternity. You would make me the happiest man alive if you would be my wife. Abby Bowers, would you please marry me?"

Abby smiled a smile that lit up even an already bright sunny day. Her smile inspired everyone there to smile with her. Then tears of overwhelming happiness flowed down her face. She paused wanting the answer to be perfectly spoken. "Robert Nance, you are an amazing and beautiful man. I would be honored to be your wife. Of course I will marry you."

With that, he took her left hand and gently placed the diamond engagement ring on her finger. Abby put it close to her face to admire it and then she and Robert fell into each other's arms as the friends and relatives clapped, whistled, and congratulated them. This was their moment in time. A moment they wanted to share with everyone. A moment they believed would last forever . . . . .

Minutes later, back in the present, Robert's mind went in the entire opposite direction. It was as though a huge pendulum catapulted him the opposite way to another scene in time. He recalled how scared he had felt about love, marriage and parenthood when it was time to come back from the war. He recalled the trip coming home from Vietnam on the large transport plane when he realized that he had been looking out the window for over 700 miles. The oddest part of that experience had been that two-thirds of those miles took place after the day had turned to night. Robert had simply shut out everything and let the circuits within his mind disconnect from his surroundings. As the plane grew closer to the California coastline he had felt more and more anxious. The thought of the responsibility involved in being a husband to Abby and a father to a child he had never met made him feel claustrophobic. Had he had the ability to alter the course of the plane and be dropped off on a deserted island in the Pacific he would have taken it. To go to a place where he would never have to disclose anything he had done and seen in Southeast Asia sounded very appealing. To Robert, the perils of war were not things you wrote home about. Thus there were no easy ways to release the horrific scenes that plagued his mind and took on a life of their own. It was like sitting in a car with the engine running in a closed garage, the invisible carbon monoxide fumes slowly consuming you until all that can be taken is your life. Yet if someone rescues you soon enough, the body survives and the mind is all that suffers. Robert's mind was suffering and he had found no way but quiet isolation to deal with it.

This was never more apparent than when he had arrived at the San Francisco airport and first saw Abby on the tarmac holding their infant son, Stephen. With each step that they grew nearer, he felt as if it was his last chance to run. The last chance to escape a future he was numb to. As he embraced Abby that day he felt it was only a physical action void of his emotions. He simply could not find a way to grasp any sense of connection with Abby or his son.

Abby sensed it as well, and Robert had seen the surprised look spread across her face after their hug. He understood her despair. She had longed for this special day for over two years. She had longed for the day that her loving husband would meet and connect with his first son. But things had changed. Robert had found it impossible to connect with anything. He felt vacant. He felt empty. And most of all, he felt guilty. He felt guilty for his time at war in Vietnam and guilty for the battle going on within him regarding his wife and child . . . . .

The sound of a dish breaking on the floor startled Robert. He jumped back from the window in an exaggerated motion, surprising and in turn frightening Abby.

"Sorry, Honey," Abby said. "Just dropped a plate from breakfast." She paused, "Do you want anything else to eat? More coffee?"

She bent down picking up the pieces of the plate. "I didn't mean to surprise you."

"It is ok, Abby. Just lost in thought."

"You do that a lot, Dear. Is it something you want to talk about?" she asked.

"No, just a lot on my mind," replied Robert. He stood up and opened the creaky side door that went to a couple of steps just outside of the kitchen. He then closed the door behind him, lit up a cigarette, and sat down.

Abby placed the pieces to the dish on the counter, sat down in a chair, and buried her face in her hands. The tears flowed freely down her forearms and onto the apron on her lap. Stephen, having just woken up, staggered into the kitchen sliding his socked feet along the linoleum floor. His small white blanket draped over his small shoulders swept the floor behind him. His teddy bear was propped under his small arm. Stephen stopped just in front of his mother, puzzled by her sniffling.

"Mommy why you cry?" he asked inquisitively.

Abby looked up at Stephen's innocent face. "What, Honey?"

"Why crying, Mommy?" He asked again as he moved closer to her.

"Honey, come here." She reached out and lifted him up in her arms, hugged him, and then kissed his cheek. Through her tears she smiled at her little man who then grinned back at her. She looked into his eyes. "Everything is ok, Sweetheart. You know I love you, Pumpkin. " You love me too?"

"Yes, Mommy. I love you lots," he answered.

"Then, little guy, we are going to be just fine." Abby replied.

CHAPTER 7

The day finally came when the visit Robert had been avoiding could no longer be put off. Robert had finally gotten up the nerve to go visit his boyhood friend, Carl, in the mental health ward of the Veterans Administration Hospital. Entering the building, he noticed the musty smell of despair, as the hospital had survived several decades and three major wars. There were also the strained expressions of many of the clientele who, in one way or another, did not totally survive those same wars, staring at you as you entered. As Robert advanced past the registration desk and moved deeper into the building's structure, there was an even more pungent stench of combined medicine, decay and dishonor. He had been told by an older lady at the front entrance where to find Carl Johnson. Slowly he walked down the long, white hallway to a large open area where many of the patients congregated. Each patient was at a different stage regarding their health, or lack thereof. The lounge was about fifty square feet. The walls were white, or at least they were supposed to be white. At the present time they were more a shade of dingy grey from the accumulation of dust, cigarette smoke, and countless handprints placed there by dazed and confused residents from years gone by.

About twenty-five individuals, mostly over the age of fifty, were scattered around the room. Some played cards at the tables, one sat piecing together a puzzle, and a few more veterans had checker games going on in front of them. Each table had several ashtrays with smoke billowing from each. There were about a dozen more people watching an average size black and white Zenith television set to his left. Four of these men were in wheelchairs. Another individual near them, but not part of the group, was also in a wheelchair. He lay, almost asleep, to one side of the chair with a slight stream of drool dangling from his partially open mouth. The only real movement in the room came from Robert's right as a man with a walker slowly moved towards him in order to exit the room. An IV on rollers trailed him with its tiny wheels squeaking as he advanced. Behind the man with the walker, about thirty feet away, Robert saw the individual he was there to see. He slowly walked towards his childhood friend.

Carl lay in a reclined gurney, draped in a white sheet up to his waist. Robert looked at Carl, starting at his feet under the sheet, and then moving up over his frail body until he looked into his glossed-over eyes. Carl had been medicated and lay in an induced stupor staring at a blank wall. The staff had told Robert that it was therapeutic for him because seeing people, trees, or experiencing any abrupt movement could set him into an uncontrollable rage. Robert was informed that on one occasion, when a steel tray had accidentally hit the floor near Carl, he had come unglued. It had taken five interns and an injection of a sedative to get him back under control. Robert thought it amazing how much power and strength a man could muster when fighting his fear.

Carl was not fighting for his life. Unfortunately, the hospital would do that for him as a duty to its government. Carl was fighting his demons from the war. Demons left over from a war fought thousands of miles away yet still going on inside his mind. Demons Robert knew all too well. The only thing different, was he could not simply stare at a blank wall as Carl had the luxury of doing. He had to walk out the door each morning and face the demons daily. Robert quietly slid a chair across the floor to sit on. He then moved closer to Carl and very slowly reached out for his hand. Carl's fingers were limp and cold.

Robert took one of Carl's hands in both of his and held it up in front of him as if in prayer. He bowed his head slightly and whispered. "Oh, Carl, I am so sorry."

He then paused, holding Carl's hand tighter in his. " I am so sorry this happened to you and so sorry it took me so long to come see you. I am just so messed up."

Robert then brought his and Carl's hands to his chest. "I couldn't deal with it all. I can't even deal with life at home. I would like to tell you that Abby and I were doing OK but I can't. I honestly can't. It isn't her. It is all me. I have a son, Carl. I have a little two-year-old boy. A boy I should adore and love to spend time with. But, Carl, I am so scared of him. That sounds so crazy, doesn't it? Scared of a three-year-old? But I am terrified at times. I just can't seem to find the way to open myself up to my wife or son. I thought when this war was over and if we survived we would just come back and have a few beers, share war stories, and joke about our childhood. Instead Mark is gone, you are here, and I am all messed up. Everything is all messed up, Carl. Everything."

Then Robert fell silent. The silence seemed to amplify the noises around the lounge. Robert looked around the room, scanning his surroundings in awkward silence. That's when he felt a slight squeeze from Carl's frail fingers. Robert turned back, looking at the hand he was grasping in his. And the squeeze came again. Robert moved his eyes up towards Carl's face to see a tear slowly rolling down his friend's cheek. The expression on his face had not changed in the slightest but the tear spoke directly to Robert's heart. He put Carl's hand down on the gurney, reached around his shoulders taking him in an embrace, and slowly rocked him as he began to cry uncontrollably.

CHAPTER 8

In the years that followed, the talk of the war began to fade. New things had become more interesting and taken center stage. Nixon had been impeached and the constant conflicts in the Middle East became nightly news. But in the Nance household, little had changed. The same emotional distance Robert used to protect himself still prevailed. They tried to do things together as a family to make things feel normal, though the loneliness Abby experienced was very obvious. In 1975, when Stephen was old enough to understand the concept of Mickey Mouse and all Mickey's wonderful friends, they decided to take him to Disneyland. The time at Disneyland actually brought a lot of happiness to Robert and Abby as they watched their son smile with intrigue at all the sights and sounds. They were entertained by his response to this child's paradise.

After a long Saturday at the amusement park, they headed out into the parking lot to find their car. Stephen was between Robert and Abby, holding Abby's hand. It was then that Stephen saw a bright red balloon skipping across the hot pavement in front of them, about fifty feet away, and he had to have it. Before Abby or Robert had a chance to realize what was happening, Stephen had broken free from his mother and was running between cars chasing after the air-filled prize. Robert began chasing after him when all of a sudden they heard the squeal of tires skidding to a stop. When Abby and Robert rounded the row of cars they momentarily stood motionless as they viewed in horror the sight of their young son laying on the ground in front of a car's fender.

They breathlessly ran up to Stephen's little body and knelt down next to him.

A man stepped out of his car and approached them. "I didn't even see him. He came out of nowhere. I am so sorry," the man bellowed.

"Just call an ambulance," Robert screamed, "Just call a damn ambulance."

Robert took his son's limp body in his arms and began to rock back and forth, crying and screaming hysterically. "No, God, no. Don't do this. Do not take him. He is only a little boy. Oh, God. Oh, God, please. Please, God, no."

Within a few minutes, which seemed like an hour, a siren could be heard in the distance. A crowd had formed and watched in silence as the grown man cradled his bloody son and pleaded with God. The ambulance slowly rolled up near them. The staff jumped from the rig in a quick but organized fashion. They took Stephen from Robert's arms, laid him flat on the ground, and began to evaluate him. Stephen was placed on a stretcher that was then pushed to the rear of the emergency vehicle. Abby also jumped up into the ambulance to be with here son on the way to the hospital. The door closed and the sirens blared as it sped off. Robert ran to his car and was escorted by the patrol car out of the parking lot and down the street far behind the ambulance.

As Robert followed the police he continued to bargain with God. "Please, God. Not Stephen. Hasn't this family been through enough? He is all Abby truly has. If you need to take anyone, just take me. Just take me. Please just take me."

CHAPTER 9

Linn Sue Nguyen was in America staying with her husband's brother and his wife. Her brother-in-law and his wife had been some of the fortunate ones who successfully fled Vietnam following the war. Linn Sue's husband, Pae, did not make the trip with her. He stayed behind in South Vietnam tending to their gift shop in the village where they lived. Pae didn't find it easy to travel, having lost a leg while stranded in a Vietcong minefield during the war. He wanted his wife to have their first child in a civilized place though, so they had made plans that during her pregnancy she would go to America to visit and have the baby. Late Wednesday night the moment came and Linn Sue found herself checking into the hospital at just after ten o'clock. She was amazed at the efficiency and professionalism provided by the staff that guided her through the process of registration and getting to the delivery room. She understood the complexities of caring for patients, as she was a nurse back at the clinic in her village. Her husband was correct; this was the proper place to bring their child into the world.

The birth went perfectly, and early the next morning Linn Sue was holding a beautiful and healthy little girl. She had chosen the name Sophia for her daughter after seeing Sophia Loren on television several times back home. Linn Sue thought she was a stunning woman and believed her little girl would grow up to be someone special as well.

When it was time to leave the hospital, Linn Sue was anxious to get back to the house so she could freely use the phone in privacy to call her husband. As she sat in the wheelchair near the front entrance to the hospital awaiting her ride, Sophia started to naturally demand the attention she desired as a new arrival into this world. She cried loudly, attracting staff over to her. And, of course, each person coming her way had his or her own version of the perfect remedy to help calm her and ease her adjustment into the world. The nurses assured Linn Sue that her cries were a normal part of being a newborn and that Linn Sue would soon become accustomed to being a new mother.

At this same time, the Nance family was about to leave the hospital through a door about twenty feet from Linn Sue and Sophia. The Nance's had been at the hospital over night finding out that, fortunately, Stephen had only badly bruised his arm, which was now in a sling, and had a concussion but was going to be OK after being hit by the car in the Disneyland parking lot. He had recovered quickly once at the emergency room, but since he had a concussion the doctors chose to keep him overnight for observation. He looked worse for the wear with the big band aids across his forehead, bruises on his face, and arm in a sling, but he was alert and talking with his parents near the doorway.

Over her crying child, Linn Sue observed the family's conversation. The parents were kneeling down listening to their son explain something to them. They both were nodding in agreement and smiling at what he was saying. The mom almost seemed to be wiping a tear from her cheek and the father put his hand on the boy's shoulder as if he was very proud of him. He then gave his son a quick wink. With that, the little, battered boy approached Linn Sue. She inquisitively watched the boy, as he got closer. He seemed to be nearing her with a sense of purpose. He stopped just in front of her and looked at the crying baby. A small smile came to his face. He then looked up at her and smiled a smile that lit up the room.

"Ma'am, my name is Stephen Nance. I stayed here at the hospital last night. I got hit by a car. I am OK though. I am really sorta tough. See this?" he said pointing to his forehead, "Eight stitches. I might have a scar they say. It is OK though. My daddy has scars from the war. Now I am like my daddy. I am a hero too. Anyway, I heard your baby crying. Is it a boy or a girl?"

Linn Sue spoke fairly good English, as she saw and spoke with many of the American soldiers during the war. She looked at Stephen and felt warmth that could not be explained. He seemed so confident and sure that he was supposed to be there talking to her and yet he could not be much over five or six years old. She smiled even more deeply. "This is my new baby girl. She is my first child. She is my angel."

Stephen looked at Sophia again. "How old is she? She is so small."

"She is three days old. And how old are you?" asked Linn Sue.

"I am five. But I will be six soon. Well, Ma'am, I heard her crying and thought maybe she could use this teddy bear more than I do. I mean I am almost a man and she is a little baby. I think she would like it. May I give it to her?"

Linn Sue continued to smile with amazement. She looked over his shoulder at the parents, seeking their approval. Both nodded in agreement. She looked back at the little boy in front of her. "I believe you are a special little man. I think you are right. She may really like the bear."

Stephen looked at the whimpering child again, wrapped in the pink blanket. "Here you go," he said as he put the bear up against her. Sophia instantly calmed and became very quiet.

Stephen looked up at Linn Sue once more with a smile, beaming with pride. "She likes it. She really likes it," he said.

" I believe she does," replied Linn Sue with a warm smile.

With that Stephen turned and ran back to his parents. Linn Sue watched the family exit the hospital. The father was holding the door open as his wife and son went through it. Before the father closed the door he looked at her and gave her a sincere and gracious wink.

When Linn Sue's brother-in-law entered the patient pick up area, the nurse pushed her wheelchair out to the car. He tossed her bags into the back seat and then helped her into the front passenger seat. As Linn Sue sat in the car holding Sophia asleep on her lap she handed her brother-in-law the gift the little American boy had given Sophia.

"A little boy that had stayed in the hospital last night gave this toy bear to Sophia because she was crying."

He looked at it and smiled. "Wasn't that a selfless thing for a little person to do for a total stranger?" she asked.

"It sure was," he replied, "but how did he know her name?"

"What do you mean?" said Linn Sue, confused.

He handed the teddy bear back to Linn Sue showing her the small little dog tags around its neck. "It says S. N., as in Sophia Nguyen. I'd say that sure is a special gift."

Linn Sue looked at the initials engraved on the small piece of metal with amazement. She then looked out the window at the trees in the hospital courtyard and whispered to herself, "It is special. Very special."

CHAPTER 10

The first part of the trip from Anaheim to Palo Alto on the 5 was quiet. There was only the sound of the occasional car racing by over the speed limit or a blast of wind from the truckers in their large semis. Stephen was fast asleep in the back seat with his head propped up on his dad's jacket. Both Robert and Abby were deep in thought, reflecting on all that had taken place in the last twenty-four hours. Robert felt an intense, internal emotional warfare of guilt and sadness. He felt guilt because of his inability to protect his son and sadness because his wife almost lost the only one in the car who truly showed her love. The reason for this sadness then brought on more guilt-filled emotions and an overwhelming sense of inadequacy, creating a vicious cycle.

Abby, meanwhile, was thinking of Robert. She had seen some flickers of hope in the hospital regarding Robert's emotional challenges. She knew though that he was beating himself up in the seat next to her. Abby gently reach over and took Robert's hand in hers. Robert looked over quickly, and then returned back to the road ahead of him.

"Robert, what happened yesterday to Stephen was an accident. You nor I could have known he was going to run after that silly balloon," said Abby, trying to pick her words wisely.

Robert looked at her again, squeezed her hand, and let out a quick unauthentic smile that revealed his uncertainty regarding the truth in what she just said.

"Robert, things happen which are totally out of our control. You have to stop doing this to yourself. It isn't fair. It isn't fair to you and it is actually selfish, Robert. You beat yourself up everyday about everything and then you withdraw your love from both your son and me. For some reason you think feeling bad about everything is to be your punishment for Vietnam. But you know what you are doing, Robert? You are taking your son and me into a battlefield that we don't deserve to have to go to. The war is over. It is over, but you want to keep it alive so you can punish yourself with it. But you are punishing me too, Robert. You are punishing your son and me. We don't deserve that." Abby lowered her head, put her hands over her eyes, and started to cry. " I love you so much, Robert, but we don't deserve that."

Robert looked over at his wife crying and then back at Stephen peacefully sleeping. It grew quiet again as he regained focused on the miles of freeway ahead of them. Everything she had said made perfect sense. There was nothing he could dispute. Abby had him figured out. It was he, though, who couldn't figure himself out. He could see it, and even quite objectively, when it was brought to his attention the way his wife just did. It was just that there was something in his mind that, when given a chance, scattered all his practical reasoning. It was like a puzzle that came together as a clear picture when someone would take the time to put the pieces in their proper places, but then, for reasons unknown to him, he chose to tear the pieces apart again. It was as if the clarity of the picture was something that scared him, so he kept it from coming together and staying together; as though on some level, he felt it better to live in the fog instead of seeing what becomes visible once the fog clears. This is what the demons of Vietnam had done to him. How could that be his fault? He looked over at his wife and back at his son again. It wasn't their fault either. As he watched each white line of the freeway disappear under the front of the car, Robert felt one tear run down his left cheek.

Abby was looking out the passenger window through her own tears. Rarely had she confronted her husband about his emotional issues, but she had to do it not only for herself but also for her little angel asleep in the back seat. He couldn't fight this battle for himself. She had to be the safe haven for him. Abby knew this was not the life she and Robert had planned when they fell in love and got married. She also realized she did not know all that took place in Vietnam that had changed him so much. She knew Carl was in the psych ward at the VA hospital, so it wasn't just her husband that was dealing with some sort of hell within his mind. Abby felt deep compassion for all that Robert was going through, and it tore her heart apart to see him such a broken man. The beautiful qualities that attracted her to him were now locked away in some hidden cavern within his soul.

Robert had been a man that knew love. From their first date until he had left for Vietnam she had experienced his love daily. The sentimental gift of the teddy bear, the laughter in the photo booth on the boardwalk, and the kisses stolen any place and at any time all indicated their love for each other. They had enjoyed being with friends and family, with Robert as the center of attention at functions and as an active leader in the church. He was a man who dreamed of playing football for Stanford in front of tens of thousands cheering fans and would have probably been good enough to eventually play in the pros. Now he chose to be alone and away from people. He avoided being a leader of anything when given the opportunity. And his not wanting to be around others had caused them to distance themselves from their families, which saddened Abby because they had been so close before. Abby realized he needed his space to think, but she also knew that these were the times that the demons frolicked throughout his mind. She loved this man. He was responsible and provided her and their son with a house and the normal amenities, but she so desperately wanted the love and affection of the man she had married and promised to grow old with.

****

One would have thought that after Stephen's accident in the Disneyland parking lot and Robert's bartering with God, it would have affected a part of Robert's soul and set the process of healing into motion. For Robert, however, it did just the opposite. It did touch him emotionally, but with that, he retreated from them even more and in any way he could. He found his escape and solitude on a small boat in the San Francisco Bay. Ironically this place of freedom, which was also in some ways his emotional prison, was in the shadows of Alcatraz. Robert felt that going out fishing after a day at work surrounded by all the other machinists, office staff, and clients was a way to clear his mind. In reality, it only added to his inability to cope with the world around him, however, he had convinced himself that if he gave the traffic at 5 o'clock a chance to thin out it would be a more peaceful trip back home around seven o'clock or so.

The marina was a mere five blocks from the shipyard and held his sixteen-foot, wooden hauled outboard with an Evinrude motor mounted on its stern. He had become a regular here, so he followed the same basic routine each day. Here Robert would park his car, grab his jacket and tackle box out of the trunk, and walk down the ramp to the dock below where his small boat was moored. The only time this might be altered, would be if he had to stop at the bait and tackle shop near the top of the ramp or to get fuel. Robert would pick up a new lure, a pack of smokes, and some beef jerky or a soda. Once in the boat, he would reach up in the covered bow area for his seat cushion and make sure no one had stolen his two fishing poles he stored there. After a few pumps on the engine primer, the choke switch set on, and the three to four pulls on the starter rope, the engine would turn over and the surrounding area would be filled with blue smoke. By the time he had adjusted the throttle, untied the ropes that held the boat in place, and started to steer away from the dock, the thoughts of work, home, and the chaos of the world behind him would begin to fade away.

The boat was not meant for speed. On a calm day it might cruise at about twenty miles per hour. On a day with choppy seas or when there were departing ships heading out to distant ports, Robert would have to cut the speed by half. Since there was never a real destination, and just him and his thoughts for cargo, speed was never an issue. Soon Robert would be out in the middle of the San Francisco Bay with the waves lapping up against the wood hull. Standing behind the steering wheel with the windshield about waist high, he found himself lost in the moment. The rhythm of the waves, the warm wind in his face, and the soothing taste of a Marlboro pressed between his lips gave him some contentment. Less then fifteen minutes later he would be at his regular starting point to drop his fishing gear. He set the two wooden poles that stretched out on each side of the boat. One lure attracted fish at a depth of about ten feet and the other at about three times that, depending on the rumors of whether the fish were near the surface or if they were running deep. Robert would then set his course just to the north of Alcatraz, a mile away, with the majestic Golden Gate Bridge in the background. Sitting sideways in the driver's seat so he could watch his lines, as well as where he was headed, he would just let his mind wander.

From this vantage point, Robert looked past the prison, and the monstrous bridge, and towards the invisible, far off land, thousands of miles over the horizon that stole his soul. The land that robbed his ability to feel, love and cope with the present world he had to wake up to each day. He heard one of the poles let out a quick and short squeal as if a fish may have hit the lure and let go before being hooked. His eyes fixed on the end of the pole to see if the fish would strike again. After half a minute of watching intently he once again relaxed and went back to his pondering. Looking over the stern of the boat, he felt a sense of sadness. Sadness rose as he blamed the mainland behind the boat for sending him to the far off land ahead of him. He was sent to fight their war for liberty and freedom, and then cursed when he returned home. Robert shook his head thinking of the word "home." When he and his comrades had returned to America they were ridiculed by the ignorant and kept at a distance by the politicians who didn't find it in their favor to associate with the veterans of an unpopular war. Slowly passing Alcatraz, a half-mile off the port side, Robert again shook his head. He took the remnants of the smoldering Marlboro from his lips and tossed it into the bay. Taking the pack from his front shirt pocket he took out another cigarette and placed it in his lips. He then took a match between his fingers and quickly flicked it causing it to ignite. Cupping his hands around the cigarette so the soft breeze would not blow out the match, he brought the Marlboro to life. For a moment, the smoke billowed around his face and then cleared, drifted away by the wind and the movement of the boat. Robert's mind was not clear though. He was a broken and lonely man, caught between two worlds at each end of the boat and with no way to fully connect with either. He was not even able to connect to the ones who loved him and accepted him the most. His wife and son were forty miles to the south and loved him unconditionally, yet he found himself identifying and bonding more with his fallen comrades thousands of miles to the west over the distant horizon.

On the nights Robert would go out in his boat fishing after work, he would get home around eight o'clock. The house was always clean and quiet with only the soft buzz of the television in the living room. He would get his plate from the refrigerator filled with dinner on it that had been prepared a few hours before. Sometimes he would warm it up, but usually he would just eat it cold, alone at the kitchen table staring at nothing in particular. After dinner he would rinse his dishes and leave them in the sink. After going upstairs to shower and put on a robe, he would go back down to the living room. He knew Abby would be there. She always was. She lay there sleeping under a small blanket her mom had made. Her head resting like an angel on the pillow with the small stains of today's tears. Robert's heart would ache as he stood and looked at his wife. This woman deserved so very much out of life, yet she had ended up with him. Robert thought how much better her life would have been had he been a casualty in Vietnam. Sure, she would hurt for a while, but eventually her heart would have healed and she could have moved forward with her and Stephen's lives. Instead, she had to cry herself to sleep early each night dealing with the burdens he couldn't find a way to let go of. These burdens were beyond what she could even begin to understand because they were things Robert chose never to share with anyone.

Robert finally got the courage to walk towards Abby and pick up her small body. She unconsciously wrapped her arms tightly around his neck as if everything was like it was in the past, when they were first married. As they passed the television he shut it off and dimmed the lamp before heading up the stairs towards the bedroom. She had noticeably lost weight over the last few months and Robert knew that was due to him. He laid her light body down on the bed and put the covers up over her shoulders to keep her warm. Abby pulled the blankets up tighter under her chin and fell into a deeper sleep. Robert sat next to her on the edge of the bed and just looked at her. She appeared so much at peace. Her beauty was so obvious and her heart was so committed to him. That thought cut his heart like a knife, as he pleaded for God to help him feel something normal and real. After a few minutes he got up and walked to the other side of the bed. Taking off his robe, he pulled back the covers and crawled under the soft sheets, bringing them up just under his chest. He lay there, staring up at the ceiling for what seemed like an eternity. Everything was silent except for the gentle breathing of his tender wife next to him. His arm reached for the lamp to his right on the nightstand, which he then turned off, making the room totally dark. As Robert lay there, not able to see a thing, he felt a tear run down his cheek and pool in his left ear. He stared up into the darkness. Abby's words echoed in his head.

"The war is over. It is over but you want to keep it alive so you can punish yourself with it. But you are punishing me, Robert. You are punishing your son and me. We don't deserve that. I love you so much, Robert, but we don't deserve that."

She was right. He knew it. At that moment he vowed to himself to find a way to get help and change. There was no other option. It was time to come home . . . home to America and home to his family.

But come morning, he had no idea how to make this change happen, and he lost the motivation to try, slipping right back into his same, ongoing pattern.

CHAPTER 11

Abby woke up in the mornings with her husband next to her, but she always felt the gap between them. This thick, daunting gap had wedged itself between them since the aftermath of Vietnam. It hadn't always been that way, though. She remembered the days when she felt his love, and held on to those memories, and the hope that it would return, to get her through each day. Putting on her slippers and heading to the kitchen on this particular morning, Abby thought back to their wedding . . . . .

Abby remembered the details of her and Robert's wedding day very well. She remembered the guests, the party, the toasts, and the food. She also remembered how the flowers were arranged and how the photographer tripped and almost fell. Abby also remembered the honeymoon night just as well.

The newly married couple left the reception and went to their honeymoon suite facing the ocean. Upon arriving through the door, Abby took a quick scan around the room. Fresh cut roses sat perfectly positioned on a center table; the room was painted in a light rose color with a huge bed. She particularly noticed how crisp and inviting the lighter rose quilt looked, draping down around the bed, but unfolded crisply and neatly at the top exposing satin pillowcases and sheets. Long, flowing curtains streamed into the room from the open window and the room smelled of sea and another smell familiar to Abby. At first Abby thought the scent was musk, and then she realized exactly what it was. It was amber. Yes, she was certain that the combined smell included amber. She knew the scent based on a perfume her grandmother wore and described as her favorite because of its "warm, alluring, yet gentle scent." Abby tried to remember the name of that perfume she swore someday she would wear, but with the excitement of this being her wedding night and the look of her love admiring her right now, she could not remember the perfume's name.

Robert had carried her into the room, gently set her down and was now patiently admiring her. Abby blushed as he gazed at her and couldn't help but to notice he suddenly looked older to her, more serious, more sure of his ways. And although he still had those same gentle blue eyes, with lashes most women would die for, she now felt as though his eyes had a more luring appeal, one that was peering deep into her soul.

Abby was proud to be able to call herself Mrs. Nance and she felt a sense of giddiness as she thought about her high school love now being her husband. As Abby's nervous giggle continued, her new husband reached out to her, pulled her in, kissed the top of her head and then her cheek, squeezed her hands, and with a deepness but sincerity in his throat, recited "Abby, my dear Abby" a couple of times as his finger moved in small circles on her shoulder.

There had never been any doubt in Abby's mind regarding Robert's affection for her, his dedication, his patience. He had always been a gentleman to her . . . just as she expected of him. Now as they stood there looking at each other, embraced, she knew their relationship was about to embark on an entirely new journey together.

In this moment, a true realization occurred to Abby that "Mr. Nance," as she had affectionately called Robert beginning on their very first date, was about to take on a new title in her life . . . . her "lover." Yes, they had kissed plenty and even made out before, but this was all new, and Abby - though undoubtedly excited - felt very anxious concerning what would happen next. She had heard from other girls about what it was like to be with a man. There were ones who described a perplexing experience that felt invasive and left them feeling wronged. She specifically remembered Janet from her high school class describing a stereotypical experience in the back seat of her boyfriend's car. The two words Abby remembered most from her tale were "awkward" and "quick." But there were also those ladies who told Abby of a fabulous experience, one of intimacy and connection, that stirred feelings these women had never known and a desire of wanting more. She was hoping for the latter of these experiences but was unsure of what to expect.

Abby could hardly believe she was sitting in this room with her soon to be lover looking at her intently. She was feeling naïve. Could he sense it? Would he be disappointed? She could barely hold his gaze, she was so nervous. Part of her wanted to run to the door, the other part wanted to stay and see what would happen next. A third, newer part arising in her wanted to take a stronger hold of him and plunge in. At the thought of this, it was even harder for her to look Robert in the eye. Did he know what she was thinking? Did he feel her awkwardness? Was he feeling the same way? Or was he really as confident as he appeared?

Robert was holding her, pulling her in ever more firmly yet tenderly. He stroked her hair, slid his hand down her cheek to her chin, and lovingly lifted her chin up to kiss him. As they kissed intently, Abby felt his hand slide down and warmly cup her breast. She first felt an exhilaration, then a panic and again shied away, not quite able to meet his gaze. As her face turned to the left she looked out the window to see a moonbeam casting its light on the water. The light was strong and reflective. The reflection from the water appeared to be aimed right at Robert and Abby. This illumination gave Abby peace, and she no longer felt afraid. Her mind shifted, and with a sigh of relief she was able to turn back and peer into Robert's eyes. This time she held strong, looking back at him and holding his gaze. He whispered kind words to her of how happy he was that she was his wife, he touched her cheek with the utmost respect and tenderness, and his look was so sincere, so warm, so manly and inviting that she could no longer be afraid. A new feeling was welling up inside of her . . . one of desire.

Robert kissed her lips, this time with more conviction. He entered his tongue into her mouth first only superficially, then deeper. Abby tasted a sweetness. She felt a tickle that started in her mouth but travelled to her toes, and she felt her own mouth return the action in a quest for more. Robert kissed her cheek, then licked her ear, then her neck and repeated this same sequence making sure both sides of her face were well taken care of. His hand pressed firmly on the curve of her low back, drawing her near, holding steady, and gently commanding every move.

Abby's breasts were now pressed securely up against Robert's chest as their bodies began to sway in unison. She allowed herself to grab his buttocks, even dig her fingers in just a bit. She had always admired his athletic build but here she was getting to enjoy it. Right then an unexpected sound came from the corner of the room, taking them out of their trance for a moment. It was a lovely sound with its own rhythm, very separate from the movement of the young honeymooners. Both were minutely startled and looked towards the corner of the room, to see a large clock standing stoically in the corner and striking midnight. How had she not seen that before? Abby started to think what the clock might symbolize at this moment, but this thought did not stay long. Quickly, easily her lover was able to get them back to where they had left off.

Robert tilted his head to kiss Abby softly then rested his head on her breast, leaving his hair right under her chin. Abby thought about how he smelled right now. She had always liked how he smelled when he had recently showered and wore a freshly pressed shirt with a collar. She would lay her head on his shoulder near the crook of his neck and take in his scent as they talked for hours. She had also secretly liked his sweaty, boyish smell after a football game although she would tease him about it at the time and never admit she actually liked it. But this scent she smelled now was very different. It wasn't exactly clean, and it wasn't exactly salty . . . no it was different, very manly, and the only word she could think of to describe it was "desire."

Abby lifted Robert's head then reached out and stroked his chest. She let her fingertips linger across Robert's rib cage, then to the ripples in his abdomen. He was built strong and capable; yet she was surprised how soft his skin was here. She found herself wanting to place her cheek here, and then her lips.

At this moment Robert gently stood, then picked her up and in one strong swoop placed her in the middle of the bed. The satin sheets and pillows felt supportive and luxurious and she let herself relax even more as she took this in, as well as the feeling of her lover's hands now moving caressingly and rhythmically across her chest. His hands then slid down to her ribs, and drifted across her lower abdomen back and forth. Abby took in every bit of his touch with love and contentment as she anticipated all that was still to come . . . .

Right then she felt a nudge, followed by "Mommy, Mommy" as she was abruptly jolted out of her thoughts from the past and back into her current reality. She looked at the unread newspaper lying out in front of her on the table, then at her young, needy son standing next to her. It took a moment for her to realize what was going on. She sighed, stood up, straightened out her skirt with both hands and walked across the room to retrieve the cereal Stephen wanted from the counter.

CHAPTER 12

Days, weeks, months routinely ran together, though the routine was anything but normal. Robert had created a systematic lifestyle which made him feel relatively safe through predictability. The issue was, as he found safety, his wife and child floundered in his neglect with sadness and despair.

One early evening after fishing on the bay, once the traffic had died down, Robert put his belongings in the trunk of his car and tossed his jacket on the passenger seat next to him. He turned the key, the car engine rolled over and started as it always had, and he began his 45-minute daily trek home.

The sky was a bit cloudy, and the fall air temperature was a comfortable 65 degrees, which was about normal for the first week of September. He reached for the radio, turning it on to the San Francisco Giants game. He looked out the window towards the stadium where the game was going on, with its lights brightly lit in the distance, then mentally disappeared into the drive home.

At that moment the silent monster that had been manifesting inside Robert let itself be known. It let him know the time had come to be dealt with. Listening to the game Robert thought of the Giants, professional sports, and his earlier dreams of football at college level and possibly beyond. He smiled for a moment and then wiped an itch from his nose. What would have happened had there not been the war? How would college football have gone? Could he have gone pro? Would he even have wanted to? Again he wiped the itch from his nose, looked in the mirror and changed lanes. How would things have been with him,

Abby and his son? With that thought he naturally bit his lower lip, as he knew the emotional pain they were going through because of his state of depression and withdrawal.

As Robert's tongue drifted across his lip he tasted an odd flavor. It was a taste so common in Vietnam on the battlefield. The taste of blood. He instantly wiped his mouth with his forearm and saw it covered with the red liquid. He then saw his white t-shirt with a large bloodstain. The persistent itch that he had been feeling from his nose had actually been a slow drip of blood that had accumulated on his chest. Shocked and a bit confused he quickly changed lanes and pulled off onto the side of the freeway. He grabbed his jacket from the passenger seat, tilted his head backwards and held it against his face.

He had rarely ever had a bloody nose. The last couple of times he could remember was once in high school football and another time when a Vietcong soldier fed him the butt of his rifle before Robert instinctively ended the Asian kid's short life with a hidden handgun. The bullet had pierced the kid's throat, leaving him gasping for his last breath, as he bled to death staring into Robert's eyes. But this was not a normal nosebleed. It started on its own and he had lost a substantial amount of blood. He turned off the radio and sat in silence waiting for the flow to cease.

After about 15 minutes, and a million thoughts, he leaned forward, saw that it had stopped bleeding, and began to clean himself up so that, when he arrived home, Abby would not see the mess and be worried. He reached into the back seat and grabbed another shirt from the several laying there. He slid it on and then tucked his stained T-shirt and jacket under the front seat. He would throw them away when he was at the marina tomorrow. It would have been odd for him to be washing clothes at home. He simply had always left that for Abby.

As Robert returned to the task of driving, he began to ponder if there was anything he was missing in the recent past that could explain the intense nosebleed. The only thing that seemed slightly out of the ordinary was a few headaches in the last two weeks, but he had simply taken a couple aspirin and chalked it up to stress. Robert pulled into the driveway, parked, and made his way to the front door. Before entering, he looked to his right, into the window, in an attempt to see his reflection to make sure there was no blood. As he walked in he heard the television in the living room. Stephen was nestled next to his loving mom as they watched an animated Disney movie.

"Hi, Hun," Abby said as she motioned towards the kitchen. "There's roasted chicken and potatoes on the stove. A small salad is in the refrigerator."

"Thanks," he replied, "I'm going to go up and take a shower. Probably go straight to bed. Not feeling very well."

"It's only 8 o'clock. Are you ok?" Abby responded.

"Yes. Just really tired and a slight headache. But thank you for preparing dinner. I will take it to work tomorrow. Goodnight"

"Goodnight, Hun."

"Goodnight, Daddy." Stephen chimed in.

"Good night, Son." With that he went upstairs, showered and quickly fell asleep . . . .

"Robert! Robert! Robert! What is wrong?"

He could hear Abby's frantic voice but it did not register. Robert could not understand why she was calling his name with so much anxiety and fear.

"Robert, talk to me. What's wrong? Why are you bleeding so much?"

Robert felt dizzy, groggy and out of touch, as if he were dreaming, but the word blood caught his attention. Still in a daze he attempted to mumble, "Call 911."

As Robert woke he was semi-blinded by the bright hospital room lights above. He turned his head to the side and saw Abby staring at him in the chair. She'd been crying.

"Hi," he said

"How are you feeling?" she replied.

"Confused." He looked back up at the ceiling now that his eyes had adjusted to the light.

"What's going on, Robert? I'm scared," Abby spoke softly.

"I really don't know. The nosebleed just started yesterday. I've been trying to figure it out myself. I've felt fine. A few headaches recently but that seemed normal. I really don't know. What did the doctors say?"

"They are bringing in a specialist. Your blood tests are not good. I will let the doctor talk to you about it. I'm just scared. "

"I'm sure I'm fine. Dry air and allergies, perhaps. That can cause nose bleeds."

Abby looked at him as a tear rolled down her cheek. "Not that much blood."

They sat in silence for several minutes. Suddenly the door opened and a doctor dressed in a long white lab coat came in.

"How are you, Mr. Nance? My name is Dr. Ambrose. Can you tell me when these nosebleeds started?"

Robert looked at Abby and then back at the doctor. "I was just telling my wife that the nosebleed just started yesterday. A few headaches lately but nothing out of the norm."

The doctor looked at Abby as well before talking to Robert again. "I've sent your blood work off to a specialist. I'm a bit concerned with our preliminary findings."

"What seems to be the problem, Doc? Until yesterday I felt fine. Just the headaches. Maybe a little more tired than usual."

"Robert, you're not the first person I have treated with these symptoms who came back from Vietnam."

"Ok. I understand that. But what's the issue? Why the concern?"

Dr. Ambrose began to walk towards the door. He then turned back. "Let's just wait on the specialist to give us his report. This is his area of expertise."

"Doc, what kind of specialist is he? What kind of doctor? Tell me," Robert spoke emphatically.

Dr. Ambrose looked at Abby again, who was looking at the floor. He walked back to the foot of the bed, never looking away from Robert. "He's an oncologist, Robert. We need answers."

As the doctor left the room Robert went within himself. He turned his head away from Abby's direction, looking out the third story window of the hospital. He felt as though wind was rushing past his ears causing a low roar. He just stared blankly at nothing in particular. There were no thoughts in his mind. It was blank. His mind was just a surreal abyss.

"Robert. Robert. Talk to me. I'm scared, Robert," spoke Abby as she broke the silence.

Slowly he turned towards Abby. "What, Dear?" he responded methodically, then paused. Robert put his arm around her, feeling her soft hair against his arm and then kissed the top of her head and whispered. "I'm scared too."

****

Abby had been staying at the hotel across the street for the last few days, leaving Stephen with her parents. There was simply too much uncertainty and a potential emotional battlefield to yet be crossed for their son to be there. She sat in the hotel restaurant sipping her coffee from the white cup she held in both hands. Quietly she reflected on the words Dr. Ambrose had said; "He's an oncologist, Robert."

She looked out the restaurant window in silence and watched the people go about their daily routine. She still had 55 minutes before the 10:00 a.m. scheduled meeting with the doctors, so she let herself drift away in thought. There really was not any way to prepare for such a meeting. No way to predict the news that the doctors would deliver. She realized that in an hour their lives would change in one way or another. She began to truly understand why Robert had stared out the window in silence seeming to be numb, because at this moment that was exactly how she was feeling too.

At 9:30 a.m. Abby paid the bill, walked across the street and into the hospital. Before she opened the door to Robert's room she breathed in deeply and mustered a brief smile of confidence and courage.

She then went in. "Hi, Honey. How are you feeling? Did you sleep alright?"

Robert looked unusually rested and almost enthusiastic. His break-fast dishes were empty and stacked neatly on the tray next to him. "I actually feel quite well. They are good people working here. They are treating me well."

She walked up to Robert, leaned down and gave him a kiss. "Are you ready for the doctor, Hun?"

"As ready as I can be."

Abby reached back and pulled up the chair next to the bed, sat and held Robert's hand. They looked at each other, both giving a quick nervous smile, and then sat in silence waiting for the doctor to arrive.

"Actually, Abby, that's not true," Robert spoke, cutting through the silence, "Yes, I am ready. I have been doing a lot of thinking in the last few days. Actually I have been thinking every single day out on the San Francisco Bay for months. Too much thinking at times. And when you think that much about a life issue like this, you can't help but visit with the Lord. Whether I found him or he found me last night I am not sure, but we definitely had a meeting of the minds you might say. I think I needed that more than I knew. I had just been fighting it for so damn long. I have resolved that this is out of my hands, Abby. It's in His hands. It's His will. Not mine. There is nothing I can do but pray and play the cards I'm dealt. I just know there are some major changes I need to make in my life no matter what the diagnosis is. It's time to stop dying and live. I haven't lived since I have been back from the war, and in doing so I have been slowly taking you and Stephen down with me. I can't do that anymore. Call it an epiphany, or words from above, but I need to change. I need to change my perspective on life, the war, and finally live. You asked me if I was ready for the doctor's diagnosis. The answer is yes. After that I will deal with the next phase of life, whatever that may be. Even if it is a bad report, the plan is to deal with it the best I can and live."

Robert looked at Abby intently then continued, "I made a vow with God to change when our child got hurt at Disneyland and never ful-filled it. I didn't do it. Instead I let my thoughts grip me again. But last night God and I solved things. I came to terms with Him, and I truly vow no matter what happens, from this point on you two have me."

Abby smiled at him, kissed his hand and rested her head on his arm. They then waited in silence.

Just after 10:00 a.m. Dr. Ambrose entered the room followed by a taller gentleman with grey hair. "Good morning, Robert. Abby. This is Dr. Macmillan. He is the oncologist I said I wanted involved in your case. He's going to share with you his findings."

Dr. Ambrose stepped aside letting Dr. Macmillan step forward to introduce himself. "Robert. Abby. I'm Dr. Michael Macmillan. Robert, how are you feeling?"

"Actually slept fairly well and had a great breakfast." The Robert got straight to the point, "So what are we dealing with, Doc?"

Dr. Macmillan looked at Abby and then into Robert's eyes. "Robert, many soldiers have been coming back from the war in Vietnam in a bad situation. We don't exactly know the cause but perhaps the napalm that was used over there is doing it. Breathing it in on the battlefield seems to be dramatically damaging. There's no easy way to say this but it's cancerous. I'm sorry, Robert. I'm truly sorry to bring you this news."

Robert's expression was neutral. Just a blank stare. Abby put her head on the bed and began to cry.

Robert then looked up at the doctors. "So what's next? What did you do to help the other soldiers recover?"

Dr. Macmillan, shaking his head, answered quietly. "I'm sorry, Robert."

Dr. Ambrose, realizing the hardship it was on his colleague stepped forward to take over the conversation. "Robert, we will exhaust every option we have. But Dr. Macmillan is being very honest. It doesn't look good. Rarely, if at all, are people recovering."

Robert looking perplexed then asked, "Then what am I looking at, Doc? 6 months? A year?"

"It varies, Robert. You're strong so let's say a year. Maybe more. Maybe less."

With that, the room became silent. The diagnosis had been delivered and the prognosis honestly shared. Not much more could be talked about. Robert put his left hand on Abby's head, gently stroked her hair, and then with his right hand he reached out to the doctors. "You're good men. Good doctors. Thorough and honest. I ask you one thing. Help me to feel good. Help me emotionally and physically to be comfortable in my final months. I will not pity myself. No more of that. I've been doing that for far too long. It's time to live. It's time to heal emotionally and live out my remaining days with my loving wife and my son that I barely know. If I need medicine or counseling then I will do it. I owe it to Abby and Stephen. My body may fail me and fall apart but emotionally I need to do everything in my power and yours to heal. To live. Until my final breath, I will show my wife and child the love they deserve. I don't exactly know how yet but please help me. Please help me. That's all I ask."

Both doctors, though surprised by Robert's direct and positive outlook, simply shook their heads in agreement before walking to the door. Abby was now looking up at Robert. Scared but proud. She smiled at him.

"I vow to make this a great year, Dear. I promise you that before I leave this world you will know I love you and Stephen with all my heart." Robert knew it may sound unbelievable coming from a man who had been so absent, but he was sincere in his vow to make this happen.

Abby sensed his sincerity and responded with, "I love you, Robert."

"I know. You always have," replied Robert, "Now it's my turn to show you that I love you. I promise." With that he smiled at her and winked.

CHAPTER 13

Keeping the vow he made to his wife upon his cancer diagnosis, Robert decided he must work on himself if he was truly going to be the best husband and father he could be in his remaining days. The doctors recommended a good counselor and Robert began going to counseling sessions one or two days a week. As he worked with the counselor, moving through his layers of grief and disappointment, it was decided that it would be good for Robert to go back to Vietnam. There he could meet and hopefully overcome the enemy, which wasn't really Vietnam, but rather the thoughts residing in his mind. When discussing this with Abby, Robert explained how much he would like to take Stephen with him on the trip so the two of them could have this experience together. Although initially reluctant, Abby trusted the bigger picture and the importance of the father/son bond, so agreed wholeheartedly.

The days leading up to their trip to Vietnam were emotionally perplexing for Robert. His new sense of value in each day of the rest of his short time remaining on Earth opened up some very deep emotional channels that he had suppressed for quite some time. Once guarded, but now surfacing, he found himself happy, excited, scared, depressed, heart broken and confused all at the same time. His emotions were like whirlpools in a swift ocean current shifting about him and constantly pulling and pushing at him in an unrelenting fashion. He and Abby had made a pact that no matter how hard it was to talk about or difficult for her to hear, let alone understand, they would fight his demons together. Opening up and sharing his thoughts and emotions with anyone was absolutely unnatural, but with the help of the family counselor that each of them saw, both individually and as a family, it already had slowly begun to cultivate more trust and understanding. Robert knew the trip to Vietnam was extremely vital for his emotional recovery, but his new connection with his incredibly compassionate and supporting wife also brought on sadness regarding the upcoming time away from her. He pondered how he would deal with the native demons lurking in Vietnam when she was not there to listen to his fears. How would he react and cope with the emotional enemy on their own playing field? Would he have a clear enough perception of reality to distinguish the horrible memories of the past from the reality of the present? Would he be pulled into the trenches of past, powerful nightmares or would he find triumph in the battle with his new-found resolve from the understanding and unconditional love he recognized Abby and Stephen gave him? He was not alone, as he had often thought since the war. He had a dedicated and loving wife and son, so deserving of his new and chosen battle with the past. He owed it to them.

Investing as much time as possible in his family in the short time he had was his ultimate goal. Some days he, Abby and Stephen would go to the park and walk the mile and a half paved path around the lake. Robert and Abby would walk slowly, talking, while Stephen ran about within their view. On other days they would sit on the wooden bleachers at the neighborhood baseball park where Stephen played Little League. His team would not make it to the playoffs, but Stephen reveled in the fact that his father was there and actually cheering for him. It was a great foundation for father and son bonding which was long overdue.

The day came when he and Stephen were going to leave for Vietnam. Abby took them to the airport. They arrived early so that they could have time for a relaxing breakfast together before the flight. They talked as they ate, and once they had finished Robert held Abby's hand from across the table. Stephen had immersed himself in a paperback mystery book he had purchased for the long hours on the plane. Robert and Abby smiled at each other as they watched Stephen quietly turn the pages.

The time came when they had to walk towards the gate. He and Abby stayed hand in hand until it was time to load the plane. Robert turned and looked into her eyes. He was mesmerized by their beautiful shade of brown.

As Robert leaned in to hold her close he began to speak, "Honey, so much is going through my mind. How each day is precious, and now I am getting on a plane and leaving you for two weeks. I realize the importance of this trip for myself and for Stephen and I together. But these two weeks I can never get back. I'm taking the short time we have left together away from you."

"Shhhh," She put one finger on his lips, "I will be fine. I am processing a lot too. This has been such a whirlwind the last few weeks. I believe this is valuable time for us as we work through everything in the months ahead. Without these two weeks apart, I would always be with the man minus what he left over there. Go, Dear. Do what you need to do to be at peace. I will be in your heart while you're there and right here when you return in two weeks. I love you more than anything in this world, Robert. I felt all the pain you were feeling because I understood what you were going through. Your pain was my pain because our hearts are connected. I married you, Robert, and I will always be here for you."

Robert could feel the tears begin to form in his eyes. "I was such a lucky man to have married you, Abby. So very lucky."

Abby leaned in and hugged him tightly. "Robert, I was the lucky one to marry that wonderful man years ago. He was the greatest man I have ever met. I counted my lucky stars and thank God for blessing me with that man years ago. I want that man back, Robert. I want that man back in my life more than anything. Please find him. Please find him and bring him back to me."

Robert held his wife tightly, whispering, "I promise you that I will find him. I will find him and bring him home to you."

Robert moved aside and let Abby and Stephen say their goodbyes. He could see her tears as she hugged her little boy. The two of them had never been apart, so it was especially emotional for Abby. As their embrace came to an end, Abby whispered a couple of words to Stephen, and he headed towards his father. Abby wiped her tears, smiled and threw a kiss Robert's way. He smiled back at her, and gave her a wink before slowly turning and heading towards the doorway.

****

Once on the plane they put the luggage in the overhead compartments and took their seats. Since it was the first time Stephen had ever flown, Robert had instructed him to sit next to the window. The stewardesses went through their usual preflight routine then belted themselves tightly in for takeoff. The plane sat at the end of the runway for about five minutes, getting final instructions from the control tower and going through their standard procedural flight protocol. Finally, the engines roared, shaking the steal beast as it slowly moved down the asphalt with increasing speed. At the last moment, the nose came off the ground and headed steeply skyward. Stephen's nose was pinned in amazement against the window, taking in the scenery outside that was slowly getting smaller and smaller. After a few minutes heading east over land, the airliner started its steep, but gradual, turn to the left in order to head back to the west, towards the vast expanse of blue ocean leading them to the other side of the world. Within the hour, food and beverages were served, and the passengers began to set up camp for the hours of travel that lay before them. Stephen pulled his book out and started to read. Robert just watched him. He was captivated by this boy. How had he subtly neglected him for so long? How could he? Then he thought of Stephen's character: It was humble, quiet, considerate, liked by all, great in school, he excelled in sports, and was even responsible enough to have a couple of weekend lawn mowing jobs, providing some extra spending cash so as to not be a burden on him and Abby. Robert was astounded, proud and a bit ashamed as he had started owning his shortcomings as a father to such a wonderful young man.

While Robert was in thought, a slight smile came across his face. At that moment, as if on cue and with God's perfect timing, Stephen put his book in the storage space of the seat in front of him and looked at his father. "Dad, can I ask you something?"

"Of course you can," Robert responded.

"The counselor and I have been talking and I realize there was a lot that happened in the war that you had difficulties with. What was that like? What was so difficult?"

Robert took a few seconds to gather his thoughts, then responded, "That's a good question, Stephen. I've actually thought about that a lot. I wasn't going to share all this with you but the counselor told me that you need to know so you understand what I am going through, that the honest truth would help heal us and in time bond us by going through it together. I will try to answer it the best I can, Son. I'm just starting to answer some of those questions myself. It's still really confusing, to be honest. Before arriving in Vietnam I thought I was a tough man. I was always the captain in sports. The leader. Very popular. So I believed that if you worked hard, were responsible and cared for and encouraged others, then everything would be fine. There were rules in life. Obey the rules and all is good. There was a sense of structure and organization. That was my true philosophy on life. But when I went to Vietnam there was no structure, the rules constantly changed, and doing the right thing didn't mean you or your buddy would not be killed at any moment. Initially I just ignored it. Tried to simply cope with it. But I couldn't always ignore it, and coping with chaos only built abnormal emotional walls that, once in place, are very hard to tear down. The next day the rules sometimes totally changed. Whether by the enemy, or the rules set forth by your commander, or even your own government. Eventually we all just did what we needed to do to survive the battle. But there was no guarantee. We may have done everything right, only to step on a land mine or be fatally introduced to a sniper's bullet. Nothing was normal. The buddies who I started out with began to disappear. New enlisted men showed up, and before I could learn their names, they were gone as well. It may have been a day or week, but eventually they were gone. In time, we chose not to learn their names anymore. Sometimes we just called them 'that guy from Jersey' or 'the big guy from Texas'. It was emotionally easier that way when they didn't return from the battlefield. I know that sounds confusing, son, and it is. There is no question about it. It's not normal thinking. That's the issue. There is no "normal" in war, just survival. You soon lose your bearing. You float so far from what you knew to be normal that perhaps you never quite find it again. That is what is so important about the time I have left. To find "normal" again. Hopefully this trip, further counseling, and us talking like this will help our family find normal together."

"Dad, I don't understand everything you said, but I want you to know I will try."

"Son, the more I talk to you and listen to you, the more I am amazed at who you are. Who you have become. Despite everything I put you through there is such an amazing person inside of you. I am so proud of who you are. Just please know that I am still trying to figure it all out. I drifted so far from where I need to be. But I will do anything I need to and share anything I need to in order for you to understand me more. I want you to know that I think you are incredible and I love you so very much. I think this trip is exactly what we need."

Stephen looked up at him and smiled, then laid his head on Robert's left side. Robert lowered his arm down across Stephen's small body, feeling the growing bond developing between a father and a son. Within moments both were fast asleep.

After a brief stop in Honolulu, Hawaii for fuel, their long journey continued. The further they headed southeast towards Asia, the more tropical turquoise blue the water became. Small deserted islands surrounded by atolls would pop up out of the water from time to time giving one a chance to get a clearer understanding of the immense size of the ocean below. In the sky around the plane were towering, white, puffy cumulus clouds that seemed to be suspended from the heavens above. Robert took in the view outside that ever so slowly changed. Stephen was still sleeping in the window seat. Robert took his focus off of the scenery outside the window and began to admire and be intrigued by the features of his son. He noted his dark brown hair groomed neatly above his ears and his eyes that randomly moved behind his eyelids. He watched his perfect nose that flared slightly with each breath and his beautiful, tanned complexion that was so much like his mom's at the end of each summer.

Robert thought to himself that though his son was twelve years old, this was the first time he had ever really embraced the essence of his son's true appearance. It was the first time he had grasped the magnitude of the perfection in this boy that he and Abby had created. He stared at Stephen in wonder and amazement causing a smile to spontaneously come to his face while deep inner emotions brought moisture to his eyes.

Robert quietly whispered to himself, "Son, I know I have neglected you over the years. I know there is nothing I can do to get those years back. All I can do is promise that with each day that I'm still on this Earth I will give you all of me. And after I am gone, well, I don't know how that all works, but if there is any chance that I can lead, guide and protect you, then I will do it; through a person's direct words, someone's subtle wink, or a warm wind in your face . . . that will be me. I will always be with you, Son. I will do whatever I can to look after you and your mom. I promise you that if there is a way, you will know I'm there with you. I promise. I love you, Son. I truly do."

Several more hours passed, and then the lush green trees of a mountain range in Vietnam came into view. Compared to California, the area below looked desolate. Mountains, hills and rivers, with an occasional art-like maze of rice paddy fields strewn about, became visible as the plane slowly began its decent into what appeared to be the depths of the vast forest, until seemingly out of nowhere, an airfield appeared. The landing was fairly routine with the obvious consideration taken into account for the low quality of the airstrip itself. Once slowed, the airliner exited the main runway and slowly cruised down the taxiway. Stephen looked at his father, his head bouncing up and down, as the wheels rolled over the bumpy terrain causing the plane to creak and moan. Finally it came to a halt. The high-pitched scream of giant turbines quickly fell silent as the locals outside approached the airliner with a sense of purpose. Robert and Stephen got their belongings out of the overhead compartments and proceeded toward the front door. The closer they got to the entrance, the more warm and humid it became. When they walked through the door, the bright sun practically blinded them. They stopped and let their eyes adjust before slowly descending the stairs that had been rolled up along the side of the plane. The asphalt radiated the heat, moisture and gas fumes up to them as they walked to the terminal, which was one long, two-story, greyish brick building that looked more like a battered hotel. The baggage claim on the right end was enclosed by glass with an overhang that jetted out about 12 feet. From the top of the building about a dozen poles with various colored flags reached towards the sky.

Once inside, many people scurried about. There had not been but about a half-dozen passengers that got off with them. Many on the plane were headed to other far-off destinations. The locals, though, were ready to help find each passenger's bags, carry the bags through customs, and get them into a waiting taxi. Robert helped the taxi driver load the luggage on the roof as Stephen found a seat in the back of the dirty and tattered jeep. Robert and the driver both got in the front seats of the vehicle. As the driver quickly revved through the gears, they picked up speed and bounced down the pothole filled road. Tall green trees and lush foliage whisked past them as they made the 40-minute trip into the small, coastal village. An occasional person in a wagon pulled by a beleaguered water buffalo, a dilapidated shack, or an old weather-beaten individual sitting near a tiny fruit stand was about all there was on the desolate road. Although, once in a while, a truck carrying everything from chickens to vegetables would ramble down the road directly towards them, honking its horn only to miss them by inches at the last second.

Stephen tugged on his dad's shirt to get his attention. He had to yell over the whining of the engine, rattling of the jeep and the noise of the wind rushing by. "Dad, is this what it looked like when you were here before?"

Robert shook his head "yes," then replied, "I was probably a couple hundred miles from here. But a lot of the places here have these same thick bushes and trees. That's what made it so tough to fight here. You could never see the enemy until they were right on you."

Robert took in everything as they moved along – the different types of trees, the colors, and the various fragrances that hung in the air – and he admired the sunlight that shined through the canopy of trees above. These were things during the war that he really never noticed. Now, with the freedom to embrace the world around him, everything seemed amplified in his mind. He closed his eyes and smiled for a moment.

Finally they slowed, as the asphalt became dirt, causing dust to billow out from behind the vehicle. They passed small shops on each side of the road. Some people walked about, while others sat near their businesses. At the far end of the village, the jeep swerved to park in front of an old hotel. The driver jumped out and started taking the luggage down from above. He carried the bags over to the front of the open lobby area.

Robert and Stephen slowly disembarked, shaking off the bumpy ride they had just endured, and walked towards the lobby. "Dad, I feel like I am on another planet. Everything is so old fashioned and dirty," remarked Stephen.

Robert shook his head in agreement and replied, "It definitely isn't California is it?"

In his wallet Robert found some money that was well over the amount necessary for a tip and gave it to the overly polite driver. He bowed several times and then jumped back into his Jeep. A couple more bows from the driver's seat and off he went in a cloud of dust.

CHAPTER 14

Robert and Stephen entered the quaint villa where they would stay for the next two weeks. It was very small but adequate, since they would be on the go much of the time. The room's carpet was olive green which somewhat matched the top of the table near the small open kitchen area to the back right. There were yellowish brown drapes covering the only window by the door. Two twin beds with a small four-legged coffee table were on the left wall. Beyond the kitchen was a closet with a built-in dresser on the right and a tiny bathroom on the left. Unlike spacious motel rooms in the states, here they had used an area about two-thirds of that to place only the vital necessities.

"Well, Son, you choose your bed," said Robert wearily; tired from the long journey and the cancer his body was fighting.

Once the beds were claimed, Robert tossed his bag on the floor next to his. Stephen left his by the door and sprawled out on the nearest bed.

"Dad, this bed is like sleeping on the floor. It is so hard."

"Better get used to roughing it. We are in an entirely different world for a while." Robert leaned down and removed his shoes. " How about we take a rest for a couple of hours then clean up and explore this little village? By that time it will be about four o'clock. We can walk around for a couple of hours before we eat. Might be safer to buy some bottled water and canned food that we can cook here. We don't want to get sick." Robert thought the rest break would do him good. Though there was much to see and explore, he had promised Abby he would pace himself and do what he could to keep his strength up despite travelling.

"Do they have restaurants here, Dad?"

"I am sure they do but we might need to talk to some people for the first couple of days and survey the situation to see what are the best restaurants. Better get used to the fact that there are no McDonald's here, Son. I promise that we will get you a Big Mac as soon as we get back home to the states."

"Why would we get sick anyway, Dad?"

"They just have different microorganisms here than we have in the states. Ones that our bodies are not used to."

"Microorganisms. What's that?"

"Think of them as very tiny bugs that you can't see. They are everywhere, Stephen. They are on the bed, in the water, on the food and on your skin. It is just that our body knows how to deal with them. We don't get sick because our body has defense mechanisms to protect us. It is called becoming immune to something. The problem is our body is not immune to the organisms in this part of the world because they are new to us."

"But, Dad, you have been here before. They are not new to you."

"True, Stephen. Very good thinking. The thing is, it was a long time ago and there are new types or organisms now that I have never experienced. Son, let me tell you something. When I first came over here for the war, I got sick a lot. Everyone did. It was almost a rite of passage."

"What's 'right of passage' mean, Dad?"

"Inquisitive today aren't you, Son? A rite of passage would be like a ceremony, a traditional act or task you perform at certain stages in your life." Robert paused to ponder an example, and then continued, "Like when you graduated from kindergarten to the first grade. You had that ceremony at the school and Mommy had a party at home for you. It is kind of like that."

"So it would be like when I first rode my bike by myself?" blurted Stephen as it clicked in his head what his father way saying.

"Stephen, I am impressed. Exactly like that," Robert smiled with a new sense of pride.

Since the war, Robert had kept his distance from people - even his son - and though he provided for and loved Stephen, he had rarely had an intellectual conversation with him. Usually his interaction was brief and direct, such as an instruction for chores but their conversation had never ventured towards mature dialog. He was starting to see his son, however, as an individual . . . a person with wonder, curiosity and opinions. Valid opinions. In the last twenty-four hours Robert had begun to see his son from a different perspective. He now began to see him as a beautiful child possessing his and Abby's physical features, as well as a boy with whom he could actually talk with and carry on a stimulating conversation. Already, he could see that this week was going to be very beneficial in so many ways.

****

Robert and Stephen had both slept for over two hours. If it had not been for the sound of a large truck passing in front of their room they might have remained in slumber longer. Once awake though, they each took showers with lukewarm water and dressed in shorts and tee shirts. Stephen wore a new tee shirt his mom bought him just for the trip. He had also brought his San Francisco Giants hat, so he put it on before they exited the room.

There were key tasks Robert thought necessary for this evening, including figuring out where to buy canned goods and water, finding someone who might know about tours around the countryside, and locating the beach so Stephen could have some enjoyable time in the water while they were there. Yes, this trip had a big purpose for Robert, but he also wanted it to be a fun experience for his son. He felt this desire heighten even more now that he had begun to feel his own protective walls lowering. He wanted to know this young person who was here with him. He wanted to grow closer to his son, and he wanted to make up for the years he had emotionally neglected such a special boy. Stephen was his son, his only son, and he wanted him to know his dad, as well. Robert desired to build a friendship between them on this trip that would last long after he was taken by this disease. He wanted Stephen to know how much he loved him. He knew there was only a little time now, but if he planted the seed maybe it would grow even stronger after he was gone. Robert would do anything to help Stephen understand love in the short time he had left. If not now, he pledged to himself he would find a way after his passing. This boy deserved to know the essence of love, and he had denied him genuine, fatherly love for far too long.

The motel was on a well-traveled asphalt road that turned to dirt just about three blocks towards the village center. Within a couple of minutes their feet were churning up light dust as they walked. As they neared the line of small shops, there were several young children running about, chasing each other, and laughing joyfully. The first shop had a barred entrance that was slid open for business. It was small and cluttered with clothing. Next was a gift shop filled with lots of native artifacts, hats, tee shirts, cards and jewelry. Finally they came to a larger area that held a grocery store. There were three aisles stocked with various canned foods, bagged goods and medicine. The wall to the right held dairy products, while the fruits and vegetables were displayed on the left. Robert fetched a shopping cart and they began their first mission of shopping for food and beverages for their stay. After purchasing the merchandise and exchanging some American money for local currency, they stepped outside with bags in hand.

"Dad, can we go in that gift shop and find something for mom?" asked Stephen, pointing towards the shop.

"Let's walk this stuff back to the motel and then come back. We can do some more exploring then, Stephen."

"Ok. Can we go to the beach too?"

"Absolutely, Son. That sounds like a wonderful way to end the day. Maybe we will find a nice card for Mom and we can write in it by the water."

"Cool," replied Stephen as he moved quickly, thinking ahead to the beach.

" I will make us some sandwiches to take, too. How does that sound?"

"Perfect, Dad. I want to walk in the water. Is that ok?"

"When we find a beach you can do whatever you desire."

They distributed the food in the proper cupboards, refrigerator and freezer. Then they made sandwiches and grabbed some chips, cookies, water and soda, placing them in a carrying bag, and headed back into the village.

When they entered the gift shop they noticed that they were the only ones there. They meandered around, looking at all the items, when all of a sudden a voice came from a doorway near the cash register.

"You are American, yes?" a man said in a heavy Vietnamese accent.

"Yes we are," Robert replied.

"Where are you from?"

"California. Near San Francisco."

"Ahhh, I see. I have brother in Los Angeles. He and his wife leave here right after war. Very lucky. Not many so lucky."

"Yes, I understand. I was in the war here. That is kind of why my son and I are here now. I need to sort some feelings out, I guess," said Robert.

"Lot of Americans come here to do the same thing. Visit and talk about past. Many tears. I think it was hard for Americans, yes?"

"Very hard. I lost many friends here in the war and many of us went home to a country angry with the soldiers who fought it. It was a very troubling time for America and especially the soldiers."

"What will you do when you are here?"

"I want to look around the countryside and see what life is like for people here. I hope to find some peace with all this. To see it wasn't all a waste of time and lives."

"May I share something with you?"

"Yes, of course."

"I think you find this trip will be beneficial for you. Life here is good now. No hostility, no anger, no regrets and no bad feelings for Americans. We simple people here. We move on. Put the past behind. Nothing we can do with the past."

"That is a great attitude. By the way, what is your name?"

"My name is Pae Nguyen," the gentleman replied. He grabbed his two canes and stepped forward from behind the cash register, Robert noting that he was missing one leg at the knee.

"My name is Robert Nance," he smiled sincerely. They both shook hands. "And this is my son, Stephen."

Stephen put down a comic book and looked over. "Hello."

"Hello, Stephen," Pae replied.

Pae could see Stephen looking at his missing limb. He turned to Robert again. "I lose leg in war. I was soldier too. Fought along side Americans against Vietcong. My friend step on land mine. He lose his life. I lose my leg. They say I am lucky one. I not sure at time but now know, yes, I am lucky one. I have wife and beautiful daughter. I lucky man. Very, very lucky man."

"Dad, look at these necklaces. They are cool," Stephen interrupted.

"Yes, they are, Son."

"My wife makes those. She and my daughter collect the small, white shells on beach and make jewelry."

"They are very beautiful. Pae, do you know how we could find a tour that would get us around to see the sights here?" Robert asked.

"No tour necessary. I think I help you with your journey. I need to take a break from work anyway. My wife watch store for a few days. I think I understand what you need. I am happy to help. I have vehicle."

"But how can you drive with no leg, Sir?" Stephen asked.

"I do not drive. I let your father drive. I just am tour guide."

"Can we pay you, Pae?"

"Is up to you. I want to help you but money is good too."

We are here for a week. How about we give you $30.00 to pay for gas and your time?"

"Is more than fair. When do you want to start? I will need to have my wife bring the vehicle to the store. We can leave from here when you want."

"How about tomorrow around 10 o'clock?"

"Ok. I have vehicle here in morning. We go then."

"Sounds like a plan. Ten it is."

Robert and Stephen found a card to send home to Abby. After purchasing it they headed to a beach that Pae recommended. It took about 15 minutes to walk there. It was just less than a half-mile east of the village. When they got near the beach, trees and bushes blocked their view of the water ahead. However, once past the foliage, there was a sandy clearing, about seventy-five feet long, that disappeared into the deep blue of the ocean. Stephen briskly ran to the water's edge and stopped abruptly just before he would have gotten his shoes wet. He then ran back laughing and completed the forward motion towards the water again. Robert slowly walked up towards him taking in the view. A hundred feet out from shore a man in a small boat was casting a net into the water and slowly pulling it in. Robert sat down in the sand just up from the water and watched his son, who had now removed his shoes and socks, and was venturing into the water up to his knees.

"Dad, it is so warm. Almost like a pool back home," said Stephen.

"Looks like you have the pool all to yourself, Son," replied Robert.

"Can I swim, Dad?'

"Yes, just stay close to shore."

"Come in with me, Dad."

Robert thought for a moment. His first inclination was to say "no" or "maybe later" but his spirit led him to a different decision. He pulled off his shirt and kicked off his shoes, then ran furiously towards the water, yelling the entire way. As he hit the water, spray went everywhere, splashing Stephen, who was now laughing out loud. Stephen had never seen his father be so spontaneous.

When his father finally came up to the surface from diving into the ocean, he let out a holler. "Yeah. This is awesome!"

Stephen swam towards his father. When he got near him, Robert grabbed him and tossed him up in the air. Stephen hit the water with a big splash and came up to the surface laughing hysterically. If a spectator was looking from a distance, the view he or she would have seen was that of a father and son playing together, enjoying each other's company immensely, and frolicking about in love and laughter. It was a beautiful sight. It was a milestone in a father and son's life that warmed both hearts. After about fifteen minutes of this joyful play, they headed for the shore. They dried off in the late afternoon sun and quietly ate the food they had brought with them.

Stephen sat in the sand for a minute with a pondering look on his face then asked, "Dad, what did that man mean when he said that it was hard for Americans. That there were lots of tears?"

"It was a tough time for us over here fighting a war. As I told you on the plane, we were just kids really not much older than you. We saw a lot of people die. We saw a lot of horrible things. People who lost limbs like Pae did. It really scared a lot of us and changed us forever."

"Were you scared, Dad?"

Pausing for a minute then choosing his words carefully, Robert replied, "Son, I have been scared for years. I was scared when I was here fighting the war. Scared to die, scared to see my friends die, and scared that I would never see your mom again. I was scared when I got back home too. Stephen, that is part of the reason we are here now. I need to resolve some things so I am not scared anymore."

"What are you scared of at home?"

"That is hard to answer, Stephen," Robert paused again to think about his words so they would come out properly, then continued, "I think our mind is an incredible thing. We remember wonderful things like my first date with your mom, the day I married her, and when I found out you were born. Those are special moments that bring my life joy. I feel happiness when I think of those times. But the mind also remembers the horrible things too. If we don't let go of those horrible thoughts then the happy and wonderful times seem to be forgotten in a way. I was scared of what I saw and experienced here and I let that take away my joy about wonderful things at home. That was very wrong, Son. Very wrong. Unfortunately you and your mother paid for my pain. I am truly sorry about that "

"But, Dad, I still don't understand what are you scared of at home?" asked Stephen even more inquisitively than before.

Silence fell over them as Robert processed the significance of the question. He thought about it and the answer became clear. It was like an epiphany, one of those moments in life when the simplest of questions is the key to finding life's answers. Nothing, he thought. He had nothing to fear at home. He had a wife that had always adored him, a son that had always been kind and considerate, and parents as well as in-laws that had always supported him. There was nothing he ever had to be scared of at home.

Robert humbly and intently looked at his son. Slowly shaking his head and smiling he replied, "Nothing, Son. Absolutely nothing." With this reply a cleansing energy penetrated Robert's soul, and he felt a burden that had been on him for years begin to break away and disperse.

CHAPTER 15

The next morning the two ate a small breakfast, grabbed their gear for the trip, and headed to the gift shop to meet up with Pae. On the walk there, Stephen was fairly quiet but Robert could tell the wheels in his brain were spinning and that he had more questions.

They arrived about 15 minutes early, placing their one combined travel bag on the small porch of Pae's gift shop. They sat on the edge of the porch and talked as had started to become so natural between them now. About ten feet in front of them was a long log sunken into the dirt road from years of past storms. This was what the front tires of vehicles rested upon as they parked.

"Dad, is it hard?" asked Stephen.

"Is what hard, Son?"

"Being here? I mean. It seems so peaceful. The sunny blue skies, the ocean, people fishing, kids playing. And Pae is so nice. All the people seem so kind. But I know you say that the pain is inside you."

Robert let out a long sigh while exhaling. "I am beginning to see your point, Son. I understand why our time here is so valuable because I am seeing what you are seeing as well. The thing is, so much happened here. I was only about six years older than you are now. We were all kids. But back then I thought I was a man. Or maybe I was forced to think I was a man by society and by our government. We were asked to do things young kids should never have to do. Now, though, I want to breath in this new feeling of peacefulness and kindness that is all around us. It gives me hope and belief in the inherent kindness within people." Robert looked around at the surroundings and then slowly back at

Stephen. "This is such perfect medicine for my soul, Son." With that, he gave him a wink then looked back around the village and repeated, "Just perfect."

The dark green pickup truck pulled up in front of the store precisely at ten o'clock, followed by a plume of dry, light dust. The truck was over a decade old, left from the war, but in immaculate condition. Rarely driven and stored in their shed because Pae had no real reason to leave the village, the odometer read less than four thousand miles. Once the truck stopped, a small Vietnamese woman stepped down from the drivers' side door, safely placing her feet onto the running board before slowly lowering herself to the earth. She nodded with a sweet smile as she scurried around the front of the vehicle and opened the passenger door. A cane appeared first, followed by Pae's one and only leg. She helped him down and he gave her a quick but sincere nod.

"Hello, Pae," Robert called out.

Slowly Pae turned towards them with one hand on his cane and the other on the truck. "Good morning my American friends. Are you two ready for our journey?" He then grabbed his second cane from the floor of the vehicle.

Robert looked down at Stephen who looked back at him shaking his head up and down.

"Yes, I think we are, Pae." Robert answered.

"Good. My wife packed everything for me last night. I think she may be trying to get rid of me." He smiled first at Robert, then at his wife.

Pae was not only a compassionate man, but he was also very wise. He sensed Robert's internal struggle with the war and the emotional pain that had lasted over a decade, wounding his spirit. He had seen it in other American men since the end of the war. It was much like an epidemic that eventually needs to be cured. Returning to Vietnam was only part of the remedy. Pae also understood it all too well himself, having been crippled physically by the war. Having to adjust to life with a handicap, and being forced to deal with what would be needed daily for the rest of his life was hard. However, with the constant love of his wife and the birth of their daughter, Sophia, he had been able to let go of the past in order to preserve the future. He wanted this for others still struggling with the events and side effects of the war.

"Sounds great." Robert responded.

Pae then turned slightly back towards his wife. "This is my wife, best friend and soul mate, Linn Sue," he said with a sense of pride and adoration.

Robert and Stephen had already approached the couple. Robert first shook her hand and said hello with Stephen following his father's lead. Robert felt he had seen her before, but being in the country during the war, a lot of the locals began to look a bit similar.

"My dear, these are my new American friends, Robert Nance and his son, Stephen. They are from California. San Francisco area. Several hours north of where my brother lives in Los Angeles."

Linn Sue bowed, as is the custom, and then said, "Welcome to our country, our village and our home. We are honored to have your acquaintance. My husband says you here during war times, yes?"

"Yes," Robert replied, "I was here. Unfortunately when I went back to America I realized that I had left a part of myself here. I owe it to my wife and son to find that part and take it back home."

Linn Sue nodded her head in agreement. "Understand. We see this often since end of war. More often in last few years. Perhaps it took time for some to heal before return."

"Yes, I totally agree. But for me, I needed to come here to help me heal. So many things happened here but also when we returned home. It was like we were despised and shunned in our own country. It was hardly a place to find comfort for healing. But now we are here and we are so happy that we found your husband who has shown so much hospitality and kindness towards us. I truly feel that is was fate that had us meet. I am going to feel so much safer with a person who knows the area, people and customs."

"It is great for my husband too." Linn Sue looked at Pae. "He needs to get out more often. With the store, my work at the medical clinic, and our daughter we simply don't go places anymore. This little trip will be good for him."

"Where is your daughter now?" Robert asked inquisitively.

Pae looked back inside the truck causing everyone to glance that way. Peering over the dashboard was a tiny little head. "Sophia. Sophia, Dear, don't be shy. Come out and meet our new American friends."

Sophia, a precious seven-year-old, slowly scooted out of the truck and hid behind her father. She held a blanket tightly under her arm with the lower quarter of a stuffed toy sticking out from under it.

"Hey, Sophia," Robert said encouragingly, "I'm Robert and this is my son. Stephen. It is very nice to meet you."

Stephen noticed the shells around her neck. "Hi, Sophia. That is a beautiful necklace," he said politely, trying to engage the little girl, "I saw those in your dad's store. Did you make that?"

Sophia sheepishly nodded her head "yes" but did not speak. She just stayed close to her father.

"Well, let's go next door to get supplies and food at the market," Pae instructed. "They have everything we will need there."

"Sophia, give your daddy a hug. We will watch the store while he is on his trip. Robert and Stephen, it is so nice to have met you. Enjoy your time in our country." With that, Linn Sue started towards the store entrance.

"Our sincere pleasure," Robert replied, "We will make sure your husband stays safe."

Sophia hugged her father and, with blanket and stuffed toy in hand, skipped to her mom's side.

"Bye, Sophia," Stephen blurted out unexpectedly.

Sophia looked back cautiously, and then ran into the store where she set down her belongings. Within seconds, she returned with an out-stretched arm, dropping a necklace made of the small, white shells into Stephen's hand. With that she smiled, gave him a quick wave, and ran back to her mother.

CHAPTER 16

Robert drove the pickup northwest, away from the coast and the beauty of the seaside village, over hills, through valleys and lush green dense jungle. The journey was treacherous and the ride bumpy.

"You sure you know where we're going? "he asked Pae with a smirk and a wink.

Pae looked back with a smile. "Not long now. Maybe one or two more hours. We stop in 15 minutes by river. We rest and eat there. Very pleasant."

With two hours behind them and one or so to go, they stopped the truck next to a river that was about a hundred feet wide and flowed very slowly. They got out, laid out a blanket and sat down to enjoy lunch. Once the food was divvied up and they began to savor their meal, no one spoke. Everyone seemed content to take in the view and listen to the birds overhead.

After some time, Pae looked over to see Robert staring at the river as if recalling past memories. It was then that he broke the silence. "Does it look familiar?" asked Pae.

Robert let out a long breath of air that he had not even realized he was holding. Without looking away from the water in front of him he replied, "How did you know?"

"I see in your face. Like a silent movie playing in your soul. Your face shares your story without saying any words."

Stephen, who was sitting between them, ate his peanut butter and jam sandwich and listened intently.

"Pae, we were just kids here in your country. I may have been right here in the same river. They all look very similar. I recall so vividly one day in particular. Perhaps this very spot. I don't know. We were ambushed as we crossed the river from a forest just like that. I lost most of my men on that mission that day. Why me? Why did I survive? And the man next to me not? Why did I go back to the mess hall for dinner and he get put in a box, draped with a flag and sent home to his family in mourning? This confuses me. I just don't understand why, and I can't find the answer."

Pae looked directly at Robert and, almost like reading a prepared script, began to share, "Answers no need to come swiftly. Answer comes at appropriate time. I lose my leg in war. I am sad. I am depressed. Some anger too. But my answer come later with my daughter. She gives me purpose. Maybe her life will become bigger than me. Maybe she change the world. Maybe I am just small part of the bigger plan. Maybe not even her but answer come with her future children. I do not believe I need all the answers. Just be part of bigger picture. Bigger plan. I may be just small part in story. Maybe your boy. Maybe Stephen figures it out. You no need to figure it out all now. You think back to wartime. Wartime is confusing time for all. War political. About fear and power. Communism and democracy. You just from country with different culture, different government and different beliefs. Is ok to have differences. Countries here think different. Is ok we think different. I believe America in war for right reason. Protect people. Protect South Vietnamese. We thank you. We appreciate. Things go wrong in wartime. Far from perfect. Without America - without you - maybe I lose more than my leg; maybe I lose my family, maybe I have no wife and no love. Maybe wife gone. Then no beautiful daughter. And maybe she is the reason. Maybe she is the purpose for something amazing in the future. Maybe she is answer. Your answer is there, Robert. Your son. My daughter. You rest your soul, Robert. You enjoy special life you have now. Look at son. Let him find answer. All you need to do is love him, love wife, love people. Have compassion, empathy. Be good man. That is your answer for now. You only need that answer now. Maybe Stephen will find answer in time. Just love, Robert." With that Pae turned his head and looked out over the river. "You love now, Robert. You rest soul, Robert. That is your answer for now."

The gentle words Pae said, though caring and compassionate, hit like a ton of bricks penetrating Robert's soul from deep within. It was as if there was an epiphany of peace surging through him. Like the warm water of the tide coming over him, he let his senses embrace this peace thoroughly. He didn't try to understand what was happening; just that something was taking place.

Stephen looked at Pae and then his father, who were both transfixed on the slow, flowing water in front of them. Pae's face was still, calm and tranquil. When he looked at his father's he saw a small smile of contentment begin to form. Then he saw something he'd never seen before from his father. It was a tear. A single tear slid down his cheek and then dropped onto the blanket.

As the tear dropped it was as if a huge burden was lifted from his father. Stephen watched him rise up and removed his shirt. Then he slowly slid off his shoes. Now only in his khaki shorts, he walked towards the river. Once he got to the water's edge, Robert turned around facing them, raised his hands out to his side, and shouted, "It is time now. Thank you, Lord." With that he turned and dove into the river. When he came up from his baptism, he let out a joyful scream. "What are you waiting for, Son?" he yelled to Stephen, "The water is incredible."

Stephen leaped to his feet, ripped off his shoes, and without even taking off his shirt, he raced down the sandy shore, dove in and came up into his father's loving arms. Both screamed in zeal as they frolicked in the water.

Pae sat and watched. His calm, peaceful demeanor changed to laughter and joyful exhilaration. He felt fulfilled, as he watched the father and son playfully enjoy this moment together. He delighted in changing Robert's memories of the past into new ones of joy, peace and love. A new story was being written on the pages of this man's soul; a story that in time would bring with it all the beautiful answers he ever needed.

The rest of the trip continued the healing of Robert's soul, which Pae had been such an instrumental catalyst for. From one village to the next, Pae introduced them to relatives and friends who treated them with dignity, honor and respect. They shared how appreciative they were for soldiers who had given their lives to protect them. They didn't know about the politics going on in America. How would they? After all, most didn't even really understand their own government. They did know that young American soldiers fought the North Vietnamese, and to them that made these men heroes. They also knew that times had changed, and even though there was still embedded pain, that they must forgive and move forward. With each new introduction came further rejuvenation within Robert. Day after day he laughed more, believed in the decency of humanity more, and saw that he and his comrades had done some good things here for these people. He felt appreciated. Robert made note of specific realizations he would share with Carl and others back at the VA Hospital when he got home. He was becoming essentially whole again . . . his senses of love and purpose more heightened. And with this came his longing to be with Abby. He needed his wife to see the renewed him. Robert. The man she married. He had found him and he was bringing him back home to her . . . just as he had promised.

CHAPTER 17

As Robert relaxed on the plane for the long trip back to California, he reminisced about his and Stephen's trip. He had been fortunate that outside of a few minor nosebleeds and some much needed naps, his body held up pretty well while they traveled. He thought about how wonderful and fulfilling the trip had been. Not only for his wellbeing and healing, but also for the incredible bond he and Stephen had built sharing in this experience. As his son looked out the window watching Vietnam slowly disappear behind them, Robert leaned over and kissed the back of his head whispering, "I love you so much, Son."

Stephen turned around, smiled and replied, "I love you too, Dad."

"This was a great trip. I learned a lot."

"Like what, Dad?

"The Nguyen's were so happy. Pae was so loving, yet he went through even more than I did. I mean, this war was in his country and he lost a lot of family and friends. He even lost his leg. Yet, everyone we met had a smile on their face and showed us so much respect. They were genuinely happy. They seemed so resilient, or maybe it wasn't even resilience but the ability to let things go before it consumed them. Let me ask you something, Son. When we first met Pae what was the first thing you noticed about him?"

"He only had one leg."

"And how did you feel about that?"

"Sad. I felt sorry for him."

"Why?"

"Because I don't know what I would do if I had one leg gone. I couldn't ride my bike, play at school or play sports."

"What was the second thing you noticed about Pae?"

"His tanned skin. It was really dark."

"True. But what about his attitude? Was he sad?"

"No. Not at all. He was so happy and loved his family a lot."

"Exactly. I see Pae with physical wounds that he has to deal with daily for the rest of his life. Yet he accepts it, deals with it, lives with it and moves forward. He is a very happy man. It is the emotional wounds that are much more devastating for a person. They consume and paralyze you if you aren't careful. Pae didn't let any of that affect him. Whatever it is that he is doing, it works. I need to grasp onto that philosophy and use it for myself."

"I do too. Sometimes I get sad. I want to be happy like they were too. I think the counselor I go to helps me with that. Thank you so much for taking me on this trip, Dad, I think I kind of understand more about what you were going through now."

Robert smiled. "How did you grow up to be so wise, Son? Yes, I needed this trip so much. But without you with me, I would never have been able to truly explain to you the essence of being here. You needed to see it, smell it, talk with the people and see how they live. We needed this time, Son. We needed time together. I know I have neglected you and Mommy over the years because of my issues. I promise every moment I have left on this earth will be spent for you two. Son, treasure this time in your life. Truly treasure it. You are still a kid. Be a kid. Enjoy your friends, sports and learning new things. Listen to people, watch people and take good advice. Be kind to others and encourage them. Forgive quickly. Be responsible and wise but don't worry about the future. It will come surely as the sun rises in the morning and sets in the evening. After I am gone, don't worry about me. I will be with God and I promise I will look over you and Mommy from above. Encourage Mommy to move forward and enjoy life too. Most of all, Son, just stay positive about life. Even on tough days, know God has your back. He has a plan for you. I didn't do that and wish I had. Now I give you the greatest advice . . . let go of the past, live in the present and don't worry about the future. Live like Pae. Live with no regrets and be happy. Always remember Pae's happiness. I will take that philosophy back home for you and your mom now. You are such an incredible young man, Stephen. I am so proud that you are my son. I love you."

Stephen leaned into his father and they hugged each other. "I love you more than anything, Dad. Thank you for being my father."

Then Stephen looked up at his father. "Dad?"

"Yes, Son."

"Mom is going to be very happy when we get home," he replied. Stephen then laid his head on his dad's chest to rest.

Robert ran his fingers through his son's hair as he looked out the window, kissing the top of Stephen's head. Vietnam had all but disappeared behind them and the United States was still on the other side of the world. Thoughts of Abby made it feel like she was practically there with him. He felt so excited to share with her the person he had found while in Vietnam again. It was as if the Robert who had left for Vietnam years ago had been lost and now resurfaced to return home to his life and beautiful wife. Robert wasn't naïve though. He realized that healing was a long process and once home they would need to continue with individual and family counseling. He was confident, however, that she would see the incredible transformation he had gone through in the short time away the moment he stepped off the plane. He knew with their first embrace that she would feel the warmth and connection she had longed to have for so long. He had kept his promise. He was bringing Robert back to her. Her love was coming home now.

CHAPTER 18

Abby sat in an uncomfortable greenish-blue chair at the terminal gate awaiting the arrival of the scheduled 9:20 p.m. flight carrying her husband and son. There were only about twenty-five people getting off the plane, since many of the international passengers were connecting to flights heading to other cities around The United States. She was a bit anxious, yet sat quietly as she stared out the window in the direction of the airport and the giant airliners taking off and landing. Their lights swiftly moved past the backdrop of the city nearby with the roar of the loud engines propelling them into the night sky or the tires screeching upon initial contact with the runway during touchdown.

It had been just over two weeks since she had seen Robert and Stephen. She, however, had gotten a call two days ago to confirm their final arrival plans back home. Under normal circumstances she would have taken this moment in stride. Since Robert had grown distant over the past years, time apart was emotionally almost better than being neglected while in the same house. Or, the same room or even the same bed. But this time it was different. During their conversation on the phone Robert seemed much more loving and attentive. Abby found herself excited but also cautious not to get her hopes up too much. Though she had her reservations, there was a sense of comfort in the tone of Stephen's voice on the phone too. He kept telling her how much fun he and his dad were having and how she would be really happy with how well Dad was doing. This news actually made her have butterflies in her stomach as if she were going on a first date with a new man.

At 9:05 p.m., a large airliner turned into the terminal and slowly pulled forward to the gate under the guidance of the ground personnel and their bright orange hand held wands. She stood about thirty feet from the door to the gate and waited. A few tired and weathered passengers, looking drowsy from their long journey, sauntered slowly through the door. Others jogged to catch their next flight. Then Abby heard laughing and joking coming from down the gateway. She recognized the voices, but she couldn't recall a time they both sounded so happy. Now the jovial tone touched her emotions deeply, causing her to bring a hand to her face as her eyes began to tear up. Just then, they came into view.

Stephen saw her and happily yelled, "Mom!" as he ran towards her.

Robert stayed near the door holding their carry-on bags and watched their embrace. Abby was holding her son held tightly in her arms when she looked up at Robert standing about twenty feet away. Their eyes met and Robert let out a smile as he gave her a wink. It was a sincere, loving wink with the depth that she had not seen for several years. At that moment she knew things had changed. She knew the man near the door was not the same man that had boarded the plane a couple of weeks earlier. She slowly got up and looked at her husband, still standing the short distance away from her. Stephen looked at her mom and saw tears start to flow down her cheeks. Abby then ran to Robert with open arms and threw herself into his reassuring embrace.

"Hi, Baby," Robert whispered in her ear. "It's me. I'm here. I found him. I promised I'd find your husband and I did. I'm here. I'm here for you, Abby. I am here for you and love you with all my heart."

Abby's face was still pressed against his chest as she cried uncontrollably. Years of pain, anguish and loneliness seemed to be coming out as she shook and hugged him tighter. Robert motioned for Stephen to come to them. Once he was there, Robert released his wife to allow their son to join in the embrace. He wrapped one arm around his son as Stephen wrapped both his arms around his dad and mom.

Stephen then said the most poignant and powerful four words of his life. "We are a family now."

Robert squeezed them both even more tightly. "Yes we are. We are a family again. And I love my family so very much. We are a family again."

CHAPTER 19

Once home, the time spent as a family was remarkable. Family and individual counseling continued but even the psychologist was amazed at the transformation that had taken place in the family since the trip to Vietnam. Though not an avid churchgoer or Christian herself, she did believe in the power of the spirit and this was one of those rare cases where she thought it was working overtime. As for Robert, Abby and their son, they were in church every Sunday, holding hands and smiling, and the wink had become commonplace again. This wink, that seemed so very subtle, was a wink nonetheless, and it was a simple, habitual gesture from the past that made Abby's heart sing, a sign that her loving Robert was back and ever present next to her. Another simple gesture that brought a sense of warmth to Abby was the smile on her son's face, as it was increasing in frequency. In the past, a smile was rare, since Stephen seemed to carry the lonely neglect from his father on his face. It had been a mirror of his father's inability to show love. Now the mirror was reflecting a totally different vision. Stephen smiled practically all the time and the joyful father-son antics played out all through the day. One minute Stephen would be holding something to help his dad with a project, and the next minute Robert would be spraying Stephen with a water hose while washing the car. Abby would wash dishes and watch them through the kitchen window as they played in the yard. Though he was very sick, Robert found the energy to play ball. Robert would toss a football to Stephen, and then gently tackle him as he tried to run by. Then they'd roll around in the yard. This would bring a smile to Abby's face, but even then she would remember they were on borrowed time. She was saddened by the reminder, but she refused to let those thoughts hinder any moments of happiness that they had left as a family.

Through September, Robert and Abby would walk hand-in-hand on the walkway around the lake in the park not far from where they lived. They talked throughout the walks, while Stephen ran and tossed a ball within their line of sight. The conversation included past memories of high school, their first date, and their wedding; and Robert was able to share more about the war now, the first time he had ever been able to share it with someone who had not actually been there or been involved with it in some way, with the exception of his counselor. This built more and more trust between he and Abby, and with this, the freedom to share and express more deeply seated emotions. They'd walk until Robert got tired and then find a bench near the lake for him to rest and talk some more.

Stephen was always nearby playing or feeding bread he brought with him to the ducks. He seemed to understand that they needed this time as part of the healing process, therefore he willingly found things to keep himself busy so they would have no distractions. His attitude seemed to say "I had my time with Dad, now it's Mom's turn."

Although Robert and Abby talked about the past, they spoke nothing about the last decade of Abby's loneliness and pain. It wasn't as if her feelings were not vitally important, but on the contrary she knew it served no purpose as the deepest, most sincere apologies had been expressed by Robert, and his profound love was now so apparent. This, in turn, gave her all the validation her heart desired. Besides, she truly forgave him. It was now time to focus on today and the future. That was all that truly mattered to both of them. Robert did share that he needed her to eventually move forward with her life. He wanted her to fall in love and remarry. He knew he had to say this or she'd never let go of him. He wanted her to be happy, and with another person she could have that happiness. It would not replace the love she had for him or all the years they had been together. It would, however, be a new chapter in her life that he wanted her to create. For Abby, thinking about the future with another person was the furthest thing from her mind. She couldn't fathom the thought of being with anyone other than Robert.

As the month came to a close, Stephen's 13th birthday approached. The three of them agreed to celebrate as a family. Although Stephen was excited for his birthday, it was bittersweet for them all. That evening they went to his favorite restaurant, then back home for what had become a customary homemade chocolate birthday cake topped with a sparkler. As they watched the small fireworks flame and spark on top of the cake, all three smiled and laughed, yet each felt an underlying resonance that this would probably be Robert's last birthday celebration with them. This thought did not keep them from over-indulging in cake though, as each devoured their extra large piece. Once the dessert plates were cleared, Robert brought out Stephen's birthday gift.

"What is it?" asked Stephen as he stared at the box placed in front of him.

"Well, you'll just have to see," replied Robert as he gestured for Stephen to open it.

Stephen dove in and opened the box anxiously to find the baseball glove he had been wanting for quite some time. "Wow!" he proclaimed as he took it out of the box to put it on his hand.

As Stephen picked up the glove, a small card fell out. He reached down to retrieve the envelope, and gently opened it revealing a message handwritten poetically from his father. It read:

Dear Son,
You are forever there.
There in times of hope,
There in times of fear.
There to show how much you care,
Just by being near.
There in times of joy,
There in times of regret.
There to tell a joke,
When I need a laugh.
You are forever there.

Remember, Son, when I am gone, I will still be forever there with you.
Love,
Dad

Stephen read the note to himself, then passed it to his mom and ran over to his dad, putting his arms around him and burying his head in his dad's chest. "You wrote me a poem," he said softly, followed with a big, "I love you."

That night, while Abby and Robert were getting ready for bed, Abby said to Robert, "I had no idea you put that poem in the glove."

Robert smiled at her and replied, "I know. The counselor told me writing would be helpful in working through my emotions, both to say how I feel and use some creativity. I had never written a poem before, but it felt right." Robert paused, and then continued, "I have one for you, too, Abby."

With that, Robert reached into his nightstand and pulled out a folded, handwritten note, which he then handed to her. It read:

Dear Abby,
You've always loved me.
There in times of triumph,
There in times of defeat.
There to lay a shoulder on,
When sadness makes me weak.
There in times of grief,
There in times of praise.
There to be my only love,
Through all my nights and days.
You've always loved me.
Even when I am gone, I will always love you from above.
Love,
Robert

Abby looked at Robert intently, gently refolded the note and set it on her dresser. She then, with one tear starting to stream down her face, walked over to her husband, sat next to him and the two hugged for a very long time, not needing to say a word.

****

October gave way to November, December and then January. It was a new year, but one that was revealing the relentless power of the cancer that was taking over Robert's body on a daily basis. He had lost almost 35 pounds since returning from Vietnam with his son. It was a noticeable 35 pounds as he had already lost a lot of muscle tone and size during the war, and since returning from Southeast Asia he never really found working out a priority anymore. Once a college football prospect with a stature at 6'2" and 195 pounds, he was now about 145 pounds and consistently heading downward. The natural effect of the illness, quietly but consistently raging inside him, simply kept taking and taking without thought or consideration to the world going on around him. It had one, and only one, task on its agenda and that was to attack and devour Robert's physical body.

By March, the walks had resorted to Abby slowly pushing Robert's wheelchair around the lake once-in-a-while. Walking any distance at all was just getting to be too much effort for Robert to handle, and for that matter Abby as well. Shortly thereafter, all such trips to the lake ceased, as the disease further engulfed Robert's withering body, leaving him to rest in his bed at home. As a family they would continue to share together, but now Robert had an oxygen tube in his nose and a simple conversation would easily tire him. As Easter drew near, it was decided that Robert needed to be hospitalized. He would get much better medical attention and more consistent care in his last days there. By now, the talks had given way to Abby holding his hand as he slept, helping to feed him, and holding his straw while he drank water from the light blue plastic cup at the hospital. On Good Friday they all could feel the end was drawing near. At 7:00 p.m. Abby lay at Robert's right side, resting on the pillows next to him as not to put her weight on his frail body. Stephen was on his other side with his head resting near his father's chest and looking at his mom as she soothed her husband with one hand on his shoulder.

Robert had moved his hand down to Stephen's head. His fingers lightly stroking his son's short brown hair. In a whisper he said, "Son."

Stephen's head tilted up and his eyes focused on his father's face. "Yes, Dad."

"Remember what I told you on the trip? That I will be in Heaven so do not be sad."

"Stephen smiled, "Yes, Dad. I remember."

"Do you remember Pae's words about having to understand everything?"

"I think so. He said we are part of a bigger story and you don't have to have all the answers right now."

"Exactly. You really impress me, Son. He also said to be a good man. To have compassion and empathy for others. But most of all to love. Do you remember the first thing you noticed about Pae?" asked Robert slowly, his voice breathy and weak.

"Yes. He was missing a leg."

"But what about his heart?"

"He was so happy and at peace. He loved his family."

"I want you to find that happiness and peace, Son. I want you to always let go of the past, live in the present and dream about the future." In a labored whisper Robert continued, "I love you, Son. I am so proud of you. You are everything a father would want in a son." As a tear came down Robert's cheek, Abby's tears began to freely flow. "You are the man now, so please take care of Mommy," continued Robert.

"I will, Dad. I promise." A tear ran down Stephen's face as he rose up and wrapped his arms around his father. "I love you, Dad. I love you with all my heart."

His words were weak but compassionate and concise, "I love you too, Son. I will always be with you. Just talk to me anytime you need to. I will be listening. I will be your guardian angel from above. I will always be there."

Robert's arm stayed around his son as Stephen lowered himself and rested his head on his father's chest, listening to his faint heartbeat.

Robert then turned towards Abby, who still lay next to him. Her eyes were filled with tears flowing down her face and dripping onto the white hospital linen. Her right hand lay lightly across his chest now.

Robert looked into the eyes of his beautiful and faithful wife. Tired and breathless, he spoke in a mere whisper his final farewell. "Abby. My dear Abby. You loved me with such a love that I can barely comprehend nor did I deserve. So unselfish, pure and true. I wish I had a hundred years to make everything up to you. I was the luckiest man on the face of the earth and didn't even realize it. Now I do. I will leave this world knowing that God blessed me with an angel on this earth. Now it is my turn. I may be gone, but I will be your angel each day watching over you. When you feel a gentle breeze, smile because it is me touching you in one of the only ways I can. When you feel the warmth of the sun on your face, close your eyes and look upward, for I will be kissing you at that moment. And when you see a bright red rose blooming in the crisp morning air, remember this is my special gift to you. When I go, remember my love will always be with you. You, Abby, I will always love."

Abby placed two fingers on Robert's lips. She knew he was exhausted and had shared everything he needed her and their son to hear. His goodbyes were a perfect gesture. "Robert, my dear, I know everything you feel. You have no need to share anymore. I always knew how you felt and I felt your pain with you. I only hurt because you hurt, I never once blamed you, I never was mad at you; I just hurt because the love of my life was in so much pain and I couldn't do anything to help. We were destined to be together. We were supposed to go through this together. We were supposed to have this beautiful son of ours. Look at him. He is the part of you I will see every day and think of you. Robert, you were always the best person and man you could be. I fell in love with you years ago, and that love will live on forever."

Abby then moved her lips up to Robert's ear and whispered, "I love you, Mr. Nance. I will always love you. Wait for me in heaven. Wait for me, my love." She then gently kissed his cheek.

Robert's last breath was a faint whisper. " I will, Abby."

Robert's chest lowered and then did not rise. His heartbeat stopped and his body became peacefully motionless as his spirit rendered to the heavens.

Abby sat up and looked at his content expression, still holding his hand. Stephen, not hearing his father's heartbeat, slowly raised his head up and looked at his mom, who had turned her gaze to him. Their eyes locked in a deep and genuine spiritual connection.

"Mom?" Stephen said with a perplexed look.

"Yes, Honey," she replied in an assuring tone.

"Mom, is Daddy gone?"

She placed her hand on his cheek. "Yes, Honey. Daddy is in heaven now." She looked back at Robert and then at her son. "But everything is going to be alright, because Daddy is watching over us from above." She leaned over and gave Stephen a kiss on the forehead, then looked into his eyes. "Daddy is our angel. He will always be with us, Son." And with those words she gave him a wink.

CHAPTER 20

Upon returning from Vietnam with her newborn baby girl, Linn Sue clearly realized she had brought a very special life into this world. It was soon apparent that Sophia was daddy's little angel, mommy's little shadow and the entire village's little princess. It was as if there was not a fiber of discontent woven into this child's tiny soul. Sophia's father, Pae, spent every evening after working at the family's small gift shop with his daughter. This war-hardened soldier quickly became a bundle of sensitivity whenever Sophia was near. Though he had lost one leg at the knee, he always had the other one ready for her to rest upon and ride like a pony. With each of her coos an uncontrollable smile broke across his tanned, weathered face. It was often difficult to determine who was happier . . . . the infant amazed with life, or the proud father immersed in the love he had for his daughter. Either way, it was obvious that this little girl brought an enormous amount of joy to the household.

As Sophia grew, she ventured away from the comfort and protection of her father's bouncing lap, loving arms and reassuring smiles. She soon followed in her mother's every footstep. When she could finally hold a feather duster in her tiny hands, she would mimic her mother doing household duties such as cleaning. By the age of five, even strangers could see the innate sense of compassion Sophia had for others, and although she was only a child and in need of others for survival, her confidence from the love she received from family and friends brought out a very unique personality trait. She had an almost uncanny innocent maturity for such a young person; although slightly shy at times, it was evident in her words, in how she held her small self, and how she responded to others. Sophia seemed to have absorbed the character of wisdom from her father and the caring for others from her mother, who was a nurse at the village medical clinic.

Sophia was an adventurous little one, as well. Often her mother would take her to the beach. Her mom had shown her the type of shells they would need to make the necklaces and bracelets for their gift shop her father ran in the village center. She'd stand for hours in the beautiful, clear water, up to her knees, filling a pouch full of the small bright white treasures. Other days she spent with her dad at the store stringing the jewelry together, and then placing the necklaces on a shelf near the register.

Sophia liked being at the gift shop because foreigners from America often passed through the town to reminisce over the past and bought things at the store to take home for souvenirs. They would sometimes give her a gift from their far away country, as well. Most of all, she liked to hear their language and funny accent. Sometimes these Americans would bring their families. Though she found herself a bit shy with the foreigners - often hiding behind her father, at first - in time, her smile would appear and find a way to bring a smile to the visitors' faces as well. This was particularly a joy when they brought their children with them.

Most of the time, however, Sophia found herself going with her mom to the clinic. This was because her father worked in their gift shop most of the day while her mom only worked half a day at the clinic. Sophia would walk along with her mother, holding her lunch sack in one hand and her coloring books in the other. Each person walking by would receive Sophia's beaming, bright smile and polite hello. Once at the clinic, she would find her spot at a table in the waiting area and contently color in her books while talking and laughing to herself. When people would enter the front door, she would look up, greet them and then escort them to the front desk of the small room. It probably wasn't necessary, but both the receptionist and the clients found it to be an endearing and wonderful routine. While Sophia walked with the patients, she would naturally assure them that they were in great hands because her mother was back behind those big doors and would take amazing care of them. As far as Sophia was concerned, her mother was in charge of the entire clinic, and although Linn Sue was actually the nurse and not the head physician, the staff let Sophia assume whatever she desired. In time, Sophia simply became a part of the clinic itself. If she wasn't there, the staff and clients felt as though something special was missing in their day. It felt as if the sun had just simply not come up that morning. Not only did everyone in the village know Sophia, but Sophia also knew their names, and eventually the names of their animals, too. And this began Sophia's passion to be a medical professional.

By the age of ten, Sophia had found her medical niche in animals. They couldn't talk like people at the clinic, but she understood them and they seemed to understand her. Animals in Vietnam had a precarious place in society to say the least; but for those who embraced them, Sophia was the person to nurse them back to health.

Behind the Nguyen's house was a fenced in area. In it was a garden, and just past that was an abandoned chicken coop. Pae understood the importance of his daughter's desire to care for animals, so he let her use this area. He even put a sign above the door to the shed that read "benh vien dong vat Sophia" which means *Sophia's Animal Hospital*. He refurbished the cages and made sure it was safe for her and all her furry patients. At one particular time, she had a rabbit who survived a confrontation with a jeep, a weak puppy who was the runt of the litter, five struggling kittens and a raven with a previously broken wing. The raven would not leave, as it had formed a strong bond with Sophia. It healed and had been released from its cage months ago but would not stay away. It would wait for its little nurse to come outside and would then follow her everywhere she went around the village. She eventually called the raven "ngu'o'i giam ho than" which means *guardian angel* in Vietnamese. The other children in the village loved to come visit Sophia, for it was the only place around that resembled a zoo and gave them the opportunity to handle a wild animal.

By age fourteen, Sophia had moved on from animals to humans. The clinic hired her as an assistant doing anything they needed her to do.

Sometimes she was the receptionist, other times she would run errands around town delivering medication to patients; however, most of the time she helped her mom and the other nurses with minor medical issues. Even though she was not able to be involved in major medical functions, she absorbed all the information she could and would use medical books to research what she heard. The staff was so impressed with her sincere interest that many times they would quiz her, which proved to inspire her even more to research the medical books and return with the correct answer. Some of the books were left by Americans during the war who had passed through the village and were, therefore, written in English. Her parents taught her English as a second language, but she was going far beyond their teaching to master the language better than even they had. The other item often left in the clinic by those passing through were Bibles, which Sophia equally studied as she, along with many in her village, embraced the Christian faith.

In school, Sophia excelled, even to the point of challenging the teachers, while remaining considerate so not to disrespect them. Often, she would stay after school to do medical research that had nothing to do with her regular studies. She learned how the circulatory system worked, the medicines they were using in the United States for heart problems, and she even learned intricacies of the human brain. Her own brain was a sponge for the information and she could not be saturated. Sophia became more and more skilled and independent as she further educated herself.

Even with her intense interest in studying, Sophia never lost the love to race home and make chicken, rice and vegetable soup for her parents. Her father may have been a very self-sufficient man, but she found it enjoyable to dote on him. She also knew that her mother worked and then cleaned the house, so cooking for her was a way for Sophia to express her deep appreciation and respect. This was important in their culture. It was part of their culture to honor and look after your elders in the family. Though it may have been viewed somewhat as a duty, it was also a way to express the love she had for her parents.

If any mother and father felt blessed to have the perfect child, it was the Nguyen's. Sophia was compassionate, driven and so very humble, that she didn't even realize how exotically beautiful she was. Her long, silky, black hair flowed down her entire back. Her soft tanned skin highlighted her dark brown eyes. And her warm smile and bright white teeth accentuated all these attributes. She had a petite, slender physique, but walked as if with a purpose which made her appear taller than her 5'1" height.

In the evenings, they would often sit outside their home as a family, drinking tea and talking about life and Sophia's dreams. From there, they would look out over the village, enjoying the tropical breeze and their bonds with each other. At times, when conversation was quiet, they could even hear an occasional crash of waves from where they sat. Sometimes other friends and family members would join them, sharing stories regarding the country's monsoons or reminiscing over loved ones who had passed on. However, conversation almost always came back around to the topic of what Sophia desired to do with her life.

At fifteen Sophia already knew. All those American medical books she had researched over time had deeply inspired her. She wanted to go to college in America and become a nurse like her mother. Then she wanted to come back home and help the family and fellow villagers. That was her heartfelt dream. Sophia realized it was a bit far fetched, but not because university admittance was a concern – her research had shown that the number of Vietnamese people attending institutions of higher learning had increased since the war from fifty thousand in 1963 to one hundred fifty thousand in 1980, and 23% of the latter were female. She was confident that with her high respect for learning and zeal for medicine she could get in. What made it a far reach was the cost. Her family had very little money for such a dream, but they had always encouraged her to dream big, which she was obviously doing.

Through the years of secondary school, Sophia worked each afternoon in the clinic taking on more and more responsibilities. She researched a couple of Vietnamese universities during her final year of school, but they were still too expensive. It was becoming apparent to Sophia, that after graduation she might have to wait on furthering her formal studies and simply continue working at the clinic as she had been. At least she was respected and able to help people, as well as serve her parents here. During her last days of secondary school, she had resolved that this was her destiny and was content with that being her future. However, the village had entirely different plans for Sophia, and these plans were about to come to her attention.

On the day of Sophia's high school graduation she was asked to speak on behalf of her class. She was the obvious choice for all she had done for the community, and the fact that her academics were far beyond those of her classmates. Honored to be selected, she graciously made it to the small podium and shared what was on her heart.

"Good evening to you all. I am honored to represent my classmates. Thank you for bestowing this privilege upon me. I also want to thank all the teachers for helping us to become good students. I respect you all so much. And I want to thank the entire community for always supporting me. I have known you all my whole life and believe it is my destiny to serve you here at the medical clinic. It has always been my home away from home, and there is nothing I want to do more than to care for those who need help. So, as long as the clinic will have me, I will be there for you all. My classmates and I understand respect and honor. Our parents have been there for all of us for so many years, and it is now time for us to give back to them. This is our time to become a more active part of this community and create more for the future generations. Mom, Dad, I love you and I want to make you proud. Thank you for giving me so much support, encouragement and love. You mean the world to me. You all mean the world to me. Thank you. Thank you all very much."

The entire room of about two hundred parents, relatives and students stood up and clapped for her as she walked back to her seat. At that moment the room grew quiet again. Then the principal of the school's voice spoke from behind her. "Sophia," said the loud but soothing voice, "would you please come back up here?"

Sophia looked a bit stunned, pointing at herself then looking out in the audience at her parents. Her dad nodded his head approvingly through a proud smile. Sophia then slowly walked back up towards the podium until she was standing in front of the principal.

"My dear Sophia," began the principal, "you have been the greatest blessing to this school and entire community for most of your short, young life. There isn't a person in this room you have not cared for while working at the clinic, and I am sure many of their animals have experienced your compassion as well. Tonight is the night this community wants to thank you and give back to you. Not only have you made your parents proud, but also everyone who has known you believes in you and your dreams. Oh, yes, we all have been aware of your dreams for quite some time now. And, yes, we all want you to serve at the medical clinic, but not simply in the same capacity that you already do, but rather as in your dream role of being a nurse. Rarely does a person like you come around; a person who can be such a vital part of the village for years to come. Sophia, on behalf of the medical clinic and everyone in this community, your nursing school is going to be paid for. Your dad has a brother and sister-in-law in Los Angeles you can stay with, and the clinic and the community will cover your school expenses to get started at Los Angeles Harbor Community College. Here you can get all your prerequisites for nursing school. Then, when you are accepted into nursing school, that too will be taken care of financially. Call it an investment in the future of our little village. We, the entire community, are so very proud of you."

The room again stood and clapped loudly. Tears freely flowed down Sophia's cheeks as she looked at her parents, who were crying tears of joy as well.

CHAPTER 21

The small Episcopal Church held about 250 people. It was about two-thirds full with friends and family. Stephen sat between his mom and Graham Taylor, his father's dear friend from the Vietnam War who had flown in from Arizona, staring out of the colored pane window. One set of his grandparents sat beside his mom, the other set sat right behind him. Mentally he was elsewhere, thinking of nothing in particular and everything all at the same time. Stephen was at his father's funeral, physically aware of his mom's sobbing and the words being said around him, yet in a surreal, displaced state of mind. He had barely known his father except for the last six months. Prior to his father's epiphany to recapture his life, Stephen had been neglected by him at best. He had felt mostly a void from the lack of love and attention from his father since infancy, but recently all that had changed.

Stephen turned to look at the casket which had been placed in front of the podium where the pastor now stood. His eyes then scanned down to Graham's arm. Just below the sleeve of Graham's black suit was a large Timex watch. Stephen watched the second hand deliberately jump from one second to the next, his eyes transfixed on its abrupt but rhythmic pace. As his eyes watched the hands on the watch, his mind drifted and fell into the journey of time. Stephen's body stiffened as his mind journeyed through the past, where there was emptiness of a father's love or adoration for his son. Through the thoughts of this sadness he felt twinges of intense anger rising up in him.

"All I ever did was try to earn your respect and connect with you, Dad, and you ignored my pain in order to selfishly embrace your own.

You chose to stay in a state of distance and despair when you could have had mom and me. You neglected our emotional needs. Each day revolved around you, your anger at life, and your pain while mom and I tip-toed around, trying to keep things afloat, finding support only from each other," Stephen confronted his father in his mind as he subconsciously leaned into his mom. Taking in her comfort, he paused for a minute, and then continued with his mental rant, "Why couldn't you care about us? Why couldn't you see what you were doing to us? Did you not have any compassion, love or hope for your own family? How selfish of you, as a grown man, not to resolve your own issues until it was too late."

The second hand of Graham's watch continued to track around the watch methodically. One . . . . two . . . . three . . . . four . . . . five . . . . the seconds ticked as Stephen continued in his mind, "the last six months were the best and worst of my life. I felt I finally I had a father. The trip to Vietnam, the healing, the support, and the loving comments were what I needed from you. Those words coming from a father to his son was what I thirsted for as I held onto every syllable with sensitivity and respect. But at the same time, watching you weaken each day until you had no more strength to carry on was sometimes unbearable."

Stephen stopped at this thought, shaking his head slightly as he felt himself start to waiver, his bottom lip quivering as he held back tears. Life with his father was like the sun finally coming out from behind the grey, stormy clouds to embrace the day, only to sink behind the horizon moments later. In Stephen's thirteen short years of life so far, he shared a loving bond with his father for a mere flicker of time. To have finally experienced the joy of a good father-son relationship, only to lose it so quickly, caused him to grieve even more pain from its loss.

Stephen was re-directed from his mental journey by an inclination in the pastor's voice, as he reminded everyone to think of the happy times with Robert. Stephen looked back at the watch as the seconds passed . . . . seventeen . . . . eighteen . . . . nineteen . . . . twenty. He was not even aware that his finger was now tracing the hand around the watch nor was he aware that Graham had been intently watching everything he had been doing the entire time. Graham had been watching Stephen touch the watch, mouth words silently, and change his facial expressions as his emotions and thoughts transferred from sadness to anger. He watched and took mental notes as Stephen sat in the pew searching for a foundation of understanding. It was as though Graham was on the journey with him. Graham felt plugged in as he interpreted Stephen's thoughts and expressions, journeying through an emotional battlefield.

****

Back home that night, after other mourners had left and the day was coming closer to an end, Abby, Graham, and Stephen gathered in the kitchen. The three sat quietly in thought, impacted by grief and fatigue. Abby was pondering her own regrets, feeling both fear and relief that the day was winding down. Stephen was still mentally addressing his questions, his anger and his sadness. Meanwhile, Graham was planning and calculating the best way to relay to Stephen what he thought he needed to hear about his father.

Sensing the time was right, Graham began, "Stephen, your father and I shared a unique relationship. We talked often about the war. We understood the many things we could not share with other people. They simply would not understand. Stephen, please understand the beauty that was your father. When I met your dad he was fearless and a natural leader. The squad looked to him for guidance. We totally and whole-heartedly trusted your father. He was serious when he had to be, but also the wittiest man when given the chance. He loved his country, his squad, but above all he loved you and your mother."

Stephen looked up at Graham, his face was a little confused, but he was listening as Graham continued, "You must look at your father as the man we knew. You see, war is a vicious animal. I saw it. I lived it. But I was only there a short time because I was shot. I would have died except your father carried my dying body for miles, saving me. Stephen, we saw and experienced things there that no eighteen or nineteen year old kid should have to go through. Your dad was there for three years longer than I was. I came home after ten months. While I was in the VA hospital I saw the anguish that this thing called PTSD brought upon many of the men who had gone to war. I was fortunate I still had my mind intact. Intact enough to put myself into counseling that is. You see, Stephen, as I said, battle is a vicious animal. It will devour one's soul. It will eat away at the inside of you until there is nothing left. One becomes a shell of who they once were."

Graham paused, realizing he had Stephen's attention and choosing his words carefully, "I wasn't strong like your father. I found help through mental therapy as soon as I got home, realizing I had no chance of conquering the beast otherwise. I believe your father saw so much and experienced so much, that the vicious beast in him had matured beyond measure. Yet, your father, since he was mentally stronger than I was, thought he could keep fighting on his own and win. The thing is, you must find a way to destroy the animal before it destroys you. In my case, I tamed it. I couldn't conquer it, so I tamed it, by accepting what I went through and finding a healthy way to cope with it. Your father was an amazing man. He was just simply fighting an internal battle with something more powerful than he was and he refused to tame it until the last several months of his life. That is when you saw the man your father was reemerge. The one who loved and adored you and your mother. He loved you both with every fiber of his soul. He told us about you two many times in Vietnam and talked about the future he was going to give you once he was back home. Remember the last six months of your father's love? That love was very real. His cancer, as hard as it was, caused him to confront the demons within himself, Christ gave him the power and spirit to accept the torture he had been through, and the trip you two took to Vietnam tamed the beast that had been overpowering him. This brought your father back to you and your mother. Just ask your mom."

"Mom, tell me more about Dad before going to Vietnam," said Stephen, turning to his mother.

"Wow, where do I start?" responded Abby taking in a deep breath, "Your father had a personality bigger than life. As Graham shared, he was a true leader. Humble to the core but a natural at rallying the team.

His perspective on life was that you live it to the fullest, dream big and work hard towards those goals. He was such a great athlete and a good student. He was accepted to Stanford and probably would have found a way to go pro in football, but his true dream was to be an engineer and raise a family. He looked at the bigger picture and was very mature and grounded in his ways. I adored him for that."

"Mom, when did things change?"

"Perhaps into his second tour in Vietnam," replied Abby reflectively, "When he came home on leave he didn't talk as much. He spent quite a bit of time thinking on his own. He had also started smoking, which wasn't his nature." Abby paused, looking at her son's response then continued, "I began to get less mail from him when he went back; mail that seemed more distant and detached. He stopped sharing things that were going on in his life over there. Perhaps I went along with it because I, too, had to cope with the names of killed soldiers on the news each night. I knowingly became a little detached as well. Mostly because I was just scared . . . especially for your father. Maybe he was too. But when he finally served his time in battle and returned, I was able to let go of the fear and reattach to him as my husband. I figured he would do the same for me, but instead, he kept his distance. He remained guarded and to himself. That's when I knew something was truly wrong. My husband was home, but in a way his soul had died on the opposite side of the world.

"Mom, how were you able to still love a person who showed you and me no love?" asked Stephen, his words poignant and precise.

"Stephen, come here," replied Abby as she held his tall, growing body in her arms, "That was not your father. It was a man who was scared and left as a protective shell from what he had been through. I hurt for him. I would hold onto the memories of our young love before he left for Vietnam. Stephen, he had been such an amazing man - your father was truly amazing - and to that man, I made a commitment to love him as his wife. In time you will read and learn more thoroughly what Graham shared with you about the war. It took so much from your father, but that protective guard is how he survived. It is how he made it through each day in Vietnam, never knowing if that was going to be his last day. As I said, he was scared, and fear does harsh things to a person's soul. I loved the man trying to find peace and fight through the fear that was still there. I wanted to hold your father and make it all right for him. What sounds so odd or strange, yet is amazing at the same time, is that if it weren't for your father's cancer, he would have never embraced his life again and found motivation to heal, accept God again, and love us again."

One tear trickled down Abby's face as she thought about the irony in this truth, then she continued, "Remember when you and your father went to Vietnam together?"

"Yes, Mom, of course I do."

"Well, when he hugged me at the airport when you returned, I felt the hug of my true husband again. I felt Robert, his soul back in him. God had sent him to Vietnam to retrieve himself, to bring him back to us. It was the most beautiful thing I have ever experienced in my life. And it was beautiful that you got to go on that journey with him. Those last months with your father healed my aching heart. Your father's illness was a terrible thing. But I would take his illness, because of the peace he found to love himself and us again for a short time, over him barely holding on and living in turmoil for the rest of his life and ours. Your father found peace, love and joy again and that makes me happy. It also makes me able to see the purpose in all of this. I loved your father with all my heart."

Abby found herself temporarily burying her head into the shoulder of her young son. As she did, Graham reached across the table knowingly placing his hand on Abby's other shoulder, and for a moment no one said a word.

After a few minutes, it was Stephen who broke the silence, pulling away from his mom and sitting back across from her in a kitchen chair. I want to know more about my father. I really only had about six months with him," he proclaimed, "He changed so much so fast. I kind of felt like I was getting to know a new person everyday, especially after we came back from Vietnam. It was like he relaxed and began to live again - which is sad - because he was also dying right in front of us. I loved our time together. He focused on me. He showed he cared. I really, for the first time in my life, felt he loved me. But to have him start living life while he was dying?" Stephen shook his head back and forth confusingly.

"Honey, sometimes it takes a person losing everything in order to wake up and see what they have. I believe if it weren't for your father's illness, he would never have changed, and we would never have experienced his loving spirit these last months. We must find it in ourselves to thank God for the change in attitude your father had, as that love, though ever so brief, will live on with you forever."

"I understand, Mom. I hurt now because Dad's gone. But I am thankful for the time we shared." With that, Stephen turned away from his mom and shifted his attention to his right. "Graham, can you continue to tell me more about my father? And if you have any photos of him from Vietnam, can I see them?" Then, just as, quickly as he asked that question, he went right back to his mom saying, "Mom, can I look at his high school albums? I really want to know my dad."

"Of course, Hun," Abby answered. Stephen looked at Graham, who smiled and gave him a loving wink.

CHAPTER 22

In the days that followed his father's passing, Stephen incorporated learning about his family, particularly his father, into all his days. He would look at photos of the buddies his dad grew up with and wonder where they were and what they might be doing now. He wondered if they all knew his father had passed. Looking through the pictures, he made a mental note to ask his mom this question. He found yearbooks from his dad's days in school. He looked at the grade school photos first, going year by year. Stephen thought his father was a cute boy. He was skinny, with a crew cut and always smiling. Stephen would slowly peer from one photo to the next, putting the pieces together in his mind.

By the time he got to his dad's sophomore year in high school, he could already see the man in his father being revealed. A narrower face and high cheekbones became evident. Longer hair, broad shoulders and muscular arms replaced the skinny boyish figure with a crew cut. His father looked very athletic, and as Stephen turned the pages he could see that he was. He was a star on the football, basketball and baseball teams even as a sophomore.

By the time Stephen got to his father's senior yearbook in 1968, his dad was a man among boys. It was apparent, combing the pages, that his dad was very popular. It was also apparent that he seemed to be very happy and charismatic. Stephen's mother started to appear in the pictures with him. All Stephen could think was that they just seemed to be so happy.

On that particular day, Stephen put the yearbook down, feeling content to have seen pictures of his parents happy. He then grabbed a white box that held one white album and one brown album. As he curiously pulled the albums out of the box, he spied an array of loose newspaper clippings under them. He first opened the white album full of photos from his parent's engagement, wedding, reception and honeymoon. His mom was beautiful and his father strikingly handsome. In every photo, the lovebirds smiled. There was no doubt regarding the incredible love they had for each other. One by one, Stephen looked at the photos revealing family and well-wishers at the wedding, cake smeared on his mom's face - compliments of his father - and pictures of a sunset on the coast where his parents had stayed on their honeymoon.

Stephen thought to himself, "This is surely what perfect love is when you find your soul mate." The pictures portrayed a vision of destiny fulfilled.

Stephen then began to look through the newspaper clippings and envelopes at the bottom of the box. Here he saw stories about the star football player at Mountainview that his father was. He read articles about his father being the number one ranked quarterback in the state of California. He saw titles to articles such as "Nance Leads Team to Victory," "Nance Watched by Many Division One Universities," and "Nance Chooses Stanford." Stephen looked through the envelopes, each with college letters expressing interest in his father attending their school. The letters were from Michigan, Texas, Penn State, Nebraska, Oklahoma, USC, UCLA, Washington, and, of course, Stanford.

The enlightenment Stephen was getting regarding his father amazed him. He hadn't seen such strength and vitality in his father, and, unfortunately, when he saw subtle glimpses of happiness towards the end, it was when his body was withering away. Stephen put the envelopes back in the box, along with the white album.

On the floor still lay the brown album. He held it on his lap and gently opened it. In it were photos of the house in which he still lived. There were photos from Colorado of his grandparents on the deck of their new house, where they had moved right after his father's high school graduation to get closer to mountains and lakes, as his father barbecued with his shirt off. Again he saw broad shoulders, bulging biceps, and a muscular abdomen. His dad wore blue jeans and had long hair in this picture. Stephen noticed in this photo that his dad had a particularly tanned body and that his posture was strong and well built. Stephen smiled as he saw how impressive his father was. And although it was just a photo, his dad seemed to exude masculinity.

He turned the pages to see his dad proudly wearing his Army uniform, with a clean-cut, chiseled face and stern eyes. There were pictures of his other set of grandparents gathered around his father and, although smiling, Stephen could detect a look of worry in his grandmother's eyes and thought she may have even been crying when the picture was taken.

The pages that followed included pictures of his mom and dad laughing at an Army function before he left for Vietnam. Another was a photo of the two of them wrestling on the couch with his father teasing her with a small teddy bear. Stephen paused and thought for a moment, recognizing the teddy bear as the one he gave away years ago at the hospital. He then came to several Army pictures in Vietnam. In the first ones his dad was smiling with his buddies. In one picture he was throwing a comrade into the river. The next picture showed the group of guys all laughing. Stephen continued turning the pages. Over and over more photos were displayed of his father in Vietnam. Some were even in battle. Then one aspect of the photos especially caught Stephen's attention. He hadn't noticed it at first, but it became more and more obvious with each passing page. His dad's smile was gone.

Stephen turned back the pages to see when his dad's facial expression had changed. He noticed it had been so subtle, yet so clear. His dad's face no longer had that Nance, ever-present, charismatic smile. It had been replaced by a burdensome expression of daunting responsibility, seriousness and even a sense of hopelessness. His eyes, previously bright and securely confident, now appeared shallow, confused, fearful and fiercely angry. Stephen's heart sank as he realized that this is what happened to his father. He saw his dad was now scared, disenchanted and in survival mode. He may not have been shot, but his father's soul was definitely dying within him in these pictures.

Stephen closed the album. He had seen enough. His father was a strong, determined leader in everything he did. He was successful and extremely happy. If Vietnam could ruin the soul of a man like his father, what chance did any soldier have?

CHAPTER 23

Stephen walked into the kitchen shortly after five o'clock. The table was set and hot spaghetti sauce rested in the center, surrounded by garlic bread, salad and a bottle of milk. He sat down and watched his mom straining the spaghetti noodles.

"Smells great, Mom."

"Hey, Stephen. You hungry?"

"Yes, very," replied Stephen.

"Whatcha been up to?" asked Abby, inquisitively.

"Just going through photo albums and newspaper clippings of Dad." Stephen paused for a moment, gathering his thoughts. "Mom, war is an awful thing," he finally said aloud.

"Yes, it is. Why do you say that?"

"Dad was an amazing man. I mean, he was so popular. He was such a great athlete. He was such a good-looking guy. He had everything going for him, and he smiled all the time. You guys loved each other – that's obvious. Graham said he was a leader and I can see that too, but the war took that away. I saw that when I was looking at the Army photos of Dad. His face changed. His looks changed. He went from happy and confident to serious, sad and scared. Looking at the photos showed me Dad losing his happiness and himself. He changed. It was like war took his spirit."

When did you get so wise and insightful? I guess you are almost a teenager," replied Abby with a tender grin.

"Well, I'm right, aren't I?"

"Oh, Stephen. I wondered when you would start having these questions. I wanted to be ready, but one never is. One just has to speak from the heart, so I am going to try."

"When your dad and I dated, then got married, it was the most magical thing. Your father was just perfect. I felt so blessed. He was so smart, so handsome, so strong and, yes, an amazing athlete. But, Stephen, your father was also humble, respectful, and compassionate to everyone, and such a loving man. When we were together, I felt like a queen and he was my king. Everyone respected your father. But you're right, he changed. At first, he would write to me and share everything that was on his heart. Then the letters became less from his heart and more matter of fact about what he was doing, then they became short and even more distant. After a while, they rarely came at all. I tried to not feel hurt and take it personally, but I began to long for your father's loving words. Yet they didn't come. Then, when he came home, I really saw the change. His love was absent. We were like two people sharing the same house, but having no connection. He never showed me affection, or held me, and when I asked him what was going on in his mind, he simply said that I wouldn't understand. It broke my heart. It was as if the war had taken his soul and ripped out his heart. It was exactly like you said, Stephen. The war took his spirit. It was so sad and it hurt so much. Not just for me, Stephen, but for you. The way it affected you broke my heart even more. I knew you were lonely for your father's attention. You were neglected. Not because he didn't love you, but because he lost the ability to love us. This is why, as horrible as your father's sickness was, it was such a gift that we were able to get him back, at least for a short time. He was able to smile again. And when you two went to Vietnam together, he found his soul again; I felt it the moment he held me at the airport, when you returned. His spirit was once again a part of him. He had found it. My loving husband was with me again."

Stephen smiled. "I know, Mom. I watched you. I watched how surprised you were at the airport. I saw you experience that magic again that you said you two shared. I'm sad that dad is gone, but am really happy that we got him back even for only a short time so that I could know who he really was."

A tear slowly ran down Abby's cheek. "Stephen, your father's spirit will be with us forever. Talk to your father when you are moved to do so. Thank God for the time you had with him. I believe that you will feel your father's spirit guiding you in life, if you choose to embrace it. In those quiet times, talk to God and acknowledge your father. They are always there for you."

Abby put some noodles on Stephen's plate and then covered them with the spaghetti sauce. "Stephen, thank you for sharing your thoughts with me. It's good for us both to talk about these things. I really love you, Stephen. You have truly grown up. Now eat, you said you were hungry."

Stephen smiled at his mom, winked, and reached for the salad. For a second, Abby was taken aback by Stephen's wink. She hadn't noticed that he had acquired that inclination from his dad, until now.

As Abby looked out the window over the kitchen sink, she smiled and whispered to herself, "I know you are here with us, Robert. Thank you. I love you."

CHAPTER 24

Learning about his father continued to inspire Stephen. Over time he asked his mom about the photos of his father's friends he saw in the yearbook. His mother shared that Mark had died in battle and that Carl was not well. She told him that Carl currently lived at the Veteran's Home. Stephen vowed to spend time with Carl whenever possible out of respect for his father and their friendship.

At first Stephen was nervous about going to see Carl. He wasn't used to these environments or being around people who were this sick or disabled; however, visiting Carl was a way he could have connection with his father while serving someone he felt was one of the forgotten. On some level, Stephen felt as though his coming helped empower Carl a bit. His hope was that his visits would give this shell of a man a little bit of brightness and love.

One sunny mid-September afternoon, Stephen walked into Carl's room, squeezed Carl's hand and reminded him that he was Robert's son. Within seconds he saw one tear stream down Carl's face. At that moment he knew he was having an impact in Carl's life and committed in his mind to coming to visit at least twice a week.

Stephen often went and just sat with Carl while he studied, sometimes reading aloud, other times just talking freely about different things he was learning or what he wanted to achieve in life. He would take breaks from his studies to read the newspaper to him and, each time he left, he would kiss Carl on the top of his head. Carl was never one to express any emotion back, but the staff let Stephen know that his overall demeanor, and even his eating habits, had changed ever so slightly since

Stephen started coming to see him. This truly made Stephen happy that he could bring joy into the life of his father's childhood friend, a man who gave up everything for his country. It was as if, even though Robert had passed, he was helping his friend through his son.

A volunteer would often bring a dog to the facility to sit at the side of Carl's bed. It was a German Shepard named Major. Apparently Carl had been a dog handler in the Vietnam War and, although this was not his actual dog from war times, having this dog there helped calm Carl when he became overly anxious and experienced nightmares.

One particular day when Stephen came to visit, Major was by the side of the bed as usual. However, Carl's appearance was different; his skin was ashen, his breathing more labored, and his vitals were weak. Stephen felt lead by something greater than himself and before he could overthink the words coming from his mouth, out they came. He simply and calmly told Carl it was OK for him to go and that Robert was waiting for him in Heaven. The words flowed as he assured Carl that in Heaven he would be healed and have peace. He then gave Carl his usual kiss on the head, patted Major and left.

A few days later, shortly after Christmas of Stephen's junior year, Carl passed away. On that January day, Stephen walked into the Veteran's Home like he always did, but this time a nurse stopped him and told him that Carl had passed just moments before. She then asked him if he wanted to say good-bye to Carl. He answered that he did, so the nurse walked him to Carl's room.

Carl lay peacefully as if he were simply sleeping. Stephen walked across the room and stood beside the bed. Reaching for Carl's hand, he whispered softly, "Hey, Carl. You look so peaceful. I'm so glad that we had time together. It meant a lot to me to know my dad's best friend. I will never forget you. Now it's time for you and my father to be together again . . . together in a perfect place, where you can be healthy and happy. Be at peace, my friend. I love you, Carl. Tell my dad I love him too."

Stephen then kissed Carl on the top of his head, and turned around to see the nurse holding a small piece of folded paper in her hand. She held it out. "This was in Carl's hand today. He never writes or draws, but today he got his point across that he wanted paper and a pen. I helped him by getting him what he needed and he made it clear in his own way that this was for you. It truly was a miracle. This is for you Stephen . . . "

Stephen took the small piece of paper, opened it slowly, and looked at it in silence. His eyes teared up. Then he looked around, shook his head and smiled. On the paper was a very rough drawing of a heart. It may have looked like a three-year-old drew it, but the message was very clear.

Stephen softly whispered, "I love you too, Carl. I love you too."

CHAPTER 25

After his father's passing, Stephen and his mother stayed in the same house and did what they could to keep routines normal. Fortunately, they had his mom's parents there to help out. Stephen stayed very close to his mother. As many sons do who have lost their father, he felt it was his role to protect his mother and be the man of the house. It wasn't anything that his mother had projected onto him, just innately how he as a young man felt it should be. He and his mom had good times. They laughed a lot together, often watching silly sit coms on "TV and popcorn night." They traveled a few weekends each year, heading along Highway 101 or to other California destinations. Stephen recalled the time he first saw the trees in Muir Woods with his mother. He also specifically enjoyed the occasion when his mom took him to the beach in Carlsbad, outside of San Diego, for the weekend. The two also enjoyed times together in the kitchen where Abby taught her son how to baste a turkey or make some of her favorite soups. He enjoyed these moments with his mom so much that cooking became one of his favorite pastimes.

Stephen studied diligently, just like his father who had had the dream of being an engineer and studying at Stanford. He worked out daily, as he also wanted to be a great athlete like his dad had been. Different from his father, though, the sport Stephen excelled in during high school was baseball. He was big, standing almost 6'3", strong, and, although quieter than his charismatic father, he earned the admiration and respect of his peers.

Stephen's strong, tall stature, good looks, athleticism and confident attitude made him popular in high school. Even with his notoriety, he avoided deep relationships though. Sure, he had friends who he hung out with, but there was a sense of protective emotional distance that he had mastered. It was a well-defined coping skill that he unknowingly used to deal with his father's latent neglect, and it continued into his teenage years, then followed him into early adulthood. This was especially true when it came to women. The ladies in high school were extremely attracted to Stephen and his nomadic, nonchalant nature only intrigued them more. It was as if they each wanted to be the one to tame this wild horse as their own.

His fear of getting hurt, being let down, or feeling pain brought on by another person made him very evasive regarding emotional connection with any young lady, especially one trying to cage him in. Through years of wanting his father's attention and love, then subsequently being let down, it made it easy to keep his emotions in check. Love was a four-letter word to Stephen, spelled P-A-I-N, and best kept at a distance. For Stephen this was as normal as the warm sun of California. On the other hand, it broke his mom's heart to clearly see how her beautiful son protected himself from love. However, Abby vowed to never force him to talk about it or to in any way push him towards having a relationship.

By the end of Stephen's tenure in high school he had been incredibly successful scholastically and athletically. With his ability to subtly, yet masterfully, sabotage fledgling relationships with the many beautiful young ladies who desired him, he was able to focus on the things he could control like grades and sports. The emotional battlefield of committed relationships fell by the wayside, which protected his heart from vulnerability or pain. And, just like the other areas in his life, he excelled at this; creating a perfectly crafted fence around his heart, so that no one had the potential to hurt him.

Stephen had many ongoing conversations with his mom through the years about his dad's illness, about what she knew regarding the war and the effects it had on his father, but it got to the point where information from his mom was not enough. He desired more and began to dive into encyclopedias, then textbooks, in search of more information about the disease that had cut short his father's life. He excelled in subjects such as Biology, Microbiology and Anatomy.

Through his personal studies outside of school, Stephen learned as much as he could about the cancer that took his father. He learned more and more about nasopharynx cancer, and its relationship to Vietnam veterans due to their exposure to Agent Orange. He thought it such an injustice that these men were sent to fight a war, were treated so poorly upon their return and then many also had to face such horrifying diseases and emotional traumas due to all they were exposed to. He felt that these men had become forgotten warriors and that the more he could learn about what his father and others had gone through physically with cancer and what had caused it, the less he was forgetting him. Through his reading, Stephen began to understand what his father had described just prior to his death regarding a buzzing or ringing in his ears, the facial pain and numbness, and the blurred vision.

Motivated by his dad's battle with cancer, Stephen desired to become a doctor. Thus, his grades were impeccable, leading him to be the Valedictorian of his class and to a scholarship to The University of Stanford. Also, as a top high school prospect in baseball, he was drafted by the Oakland A's. Though honored by the accolades of a possible baseball career, he knew his heart was being entirely pulled towards becoming an oncologist in order to understand his father's life, illness and passing. The burning desire within him to connect in this way to his dad, who he only really knew for six short months, beckoned for completion.

Stephen did walk on to the Stanford baseball team, which, for the coach, was a gift from God above. The coach had been hearing of this local kid for a couple of years, but had also learned through a San Francisco Chronicle article that he was going to focus his attention on getting into medical school, so the coach had decided to take a pass on offering the young man a scholarship. Anytime the coach would watch Stephen standing on the pitcher's mound, it pleased him how events had turned out. The coach would simply smile with satisfaction as he basked in the warm California sun, watching Stephen Nance throw, knowing that he had obtained a great pitcher, without having to let go of a coveted scholarship

For Stephen, the academia of college life at Stanford was a perfect fit. Pre-med classes required nearly one hundred percent attention, and he was willing to put the time in. This said a lot about his focus, considering all the beautifully tanned California ladies that could have been a powerful distraction for a healthy young man. However, baseball gave him enough of a social life that he didn't feel he was missing much. He did have female friends though going through pre-med with him, whom he hung out with in a non-demanding way. Stephen felt very content, and liked how he had successfully created a productive and structured world.

He became a teacher's assistant in the microbiology lab. The female students would come into the lab on the first day of class, delighted to set their sights on their handsome TA. They would line up to ask him questions, sometimes even irrelevant ones, and do petty things to try to get his attention. It didn't take long for them to realize, however, that he really did want to talk more about Gram-positive versus Gram-negative, or whether or not they were able to identify the squamous cells through their microscopes, more than anything else. He could care less about their upcoming sorority mixers or hints as to whether or not he had a girlfriend.

It wasn't as if Stephen didn't notice the ladies that passed through his world daily. He had become very good friends with some; even deeper friends with those that somewhat understood his nomadic nature. If they understood that he was not theirs' to trap or fence in, he was a great and loyal friend, but the relationships didn't go much beyond that. In fact, only a few women had that ability to let him be himself - usually those were women who also wanted to get into medical school and didn't want to be wasting time on the demands of a relationship – and these symbiotic relationships were mutually beneficial and blossomed into great friendships. The others simply died on the vine.

After four years of playing baseball at Stanford, Stephen chose to retire from the game and put all his focus on his future medical career by accepting an offer at The University of California, Los Angeles School of Medicine. He chose UCLA above other offers because of its affiliation with the VA Hospital System. By this time the Veterans Administration Affairs was in place, and more emphasis was being placed on improving the quality and efficiency of care within VA facilities. This pleased Stephen because it was something he wanted to take part in, especially following his experiences with Carl.

Again, the demands of medical school fit well with the overly structured world Stephen had created. And with no baseball, his complete focus went towards school, and school alone.

There was one occasion, however, during his residency when he did find one particular woman attractive. As part of the residency program, he was asked to do some guest speaking at California colleges providing prerequisite courses for pre-med and nursing. On this day, Stephen was the guest speaker at a community college in Los Angeles. Dressed in a white shirt, dark slacks and a tie, he stood at the front of the lecture hall as the professor introduced him.

"Everyone, welcome Dr. Stephen Nance from the UCLA School of Medicine. He will speak to you on his chosen field of oncology, and what led him to medical school, as well as that choice of specialization. Welcome Dr. Stephen Nance."

Stephen walked onto the stage in front of about 70 students. Initially he was a bit nervous, and he didn't really see any of the people sitting before him. Yet as he relaxed and his presentation began to flow, the students slowly came into focus. As he shared that he had lost his father to cancer, and explained that his dad had been in Vietnam, a beautiful Asian woman wearing a dark blue dress and a classy, light blue scarf in the front row perked up and their eyes met. For a moment, Stephen was transfixed on her natural beauty, before he caught himself staring and looked away. His gaze continued to be drawn back to her as he spoke, and it seemed like she was always looking right back into his eyes. After forty-five minutes of sharing, his presentation ended and the class gave him a respectful applause. He walked up to the professor and shook his hand, then left the room. He stood outside the lecture hall contemplating going back in or waiting for the Asian woman in the dark blue dress to come out, but right then his pager went off, beckoning him to return to a patient. He took a deep breath, feeling a sense of disappointment and made his way to the elevator.

Stephen finished medical school as one of the top in his class. Once completing medical school, he went on to UCLA Medical Center for his residency. He enjoyed the vigors of being a resident at a large institution, and continued to excel by being chosen Chief Resident by his peers. After Stephen easily passed his medical boards, he continued on, completing a fellowship at this same institution. By the time his training was complete, he was an oncologist for the UCLA Health System, one of the most advanced and comprehensive health care systems in the world. A couple of years later he was recruited by and accepted a position as a staff oncologist at The Fred Hutchinson Cancer Research Hospital in Seattle, Washington. He accepted the position, however, on the stipulation that he could have a few months to relax and prepare for the rigors of being an oncologist for the rest of his working life. The hospital granted his desire and actually saw it as a very mature career move for such a highly sought after doctor.

CHAPTER 26

June slipped into July, which quickly turned to August. Sophia was scheduled to leave for Los Angeles on Sunday morning. On Friday, the village basically shut down to celebrate and wish her a safe and fulfilling journey. Over a hundred people from her village and the surrounding area congregated on the sandy shores of her favorite beach not far from where her family lived. The aroma of pig and chicken roasting over a fire pit lingered in the afternoon air. Fruit and vegetables were organized neatly on the numerous tables scattered about, each table was adorned with colorful native flowers. And music from an outdated portable stereo filled the air. Children running on the beach and frolicking in the water only enhanced the festive atmosphere. The weather was sunny, the water was a deep blue, and the distant, puffy white cumulous clouds majestically floated in the sky. It was nothing short of a perfect day.

Sophia was observably happy as she joyfully visited with the guests. Some faces were those of people she had only seen in the clinic, coming from miles away. They, too, wanted to express pride and appreciation for the young woman who had so kindly served them over the years. This was a special time for Sophia and her family, as well as the entire community. The afternoon was spent in a wonderful celebration of thanksgiving and hope.

By sunset most of the crowd had retreated back to their homes after a long and enjoyable day. Some of the closer acquaintances stayed to clean up, returning the beach to its regular pristine tropical look. Finally alone, Sophia and her parents sat under a few palm trees near the water's edge. It was quiet now, except for the lapping of the small, yet consistent waves against the shoreline and the occasional voices and laughter from the village behind them. They all sat quietly for a while. They just smiled and looked out over the calm waters along the peninsula, admiring the colors of the sunset, as the glowing round sphere slowly lowered itself behind the horizon. It had been a beautiful day, but behind the smiles, each felt a sense of sadness that came from knowing that within the next 48 hours they would be saying their good byes. There had rarely been a day in Sophia's life that the family had not been together as a unit. It was simply the nature of their culture. Sophia respected and honored her parents and they in turn were very proud of their daughter. It was the fabric of their family.

Now, however, the design was changing. Once a little girl, Sophia was now an incredible, beautiful young woman with a pleasant disposition. She was truly special. One might say that she had it all. What made her even more special was that she didn't even realize her near perfection. What all three of them did realize is that it was time for this young woman to become more independent and move away from their close-knit, nuclear family, at least for a while.

Sophia softly reached to either side, grasping both of her parents' hands. In a gentle voice she said, "I love you both so much." She then felt each of them squeeze her hand simultaneously and saw sentimental smiles come across their faces. Neither said a word, but their smiles said it all. With that, they all looked back at the sunset, each dealing with their own swirling emotions within.

Sophia spent the following day fervently packing. She had been given a set of luggage as a gift from the clinic, yet the medium and large suitcases were barely going to be sufficient. The bags lay at the end of her bed surrounded by a pile of neatly stacked clothes, the necessary documents she would need, books and memorabilia. Sophia wanted to take with her things that reminded her of home, so she thoughtfully selected items she thought would fit. She had a picture of her parents and her when she was just a baby. She was wrapped gently in a blanket in her mom's arms. Another item she selected was a picture of her on her dad's lap at the age of about six. The third she selected was of her in her blue graduation outfit standing between her dad, nicely dressed in his black suite, and her mom, in a cream colored, conservative dress. She wrapped each item delicately with cardboard, secured them with twine and placed the items safely between the clothes in her suitcase.

As Sophia was packing, her mom entered the room. "Sweetie, are you OK?"

"Yes, Mom," she replied. There was silence for a moment then she continued, "I must admit I am dealing with a lot of emotions right now."

"That is to be expected, dear. This is a big moment in your life. In all of our lives."

"Yes, it is. I have dreamed of the day I would grow up and move away. I didn't know what I would be doing or where I would be going, but I knew one day I would be saying good bye to you and Daddy."

Your daddy and I knew this day would come too. We knew it would be sad but we also knew it would be happy because it means you are moving on to a new part of your life that we wanted for you."

"Yes, Mommy. It is just that everyone in the village has given so much to me and I am so grateful. It is all so amazing, but I also feel such a sense of burden. Much of their hopes are in me; what if I let them down?"

Linn Sue watched her daughter's expressions closely and chose her response thoughtfully. Though she had wondered if Sophia might be feeling this, it was the first time she heard her daughter express that she might feel pressured or overwhelmed by the endeavor ahead of her. Making sure she responded appropriately, she spoke back to her daughter slowly and gently. "Sophia, they are all with you in spirit because they love you. Everyone helping you has seen you give so much of yourself and do so unselfishly for many years. They have watched you grow from a little girl to a woman who cared for them in the clinics. Everyone gave freely from their hearts, just as you did for them for so long. Sophia, when you gave to them did you have expectations in return or did you give because you simply felt compassion?"

"Compassion, Mommy. I just like to help people and see them happy."

"My sweet, Sophia, you did make so many people happy. And now their gift to you is to help you and see you happy." Linn Sue paused, and then went on, "Wherever that may take you, your debt, my precious daughter, was paid long before any donations were given." Linn Sue caressed Sophia's hands in hers. "You have given others a sense of hope, a sense that there is more out there, and you helped to inspire them. That sense of hope is instilled in all of us through fostering you and is something we all want to feel. You give this entire village an opportunity to give to something that makes them feel good. That feeling alone is their reward, so I don't want you to feel burdened or take on too much emotional weight. No matter what you do or where you end up, you gave them hope, happiness and purpose."

Sophia's eyes began to tear up. "Thank you, Mommy. I needed to hear that. I want to learn all I can and then come back home and use it to continue to help our community. That is what I want to do. I guess I am just overwhelmed with leaving home. I miss you and Daddy so much already."

Linn Sue leaned over and hugged Sophia. "We will be right here for you, Dear. You will be with your aunt and uncle there, so you will still be with family. That will keep you safe and loved. Then you will be home next summer. Remember that is less than ten months away from now."

"I know, Mommy. It is just that you and I talk. We share everything. You are like my best friend. I have never talked to Auntie like that. What if I can't?"

"Baby, you will be busy. I am sure with love, honor and respect you two will get along just fine. Your auntie is a wise woman. She has been in America for a while now and people talk more openly there. She will become not only family but a close friend too, I am sure."

The word honor stuck in Sophia's mind and in turn made her think of her father. "Mommy, is Daddy doing OK?"

"Honestly, Dear, he is probably taking it the hardest. You have always been his princess. He is so proud of you."

"Where is he now, Mommy?"

"I believe he is sitting outside watching the ocean as he loves to do. I am sure he would love to spend some private time with you." With that Linn Sue stood up and gave Sophia one more hug. "I love you my precious daughter."

"I love you too, Mommy," replied Sophia. Then her mom quietly walked out of the room.

When Sophia walked outside, her dad was resting quietly in a chair, a cup of tea sitting on the small wooden table next to him. On the other side of the table was another chair that her mom usually sat in while her parents talked at night. Pae was gazing through a clearing in the trees, where one could then see a bit of the vast ocean in the distance. There was a slight breeze moving his thick hair.

"Daddy," said Sophia.

Pae turned slowly towards Sophia and gave her a smile. "Hello, Princess." He motioned for Sophia to sit in the empty chair. "Come join me." Sophia sat down, feeling the warm breeze on her face.

"How is my angel doing?" said Pae.

"I am fine, Daddy. A little emotional, but Mommy and I talked and now I am doing better."

"Ahhh. Emotions." He nodded with a smile. "Sometimes we love them, and sometimes they scare us. Emotions are normal, Princess. Just realize what an incredible experience lays before you. You are such a special girl, Sophia. I know you will work hard, but also remember to enjoy your experience in America. It is a very good country. There are so many opportunities. Embrace them."

Pae paused and then went on, "We are a fortunate family, Sophia. It may sound strange coming from your dad who is old and only has one leg, but we are. We have our home, our gift shop, and your chance for an education in America. But most of all we have each other." Pae reached over, patted his daughter's forearm and then continued, "We love and respect each other in our family which means a lot. Having that closeness is what life is ultimately about. Anything else is extra. So please, my princess, we want you to enjoy America. And don't worry about us back here. You are a special girl and will always be my princess."

Sophia reached across the table, grasping her father's hand. She could see the moisture in his eyes. "I love you, Daddy," she muttered between sobs.

They both smiled and looked out towards the ocean as they continued to hold hands.

CHAPTER 27

The drive to the airport was very quiet. The luggage had been placed in the back of the pick-up and now Sophia was sitting between her two parents. In her hands was the small brown teddy bear she'd had since she was a newborn. There had not been a time in her life without the stuffed bear, and there were many times as a child that this little bear had consoled her tears and frustrations. She had enjoyed hearing, again and again, the story of how she got the bear from an American boy as she and her mother were leaving the hospital three days after her birth.

Pae guided the pick-up truck down the bumpy road in the direction of the airport, while Linn Sue appeared to stare out the passenger side window at the passing trees. She was actually seeing absolutely nothing except the memories of her daughter's life reeling in her mind.

Finally, they pulled up to a large building that was the terminal. Only one jetliner sat on the tarmac, its stairs down, leading up to the door near the front of the plane. Sophia felt her chest swell up some. The building and the plane looked like monstrosities to her, and she could feel herself start to become overwhelmed by it all. Her father awkwardly got out of the truck and waved to a young man for assistance with the two large suitcases. The young man took the bags to the ticket counter. Linn Sue pulled her daughter's ticket from her handbag and handed it to the lady behind the counter. The lady behind the counter gave Sophia her boarding pass, put the baggage tags on the bags and, with a smile, pointed them to a seating area just down the way. Sophia sat between her parents with her handbag at her feet. Her father had his hand placed lovingly on her back. Her mom was holding her right hand gently yet firmly. In Sophia's handbag sat the small teddy bear peering up at them.

"I remember the day you got that teddy bear, Dear," her mom said. "You were just three days old." Linn Sue smiled. "Now that little teddy bear is going back to Los Angeles with you. I don't remember the boy's name but I wonder what ever happened to that little boy who gave him to you. He is all grown up now like you are, Dear. He would be a young man now." They all smiled at this. Then a voice came from behind then letting them know it was time to board.

Pae, Sophia and Linn Sue all stood. As Sophia and her mom hugged, her dad just watched, balancing himself on his hand held crutches. Tears flowed freely from both Sophia and her mom. After a couple of minutes both let go. Slowly Sophia turned to her dad. He had been able to contain his emotions up to this point, but as his daughter gently leaned into him, then squeezed more tightly with persistent sobs, he could not stop the one tear that began to run down his cheek. Linn Sue moved closer, placing her arms around both of them.

The sound of the two women softly crying was audible to those around. Pae sensed this, as well as the need for his daughter to depart. "It is time now," he said softly.

One final hug and Sophia picked up her bag, then turned towards the door leading to the airplane outside. She restrained the urge to throw down her bags and run back to her parents for another embrace. Instead she gave them a soft look, a quick wave good-bye and she was gone. Sophia's parents watched her walk to the plane, ascend the stairs and disappear from view.

The two held each other proudly until Linn Sue finally said, "We did good, Dear," as she lovingly rubbed her hands across her husband's back.

Pae continued to look at the aircraft as he replied, "We sure did. We did very good."

CHAPTER 28

Sophia had never been on an airplane before. This was more than just a small airplane, it was a large airliner. It was the biggest transport vehicle she had ever seen up close. This enormous, mysterious aircraft was going to take her from a small, obscure part of the world to America. America was a place she had only heard about on their old, outdated television, from talk in the village as people reminisced about the war, or Americans passing through. Sophia entered the plane with her ticket stub and handbag. The ticket stub read 17A, which meant very little to Sophia. The flight attendant recognized this and guided her to her seat next to a window. She put her bag under the seat in front of her as instructed. The flight was notably not very full; she was only one of five people that got on at her stop. The plane had come from Singapore, stopped at Vietnam, would stop again in Tokyo, and then head to LAX Airport in Los Angeles. Sophia began to settle in, dealing with her anxieties. Part of her was excited for the chance to go to America while another part of her was being torn apart about leaving her home, her family, her friends, and the only life she had ever known. She sat looking out the window at the tarmac and the workers scurrying around as she processed this.

"Hello," came a voice from a man who was now sitting down in the aisle seat and fastening his seat belt.

"Hello," Sophia replied.

"I had to stretch my legs before the next leg of the flight. My name is Graham Taylor."

"Hi, I am Sophia."

Graham Taylor was a very nice looking forty-five year old man. He had thick, sandy-gray hair combed straight back and his face was clean-shaven. It was apparent he took care of himself through diet and exercise so his six-foot frame was well proportioned. He was wearing black slacks and a light blue, tailored shirt. Graham was confident, and yet unassuming, with a captivating smile that made him easy to get to know. He had passed through Vietnam several times on business, however his deeper connection to this land was that he would have died here years ago as an injured soldier had he not been carried off the battlefield by his dear friend Robert from California. Now Graham was in corporate real estate and had been in Singapore on business. He was traveling back to Phoenix, Arizona where his business office was located.

"Sophia. That is a nice name. Where are you headed?" he asked.

"I am going to Los Angeles for school to be a nurse," replied Sophia.

"Have you been to The States before?"

"Well, I am told I was born there but I don't remember that. This is my first time away from home."

"And you are heading to Los Angeles?" Graham said aloud as his inner dialogue pondered this choice for the first time away from home in addition to the first visit to the United States.

"Yes, I am going to stay at my aunt and uncle's house and go to community college until I can get into nursing school," Sophia responded innocently.

The more they talked the more Graham realized Sophia was naïve to the fact she was going to get a real culture shock. Of all the American cities to be thrown into, Los Angeles has to be near the top on the "most shocking" list.

The jet pulled away from the building and was being towed a safe distance from the terminal. It then slowly proceeded and stopped for final take off instructions. Sophia kept looking out the window. She could see the building - far away now - where her parents said goodbye. She could not see them, but she knew they were there watching. This moment was as tough on them as it was on her. She was certain of that.

Right then the jet engines began to roar causing Sophia to grab onto the armrests for security. The brakes released and the great machine lurched forward picking up speed with each passing moment. Sophia watched as the ground moved so fast beneath her, that it soon became a blur. The nose of the plane came up and the surface of the earth fell further and further away from her. Within a minute they were inside the clouds, and the view was a murky gray rushing past with incredible speed. She glanced at Graham for a brief moment, searching for any sense of security. He looked back at her with a smile.

"Sophia, you will be just fine. Trust me," he said calmly.

With that, Sophia looked back out the window, taking in the full experience as her father had recommended. The gray was growing lighter, and then the plane suddenly broke through the top of the clouds, instantly revealing the almost blinding, shimmering white from the sun. It was as though someone had just turned a bright light on, and now she was in an entirely different world, separated from the earth somewhere far below. Sophia smiled out the window as she pondered the new and exciting world she was embarking upon. America was a dream come true. Feeling blessed, she sat back in her seat and closed her eyes, said a prayer, and then fell asleep.

Sophia was awakened by a gentle tap on the shoulder from Graham. "Time for lunch, Dear," he said in a fatherly tone.

She stretched for a moment while Graham politely pulled down the table from the seat in front of her. The flight attendant sat a tray down on Sophia's table before moving down the row.

"I think it is chicken but I am not putting my money on it," Graham said with a smile. Sophia smiled back, appreciative that Graham had helped her manage the meal process on an airplane, for she had no idea herself.

When Sophia finished eating, she put her napkin on the tray and then turned to look out the window. It was now late afternoon, sunny and with little-to-no clouds to be seen. All she could see was the deep, blue expansion of ocean six miles below, the blue waters captivating her and putting her into a sentimental state of mind. She thought of her mom and dad back home, wondered what they were doing and how they were going to handle the separation for the next ten months.

Her stream of thought was suddenly interrupted by Graham's voice. "Sophia, are you alright?"

"Excuse me?" Sophia asked, a little dazed.

"You seem sort of sad."

"A little, I guess. I have really never been away from my family. We are very close. My mom is my best friend. And as for my dad, I just love and respect him so much. I knew I would miss them, but I did not know it would hurt this much or start so soon."

Graham looked at her kindly and replied, "Sophia, it is natural to miss them and for your heart to hurt. Don't fight it. Accept it because it reflects the love you share with each other. It is really a beautiful thing."

"Thank you. I know you are right. This is just a very different experience for me. Every day I can remember, they have been there," she said between light sobs, "It will be a challenge not to see them each day."

"You are right, Sophia, it will be tough. But you will grow from this experience. Part of life is learning to do things on your own. It sounds like you have a special bond with your family. That will always be there. As much as you will miss them, you are doing something very worthwhile in your life. And as much as they will miss you, I am sure that they want you to live this experience to its fullest."

Sophia felt like her parents' words were coming from her new acquaintance's mouth. At this moment, she felt as though Mr. Taylor had been hand-picked by God, and placed right there in the seat beside her to console her and guide her through this flight. "I know you are right, Mr. Taylor. Thank you for being so kind."

"My pleasure. Sophia, can I share a little advice with you?"

"Yes," she replied.

"The United States is a wonderful place, but it is also a little cruel at times. Especially a city like Los Angeles. You have to be very careful. You can't trust everyone. Back at your home everyone knows you and will protect you. In a big city like LA, you just can't expect that people will look after your best interest. There are people that try to take advantage of others. Do you understand what I am trying to tell you, Sophia?"

"Yes. I think so. I need to be careful of people."

"Yes, but more than that. People there may try to manipulate you to get what they want from you. " Graham tried to be tactful but decided to be more direct for Sophia's sake. "Sophia, you are a beautiful young woman and American men will be attracted to you, but not always with the most sincere intentions. It is a very different culture than you are familiar with. It is very open and aggressive compared to what you are used to. I just want you to be safe. Enjoy the experience of America but be very careful. OK?"

Sophia smiled brightly, "So are you being my new American father now?"

Graham laughed. "Why? Do I sound like I am being overly protective?"

"Yes, but I admit it is nice to have a new American friend already watching out for me. I really do appreciate your concern, and I will take it to heart. I really will. You have a very caring spirit and that is nice to have in a new friend. Thank you very much, Mr. Taylor."

"Please, Sophia, call me Graham. We are friends, right? First names are fine then."

"Ok, Graham. Thank you very much."

In Tokyo, Graham and Sophia were both scheduled on the same flight again since Graham had to change planes in LA before heading home to Phoenix. This seemed like fate to Sophia. Not only did she have a new friend who treated her like a daughter, making her feel safe and protected, but Graham was also very well travelled and there was a lot she could learn from him. The two had several hours to waste during the layover, so Graham found a nice restaurant at the airport and bought Sophia dinner. Over their meal, Graham gave Sophia a lot of practical advice about the United States and LA in particular, including how the stoplights worked, areas to check out and areas to avoid, the ins and outs of public transportation, popular foods and the money system. Sophia asked Graham to make up real life scenarios where she would need to determine how much items would cost in American dollars and calculate her change, for which Graham was happy to comply. He even threw in information about US history, the government, and the educational system, which Sophia enjoyed learning.

The two talked until about eleven o'clock that night, at which time they boarded their next flight. This time, however, their seats were not together, so Graham used his charm to switch seats with another passenger, in order to continue talking with Sophia on the way to LA. It was very late, however, by the time the airliner taxied into position, and after having had a great meal and conversation, both of them found it time to get some rest. Graham tossed Sophia a pillow and blanket from the above storage compartment, and she settled in for the long flight ahead. Within a few minutes after take off, both Graham and Sophia were sound asleep.

Sophia had slept for several hours surely exhausted from all the emotions she had endured over the last several days. When she woke up, it was getting light outside, and although she did not realize it, she had passed through multiple time zones. She felt as though she had slept a full night's sleep, yet it was only early morning. It would be several more hours before the plane was to touch down in Los Angeles. Graham was still sleeping, but she noticed an empty breakfast tray in front of him. Sophia smiled as she realized she had slept so hard that she missed the meal served earlier. It had been nice, however, to have finally been able to rest that hard and wake up with a clear perspective regarding the journey ahead. After her conversation with Graham and a sound night's sleep, she felt more settled and at peace. Enjoying this sense of contentment, Sophia reached down and grabbed the teddy bear from her handbag. She held it close to her and lightly patted it. At this moment Graham shifted in his chair and woke up just enough to see Sophia smiling gently as she cuddled a tattered teddy bear.

Sophia then retrieved her journal, set it on the table in front of her and began to write down her thoughts. She began by expressing to her parents how much she loved and missed them. She also thanked God for the comfort of such a wonderful man as Graham, who gave her a sense of security. He had seemed to be placed by God as her guardian angel. While she was deep into her writing, the flight attendant asked her if she wanted to have her breakfast. She nodded yes with a smile and placed her journal back into her handbag.

As she began to eat, she felt a sense of distance from her homeland and a building excitement about nearing the United States of America and living in Los Angeles. She had only seen pictures of the City of Angels from photos sent by her aunt and uncle, whom she had not seen since she was 12 years old.

Graham finally started to stir. He rubbed his eyes and then looked up to see Sophia smiling. "Did I snore?"

"Not too loud," she answered with a smile.

"Are we almost there?"

"The captain said over the load speaker a while ago that we were about two hours away. I would imagine it's about an hour now."

"Great," Graham replied, "I feel like I have been on this plane for about a week now."

Sophia smiled at his quick wit.

"How are you holding up, Sophia?"

"Better now that I got some rest and food and was able to collect my thoughts and put them down in my journal. So much has been going on in my head for the last few days. I really did need a friend like you to talk to. Thank you, Graham. I truly feel you were heaven-sent."

Graham reached into his pocket and pulled out a business card. "Sophia. I am going to give you this card with my name and contact information on it. I want you to feel free to call me anytime. Let me repeat that because I know you will feel you are overreaching and bothering me, but you truly are not. I, too, feel I was supposed to meet you and to look out for you in some way. I want you to feel you have that friend in America that cares about your safety and well-being. Please call any time."

"Thank you, Graham. I appreciate that so much. You are so kind." She took the card, reached for her handbag and placed it in her Bible.

At that moment, the engines to the airliner slowed and the gradual decent into Los Angeles began. Sophia looked out the window to see the coastline come into view several miles ahead.

"America," she whispered to herself.

As they got closer, more and more buildings and thousands of closely-knit houses came into view. The freeway had four or five lanes with cars racing in every direction during the late afternoon rush hour. It amazed Sophia to see so much humanity moving around like millions of meandering insects.

As they passed near LAX setting up for a landing, she could see hundreds of jets and small planes. Some parked, some taxiing, some landing, while others leaped from the airstrip into the sky. Soon they turned onto final approach and began to line up for the landing. The aircraft swayed back and forth and then the wheels grabbed the pavement and slowed it down. As the captain welcomed them to Los Angeles, they began the long taxi to the terminal. After about 10 minutes, the jet pulled up to the loading ramp, a bell rang and the passengers jumped up for their luggage.

Graham and Sophia got to their feet, retrieved their bags and followed the other passengers towards the exit. As they left the plane, Sophia could feel some of the warm California air blast through the open door. She sighed partly out of relief to be off the airplane, and partly out of anticipation regarding what may be ahead of her. Once they entered the terminal, there were thousands of people, shops and places to get food. As they followed the signs to U.S. Customs, Sophia looked around her apprehensively.

Graham could see that she was quite overwhelmed. "Don't worry, Sophia. I won't leave you until we find your family."

Relieved, Sophia beamed a nervous smile and then refocused on the task at hand.

Once through Customs, they finally ventured to the carousel to find their bags. Sophia had been amazed by her surroundings while waiting for her luggage, marveling at the hundreds of people scurrying around the area and the hustle and bustle of LAX, as a whole. Unlike the small terminal in Vietnam, the airport in Los Angeles was a universe within itself. She had watched in awe as bags, suitcases and boxes of every shape, size and color whisked robotically around the several enormous carousels. People crowded around the area, surveying and reaching for their luggage as it slowly moved by. Sophia had little faith that of all the bags in front of her, hers would magically show up, and then lo and behold, just like clockwork, it did. Her bag had dropped from the conveyor belt onto the carousel, slowly coming towards her as if on its own journey to find its rightful owner.

Graham checked his bag for his connecting flight to Arizona. He then followed her to the area where she would meet her family. As they came through the door, her aunt and uncle spotted her and waved with a welcoming smile. Graham followed closely behind her with her bags.

"Sophia, oh it is so nice to see you. You are so beautiful," her aunt exclaimed with a hug.

"Thank you," she replied.

Her uncle followed with a hug as well.

"I want you to meet my guardian angel, Graham Taylor. He has been an absolute blessing from God. Without him I may have not gotten here. Graham this is my aunt and uncle."

"Very nice to meet you. You have a delightful niece."

"We are so grateful for you looking after our dear Sophia."

They all talked for a few minutes, and then began their goodbyes.

"Sophia, remember that you have my business card. I am here for you. It was such a pleasure to meet you; you are a very special young lady. Good luck in school; I know you will do great." Respecting her culture, Graham reached out to shake her hand.

Sophia, however, leaned in and gave him a hug. "Thank you, Graham. You were a gift from God. I will never forget your kindness. Bye. Be safe."

Graham then turned and walked towards his gate, while the Nguyen family headed to the parking area.

As if the baggage area had not been surprising enough, the trip to the parking lot was a shock to Sophia as well. People were everywhere.

Cars, buses, and taxis were all over the place in their own version of organized chaos. Once past the four lanes, they entered the multilevel parking lot. They found her uncle's Toyota Camry, loaded her two bags into the trunk, and got into the car. Sophia's aunt had instructed her to ride in the front seat in order to get the full affect of her new city. Sophia, dazed but taking everything in, complied.

From here, they slowly meandered down the levels of the parking lot until they reached the street that led them towards the highway. Once on the 5, the traffic was stop-and-go during the afternoon rush hour, an endless sea of vehicles. Sophia watched as cars struggled to change lanes, listened as cars honked, and smelled the exhaust fumes coming from the cars in front of them. She took it all in with astonishment, as she felt herself occasionally clutch her seat extra tight. The airport baggage claim and parking lot were nothing compared to the culture shock of experiencing California traffic.

Once off the highway, the busy streets were lined with businesses on each side. Every culture was represented on the streets around her. "America truly is the melting pot of the world," thought Sophia to herself. It actually gave her a sense of comfort seeing all the diversity around her; however, this comfort teetered in her mind as she remembered Graham's protective comments.

After the one-hour commute to her aunt and uncle's home, they entered a nice neighborhood. It was nothing too ritzy, but quiet and clean with small houses and green yards. The car slowed and pulled into a driveway, stopping just in front of a garage. Sophia got out and stood next to the car. She looked around and noticed that all the houses were similar. A subtle, flowery fragrance floated in the afternoon breeze - the air wasn't thick with moisture like back home - it was 72 degrees with a humidity that was very comfortable. Sophia also noticed the singing of birds, both near and far. Compared to the overwhelming shock after landing at LAX and the highway gridlock, Sophia now felt like she had been placed in her own little corner of paradise. She immediately liked it here.

Her aunt and uncle's house had a small, well-manicured, green yard with rose bushes around its perimeter blooming in shades of red, yellow and pink. "Oh, this is so beautiful," Sophia said, pointing towards the flowers.

"Thank you," replied her aunt, "Your uncle likes to spend time in his small yard and garden. Most of the people in this community are the same. Property is expensive in California, so you do whatever you can to make your little lot look nice."

Her uncle unlocked the door, which Sophia took note of, as locks weren't used back in her village; they simply weren't necessary. Again, Graham's cautionary words came to her mind, as they entered the house. It was a quaint, single level structure - about 1000 square feet - as were most of the houses nearby. There was a neatly kept living room, with the dining room and kitchen attached. To the left was a hallway with a bathroom and master bedroom on the right side and a guest bedroom on the left.

Sophia's aunt smiled and waved her to the room on the left. "This will be your room, my dear. We put a desk in here for studying. You also have a phone in which we all share a common line." Her aunt paused then continued, " We will also share the bathroom across the hallway from you. Please make yourself comfortable. We are so happy that you will be with us. It makes us feel so much closer to the family back in Vietnam having you here. It really is special for us to be a part of this journey with you."

Sophia crossed the room to her aunt and hugged her. "This is perfect," she said aloud. She then went to her uncle, hugged him as well, and said, "Thank you so much."

"Dear, why don't you unpack and get settled in. I will prepare a meal and then I'm sure you will need some sleep. It will take about an hour or so for me to make dinner. Your uncle has placed some towels in the bathroom if you would like to take a shower before dinner," her aunt said gently then continued with a smile, "We are so happy you are here."

Sophia sensed the sincerity in her aunt's voice. After she walked out, Sophia closed the door and sat on the bed next to her luggage. She had a nice bed, a desk, dresser with a mirror, and a small closet. The bedroom was painted a pale blue with white trim. She sat quietly for a few minutes scanning her little blue bedroom, pulling out her teddy bear from the top of one of her bags, and holding it close while she smiled to herself. Though tired and somewhat jet lagged, she was happy and excited. This was perfect, she thought, to herself, as an enormous sense of peace engulfed her.

CHAPTER 29

Blending into life at her aunt and uncle's was very natural for Sophia, as they had kept many of their Vietnamese customs and traditions intact, having found that the American culture had given them the freedom to do so. When it came to school, Sophia was a little more worried; however she had already addressed this concern by setting up a meeting at the community college with a guidance counselor. The goal was to make sure she was registered for the proper classes that would meet requirements for nursing school.

The next step was adapting to the city of Los Angeles. Getting to campus was going to be an entirely different animal for her to conquer. Sophia's home village was small. It had the basics that the villagers needed to survive and enjoy life, but there were no extras. Here in Los Angeles, her simple little village could be consolidated to less than two city blocks. And the blocks in LA continued on and on forever. There was just so much more in LA, more of everything.

Sophia's aunt and uncle took her to campus on the day of her meeting with the counselor. The counselor, who was also an Asian woman, was a tremendous help. Sophia felt she had gotten the five classes including English, Biology, Chemistry, Physiology and Pre-Nursing that she needed most. The classes intrigued her and she looked forward to them with eager anticipation. She decided to wait and take her Math requirement the following year.

After the meeting they drove to the mall so that Sophia could get some new clothes. The village's sponsorship fund had unexpectedly sent over some spending money which was entrusted to her aunt and uncle to dispense however they felt was appropriate and necessary for Sophia's happiness and peace of mind. Sensing Sophia's nervousness about the city of LA and starting a new school, they thought some new clothes would be a great way to help promote her confidence and feeling of beginning to fit in.

Yet again, Sophia felt astonishment by the scope of the mall. There were two levels, each having more stores than she could see while standing in one place. "Why do American's feel they need so many options?" Sophia whispered to herself as they scaled the mall and she tried to make decisions on which stores to even go into.

After a couple of hours of shopping with her aunt and very patient uncle, the three of them had dinner at a traditional American hamburger joint in the mall. Sophia was so happy. They had all easily bonded in such a quick time, and she so appreciated how they were trying to make her feel comfortable and give her experiences common to a girl her age in the United States.

By the end of the week, Sophia had thoroughly studied the local bus schedule, so as to not burden her uncle with driving her around. With school starting the following Monday, she actually felt that she had a comfortable grasp on how to get to and from school. She even did a practice run the Friday before to time things out. She was so close to embarking on her journey to become a nurse, which made her feel exhilarated and proud!

Sophia had talked to her parents the day she arrived to let them know she had gotten to Los Angeles safely. They planned to talk weekly after that, both to save on money and so that Sophia could focus on school. During their most recent conversation Sophia shared the size of the classes, describing auditoriums with fifty to one hundred students filling the room, while a professor walked back and forth on a stage below. From the other end of the phone, her parents marveled over what the school was like and how quickly Sophia had learned so much. Each time she talked to them, Sophia did feel a pang of missing home, but it was easily overcome by her excitement regarding the days ahead.

Sophia loved her classes and would sit in the front row in order to hear every word from the instructor. She immersed herself in her studies. At night she'd eat dinner with her aunt and uncle before retreating to her room, opening her books on her desk, and - under the watchful eye of her teddy bear - study vigorously for a couple of hours. Around 8:00 p.m. she would come out and join her loving hosts to watch television for about an hour, then head back into her room to do some more reading before going to sleep around midnight. It was a schedule that worked for Sophia, and she liked the routine, so she systemically stayed with it.

This lifestyle wasn't work to her; she loved every minute of it. She had set out to become a nurse, and now was exactly where she wanted to be. The professors were so intelligent and knew exactly how to engage a student that was there to learn. That surely described Sophia and the professors sensed this in her. She truly loved the biology labs for pre-nursing students. It was her first experience seeing a cadaver. Once she had worked through the emotion of this being someone's loved one who had passed, she found herself fascinated with all that was presented in front of her to learn. She found herself up in the early morning hours, when it was only she and her teddy bear, reviewing extra credit research articles the instructor had shared the previous day. Sophia's passion and commitment to her goal of becoming a nurse catapulted her to the top of all of her classes. It all seemed so natural . . . as if this was what she had prepared for her entire life. She was so excited about reaching her goals and returning to her village as a real medical professional, that she even chose not to return home the following summer as planned. Wanting to apply to nursing school as soon as possible, she decided to stay and take classes during June and July.

Sophia had little in common with those at the college who did not share her ambition. She wasn't interested in a lot of the buzz she heard from other girls around her, who were more focused on whether or not a certain boy was interested in them, or what each girl was going to wear to an upcoming mixer. Sophia had, however, made some friends in class, as they would routinely have group study sessions.

Most of the people that she aligned herself with were committed like Sophia, but some in the study groups were taking prerequisites to simply fulfill university requirements. One such student was Matt Chambers. Matt was in her English class on a pre-law track. He wasn't a good student, but came from a demanding, wealthy family. He was the son of an overbearing father who ran a very successful business in Los Angeles and had expectations, whether realistic or not, to eventually have Matt become a partner. He insisted, however, that Matt receive a degree first. Matt wore designer clothes and drove a nice, late model BMW. He certainly looked the part of being on the road to big things, but money and pride stunted any real ambition to diligently work hard and achieve true success. To put it bluntly but accurately, he was a lazy, self-centered, and entitled kid with no real, significant reason to change his ways.

Matt had arrogantly approached Sophia in the library one afternoon as was his trademark way. He attempted to charm her with his irrelevant, materialistic lifestyle. Though Sophia excelled in her scholastic skills, she still lacked in social understanding of American men, despite her earlier warning from Graham Taylor. Unknowingly to Sophia, Matt was exactly the type of guy Graham had warned her about, the type of person who saw her as only a conquest, or prey. Although he was certainly intrigued by Sophia's Asian beauty, to him she was simply something his ego needed to conquer. Her quietness, according to his twisted, selfish mind, justified him the opportunity to fill in the blanks with fantasy at Sophia's expense. And, unfortunately, his artificial charm and salesman-like ways often succeeded in drawing his prey in with little resistance.

Throughout the month of June, Matt spent a great deal of energy pursuing Sophia. He sweet-talked her into going to dinner with him on two occasions, which Sophia appreciated. To her, it was nice to have a new friend to do things with outside of school. She thought it was helping her balance life, which seemed to be a good thing. Matt spent time explaining to her why Americans do what they do, and he would listen intently as she spoke of her aspirations to be a nurse and what she had most recently learned about the human body. He even seemed sincerely interested when she spoke of her village back home and her parents. Although it was apparent that Matt had attempted subtle advances towards her, Sophia was able to jokingly play them off and focus on how kind Matt seemed to be towards her. It was innocent enough to her, but Matt was becoming more frustrated and obsessed with her each time she did not return his advancements.

These advances all came to a head one evening after Matt and Sophia had gone to a movie together. The drive to her home was normal enough, but once the car was parked in front of the house things changed. Matt reached over and placed his hand firmly behind her head pulling her closer to him as he forcefully kissed her. To Sophia, this came out of nowhere, and it was only at this point that Sophia smelled the alcohol he had somehow secretly been drinking that night, as his other hand quickly and abruptly grabbed her breast.

"Matt," she shrieked, "No. We are friends. That is all."

Matt let her go and angrily turned towards the steering wheel shaking his head in frustration. "Why the hell can't we do more? I take you out. We have fun. Why can't we have a little more fun? You can't really be that prudish?"

"It isn't prudish, Matt. It is knowing my boundaries," replied Sophia.

"Boundaries? The hell with boundaries. You only live once. Why not enjoy it? You can't study all the time."

Still caught off guard, but remaining calm Sophia responded, "We are apparently two different people, Matt, with different priorities. Can't you see that?"

"Being different doesn't mean you can't have some fun."

"We went to a movie, Matt. Isn't that fun?"

"Are you that naïve, Sophia? You go on some dates and then it is natural for things to happen. You are a woman. I am a man. It is normal."

"What is normal?"

"Being close. Kissing. Touching."

"I'm not like that, Matt."

"What? You've never been with a man? Are you kidding me?"

"No, I haven't and I'm proud of that. I will honor my future husband with the gift of intimacy." Then realizing Matt was only getting more perturbed, Sophia continued, "I need to go."

With that, Sophia opened the door and walked up to the front porch. As she unlocked the door to the house, she heard the engine to Matt's car accelerate and the wheels shriek on the pavement. In the distance, she heard the car squeal once more around a corner and then all went silent.

Once in the house, Sophia walked into her room, grabbed her teddy bear, and lay on the bed staring at the nightlight. After a few minutes a knock came upon the door. "Come in," said Sophia.

Sophia's aunt opened the door slowly. "Are you OK? I heard the car noise so wanted to check on you."

"Yes. Just tired. I am going to go to sleep."

"Ok, Dear. Sleep well."

"Thank you. Good night," responded Sophia softly. With that her aunt quietly closed the door.

Sophia hugged her bear and felt tears roll down her face. Within minutes she had cried herself to sleep.

CHAPTER 30

After the unfortunate turn of events with Matt, it was easy for Sophia to focus all of her energy back on school. She let the social life, especially with men, go totally by the wayside. She did have a couple of classmates, named Jenny and Susie, who had become friends. They still met periodically to study or grab a bite to eat, but social life was a far second to Sophia's studies.

Another thing Sophia found that she liked about school in The United States was the resourcefulness. The school found ways to incorporate individuals from the working world to share their experiences with students at the college. One example was for resident doctors and nurses already in the hospital setting to be able to teach lectures in the classroom. They shared pertinent information with pre-med or pre-nursing students who hadn't yet had the opportunity to be in the hospital setting, thus helping the clinicians learn teaching skills while also motivating the students they were addressing.

One day in mid July, Sophia wore a nice dark blue dress and a decorative light blue scarf tied around her neck, hanging gently down her front. Her school counselor had set up an appointment for her later in the afternoon with a local hospital interested in top students desiring to pursue a career in nursing. They provided scholarship opportunities for exemplary students accepted into their program and gave special consideration to students agreeing ahead of time that they would be their employer. Although Sophia was eager to get back to Vietnam and serve as a nurse, she knew she should explore all opportunities to get accepted into nursing school. This was her opportunity to get her foot in the door, ask questions and possibly get acquainted with some of the people handling the selection process.

Sophia wanted to impress those she was meeting with later that day by looking professional, so she took extra care getting ready that morning. Her hair laid perfectly down her back and she had applied blush, lip-gloss and a layer of mascara giving her face a polished, vibrant look. Sophia felt good about herself as she walked down the hall of the community college thinking about how she would greet the people from the hospital later that day and the questions she would ask them. She turned the corner and entered the lecture hall. As always, Sophia then sat down in the front row.

Within a few minutes her professor introduced that day's guest speaker who was a resident from UCLA Medical Center. Sophia didn't hear the doctor's name as her thoughts were still on her upcoming meeting, however she pulled out her notebook and readied herself to take notes.

At that moment, Stephen came onto the platform and began his presentation. Sophia casually looked up from her notebook at just the right time. Their eyes met. Sophia, being the sensitive, shy Asian woman that she was, normally would have looked away and blushed, but something compelled her to hold his gaze. He was tall, built nicely, had a slight tan and cleanly cropped hair. He wore dark slacks, dress shoes, and a white shirt with a stylish tie. He looked like he could have been on the cover of a GQ magazine. Sophia intently listened as he began his lecture. The young doctor's eyes frequently caught hers as he spoke, then he would comfortably and professionally look away to engage others in the class, and then would come back to Sophia. Needless to say, Sophia was mesmerized, and although she was very interested in what he had to say that day about being a medical professional, the organs and systems within the human body, and how they interrelate, this was one day she was interested less about her studies and more about the individual presenting them.

The class sped by as their eyes met time and time again. Once the class was over, the students applauded in appreciation. Dr. Nance smiled with gratitude and, after a brief wave, exited the platform off to the right and continued out the door. Sophia sighed and wondered if she'd ever have the opportunity to meet this handsome young doctor again.

Sophia gathered her books, hoping that with any luck, the young doctor would be in the hallway as she exited the lecture hall. Sophia was filled with hope as she looked intently down the hall to the right, then turned quickly to the left, but with an odd sense of disappointment, she realized he was gone.

CHAPTER 31

July came to an end and finals were complete, giving Sophia a chance to relax after a tough summer session. While sitting at home one afternoon, the phone rang. "Sophia, it's for you," her uncle said holding out the kitchen phone.

Sophia grabbed the receiver and gently rolled the telephone cord around her hands as she said, "Hello. This is Sophia."

"Sophia, it's Jenny. What are you doing tonight? Some of us are going to a small party to celebrate the end of classes. Please come with us. We want you to come. I can pick you up at 8:00. I know you aren't much of a partier, but it's not far from you so if you want to leave I can just take you home."

Sophia paused for a moment. Her initial response would normally be to decline, but she thought about how hard she had been working in school, and after all, she was on break now. Hanging out with some friends may be good for her. She was touched that Jenny reached out to her and wanted her to come. She decided since she would be with girlfriends, it would be fine.

"OK, Jenny, I will be ready at 8:00. Thank you for inviting me." Sophia hung up the phone and looked at her aunt cooking in the kitchen.

"I am going to go out with Jenny for a little while tonight," she said to her aunt.

Have fun, Dear, you deserve it," she replied, smiling understandingly.

****

Jenny was there promptly at 8:00 p.m. wearing a short skirt and makeup to the hilt. "She certainly is ready to blow off some steam from the difficult semester," thought Sophia.

Within seconds of getting in the car, Jenny pulled out her makeup bag and signaled for Sophia to lean in towards her. Sophia agreed to let her apply some extra blush, eye shadow and lipstick. She then let Jenny persuade her to do a slight tease to her hair and add hairspray.

"Wow," said Jenny, "You look great!"

Sophia pulled down the car's visor and looked in the mirror. A little surprised at what she saw staring back at her, she reluctantly decided to just go with the look.

When the two girls arrived at the house, it was obvious that it was not actually a small party as Jenny had described on the phone. Cars were double parked down the long street, the music was loud, the place was very crowded and alcohol was readily available. Jenny saw more of her friends and let out a shriek of exhilaration as she hugged them and was promptly handed a drink. Sophia smiled politely at Jenny's other friends, nodded at their dramatic stories, but found it very hard to relate. Sophia observed as drinks one and two went down for Jenny like water to a parched traveller in a hot dessert.

Sophia surveyed her surroundings. It was a large, beautiful house but there wasn't a person over 22 or 23 years old in sight. She stayed near Jenny most of the time and sipped on a ginger ale while her friend partied and drank. Within an hour Jenny was dancing and singing with her other girlfriends and some guys in the living room. Sophia watched the activity going on around her, when a voice came up from behind.

"Hey, what's a girl like you doing in a place like this?"

Startled, Sophia turned quickly to see Matt looking directly at her. This was the last person she wanted to encounter tonight; especially in a place and situation like this.

"Just here to get out of the house with friends," Sophia answered.

"Who you with?" asked Matt, scanning the people around Sophia, including the guys in particular. He felt a hint of rage swell up in him thinking about how dolled up Sophia was with her hair and make up around all these other guys, when she wouldn't think of being like that with him.

"I came with Jenny," replied Sophia.

Matt let out a laugh. "The odd couple. The bookworm and the party girl! Looks like Jenny is already hammered."

Sophia looked over at Jenny now dancing very closely with a guy who was all over her. She then looked back at Matt and said, "Yes. Kind of looks that way. I think I will give my aunt and uncle a call and have them come get me. This is a little too much for me."

Seeing an opportunity, Matt replied," You don't need to call them for a ride. I can get you home in ten minutes and be back at the party before anyone even realizes I am gone."

Feeling a bit uncomfortable after their last encounter, Sophia shifted from one foot to the other and replied, "No. That is OK. They are happy to pick me up."

Matt decided there was no way he was going to lose this opportunity so he turned his tactics up a notch and replied with what came across as a sincere voice, "Sophia, it's 10:00. They are probably in bed. I can have you home in ten minutes. I have felt horrible about what happened last time we were together and have wanted to apologize and try to make it right. I am sorry, Sophia. Please let me do this for you to show I am sorry and try to make things right."

Sophia's intuition first told her no, but the more she thought about it she began to appreciate the fact he was apologizing and wanted to make amends. And besides, he was right. Her aunt and uncle probably were in bed. Yes, they'd be happy to come get her anytime but why inconvenience them? After all, she really didn't want them to have to come and pick her up from this environment anyway. Matt could have her home in minutes.

"OK," Sophia told Matt, "Let me tell Jenny that I have a ride home." With that Sophia walked away to talk to Jenny. Matt glowed with pathological pride realizing that his act of remorse had done the trick.

As Sophia walked away Matt's eyes fixated on her small, shapely figure. Seeing her bare legs under her black skirt and white summer sweater were intoxicating to him. His mind wandered towards his desire to have her. He felt his need for her tighten in his jeans. He took a big swig of the drink he had placed on a table, paused, and then slammed the rest down.

Drunk and his ego bolstered, Matt smiled at Sophia as she returned. Under his breath he told himself, "You're mine tonight. I will make a woman out of you once and for all."

As they walked to the car, Matt let her walk in front of him so he could watch her hips move in anticipation of knowing he'd have her soon. It turned him on even more to know that she had no idea what was about to happen.

As they approached his black BMW with the tinted windows, Matt reached for the door to let her in. She sat inside the car and as he shut the door, the streetlight caused his reflection to show up on the window, mirroring back at him. Seeing his own reflection, he smiled a big smile back at himself. He was full of narcissistic admiration over nearing his conquest. Sophia, from inside the car, saw his smile and, feeling it was a gesture of sincerity, she smiled back in gratitude that he was giving her a ride, and in hopes that maybe they could be friends again.

Matt rounded the front of the car and got into the driver's seat, started the car and began to drive. He put in a hard rock CD and stared straight ahead, not speaking to Sophia at all. She had seen that look before. As the rhythmic pounding of the music continued and the dashboard lights glared in her face, Sophia began to feel more and more uncomfortable.

"Matt, can we turn that down a little?" she asked.

He reached for the volume and turned it up. That was an instant message. Then, all of sudden he swerved the car down a road with no streetlights. He pushed the accelerator and recklessly drove down the abandoned street.

"What are you doing, Matt? Take me home," begged Sophia.

Matt said nothing still. By now the evil in his eyes was apparent. He had no expression and it was as if he was someone else. The car came to a drastic halt. Music still filled the air.

"Matt, what are you doing?"

"It's time, Sophia," was his reply.

"Time for what?"

"Time for you to experience a man. Especially as much as you have been shaking it tonight with all your hair and make up done," he said as he removed his jeans.

Matt then reached over and made Sophia's seat fall backwards with an abrupt bang.

"Matt. No. Please. No," Sophia pleaded through tears as she tried to open the locked door.

Matt put one hand over her mouth, and with the other hand ripped her underwear off her hips. Held down hard by his grasp, Sophia screamed into the loud music as Matt rolled on top of her. She cried out in agony and pain, as she struggled, then limply gave up to his size, strength and cruel desires. She was overpowered . . . powerless. Her eyes closed and she tried to make herself invisible.

Within minutes, the horrific nightmare was over. The beast was satisfied. He proudly zipped up his pants, started the car and headed to Sophia's home. She pulled her underwear up and put her skirt down. She stared out the passenger side window as tears still flowed down her face. She felt excruciating pain between her legs from the attack, however the shock made the rest of her feel completely numb.

Finally, the car slowed at the curb of her relatives' home. "Sophia, I'm sorry. I don't know what came over me. But we both needed that," said Matt.

Sophia, for a split second came out of numbness and pain, harvesting anger so deep from within that it surprised her. She slowly turned toward Matt. Her eyes glared with disdain. Before she knew what happened she slapped him, fingernails penetrating his face. The surprise startled him and before he knew what hit him Sophia was already out of the car and heading to her front door.

As he drove off, Sophia slowly sat down on the top step. Severe confusion set in. She could do nothing but bury her face in her hands and sob. As she took her hands away from her face and looked up at the moon, the tears caused rays of light to fill her eyes.

"Lord, why? What did I do to deserve this? I'm always careful, Lord. Please help me. I don't understand. Why me?"

She sat there for about 15 minutes. She didn't want to go inside and have her aunt see that she had been crying. She was sure her eyes were probably red and puffy, but her sobbing finally was under control so she stood up, wiped her eyes one more time and unlocked the door. She quietly opened the door into the silence of the house and softly walked to her room. She fell onto her bed, landing on her teddy bear, and stared into the darkness. She wanted to fall asleep and forget any of this had ever happened, but she knew it was real.

After a few minutes went by, Sophia sat up, turned on the lamp on the nightstand and got up to look in the mirror. Her eyes were still puffy and her shirt ripped in the struggle. She thanked God that her aunt had not woken up to see how battered she looked. She went to her closet and got her nightgown. The best thing she knew to do was to take a shower. She so terribly wanted to be clean. When Sophia removed her sweater she noticed marks on her neck, stomach and sides. The adrenaline and confusion from the attack had made her oblivious to the wounds. She had only felt the excruciating pain of Matt violating her, and then the numbness of realizing there was nothing she could do. She looked down and noticed a blood stain on her underwear and thigh. This shocked and scared her. Awkwardly she got into the shower to clean herself and wipe away the blood and, hopefully, some of the confusion and shame that were invading her now.

In the shower, Sophia could not clean her body well enough. She wanted to scrub harder and harder in an effort to wash away what had happened, but the rational side of Sophia knew this would not erase her wounds. The warm water of the shower stung her scraped and scratched body, but she let it run over her anyway. As she stood in the shower, she visualized the water cleaning away her struggle, soothing her soul. With each minute in the water and with each breath she took, she then began to feel more cleansed. After what seemed like forever, Sophia got out, dried herself off and put on her nightgown.

She walked back into her room, grabbed her teddy bear and lay underneath the cool blankets. She wished her mom were there to hold her and help her through this. Sophia wished she hadn't come to the United States. She wished she hadn't been so naïve. She wished she hadn't gotten in the car. Since her mom wasn't here, and she couldn't do anything to change the rest of it, she turned to God and talked to Him. She asked that He would see her through this and help her with whatever she needed to do. She asked Him to guide her through what was happening. She asked Him to give her understanding. She prayed and prayed until eventually she fell asleep.

CHAPTER 32

Many nights in a row continued the same for Sophia. Lying under the soft light of the lamp on her nightstand, Sophia would whisper, "Oh, Dear God, please be near me now. I feel so hurt. So empty and ashamed. I know Romans 8:28 tells us that everything has a purpose but how can good come of such an evil act that has happened to me? I struggle to understand."

Turning and grabbing her teddy bear, she would continue, "I beg you to be close to me now. I don't know what to do. My body hurts. My heart hurts. Please heal me. Please forgive me for being so naïve." Then, reaching for the switch on her lamp, she would push it, casting the room into darkness. Sophia would then roll onto her side and tighten her lips as tears moistened her pillow. Eventually she would fall asleep feeling empty, damaged and alone – alone, that is, except for the comfort of God and the bear squeezed against her chest.

As the days passed after the incident, the physical pain subsided, and the constant grief faded. Though she told no one except The Lord about the attack, her demeanor changed. She didn't smile as much when school began in September. She socialized with no one. Sophia had lost her sense of trust. She would go to class and come back to the house to study and do research. No longer did she want to be at the library during the evening hours or with the study group. The whole ordeal made her focus on getting her nursing degree and going home, and these two things only. To her, home meant family. It meant people who protected and cared for her. It meant people she could trust. Home was a village. And Sophia knew if not only for her own desire, the village needed her as well.

Sophia did continue to excel in class during the first part of the semester. In early October, however, she began to find herself losing focus. She also felt a relentless fatigue that she just couldn't overcome. She was very stressed. Not stressed with her course load, but very uneasy with the reality that she had missed her period for the second month. In typical Sophia fashion, she researched details on pregnancy and read how there are times when stress can cause a woman to miss her cycle. Sophia hoped this was the case for her. She prayed and prayed but finally decided it was time to take a pregnancy test.

On a quiet Saturday morning, Sophia went into the bathroom and pulled the newly purchased instrument out of its wrapping. As she held it in her hand she bowed her head and prayed. "Oh, Dear Lord," Sophia whispered, " I am so tired, so afraid, but I pray Your will be done."

Sophia took the test and waited. Five minutes felt like five days, however at the end of the five minutes, she saw the result she feared. She was pregnant.

Sophia's mind swam with thoughts and emotions. "What now?" was the question she kept coming back to. With no idea of what to do next, she stuck to what was right in front of her. She fervently disposed of the pregnancy test and cautiously walked to her room. Lying on the bed, she rolled to her side, and stared across the room for what could have been minutes or could have been hours. She lost track. Her eyes gazed at the wall, then at the picture of her parents on the dresser, then back to the wall as she whispered, "What next?"

****

Sophia decided that after church the next day she had to tell her aunt and uncle what was happening, then call home and explain things to her parents. When the next day arrived, the drive home from the chapel was quiet. Sophia could feel her stomach churning with nerves. Her aunt and uncle spoke to each other occasionally, but Sophia was deep in thought while staring out the window at the passing scenery. She remembered back to the first day she had arrived here in LA and contemplated how things had changed. An incessant haze began to overtake her as she thought through each step of the past months. She fought through this gloom knowing she had to keep her mind on the task at hand today. When they arrived home, Sophia helped her aunt prepare the usual meal they shared together on Sunday afternoons. After a short prayer by her uncle, they began to eat. The meal seemed to last forever, as Sophia pondered over the words that she would use to describe the events that led to her current predicament. When they were all through eating, Sophia knew the time had come that she had to share her story. It wasn't going to be easy, but it was something she had to do despite the growing lump forming in her throat and the confusion swirling in her head.

"Um, I have something I need to share with you," Sophia quietly sighed. She felt a gagging feeling in her throat and her mouth felt very dry. "First I want to thank you for having me here the last year or so. You have been so kind. What I am about to tell you has nothing to do with you or anything you did or didn't do. It just happened." Sophia hesitated. Her eyes began to swell and her head began to spin.

"Honey, are you OK?" her aunt asked, seeing that she was in distress.

"No auntie . . . not really . . . to be honest . . ." tears began to roll down Sophia's cheeks and drop at her chin.

Her aunt moved over to the chair next to her and took both Sophia's hands in hers then began rubbing them. "What happened, Dear?" We are here for you. What is going on?"

"I know . . . I know you are . . . I should have told you sooner but I was so confused and scared . . . and I wanted to pretend it didn't happen."

Sophia's uncle chimed in, "Sophia what is it? Did someone hurt you?"

"Yes . . . a couple of months ago. Someone did. He hurt me pretty badly. But I thought in time it would just go away. And I could forget. But . . . but . . . now I am pregnant."

At first Sophia's aunt and uncle weren't completely sure what Sophia meant when she stated that she had been hurt "pretty badly". However, it didn't take long to realize the magnitude of what she was talking about. As Sophia continued telling more about the incident, though still not every detail, they understood more and more.

When she had revealed the necessary details about the ordeal, Sophia began to cry uncontrollably. Her aunt pulled her in and hugged her tightly, letting her release her pain. Her uncle joined them, wrapping his arms protectively around his wife and his wounded, frightened niece.

Her uncle's heart ached. Though his Asian culture might normally tend to feel dishonored, he found himself more upset that he hadn't protected Sophia better. How would his brother and his brother's wife back home take this? They had trusted him with their daughter, putting her safety and future in his hands. She was living in his home when this happened. He didn't say it out loud, but he felt he had let them all down. He had much he was concerned about right now. Yet, he knew he must stay strong for Sophia and his wife.

"Sophia," her uncle said with a fatherly voice, "We love you . . . it will all be OK. Let's give your parents a call. They need to be a part of this conversation."

The three of them cleared the dining area, then sat down in the living room. Sophia sat between her aunt and uncle on the couch. The phone sat stoically on the coffee table in front of her. Sophia felt her hands quiver as she picked up the receiver and dialed the number.

"Hello," her mom answered.

"Mommy," said Sophia, softly.

"Sophia!?" responded Linn Sue, pointing to her husband to get on the phone too.

"Yes."

"Sophia, so good to hear your voice! How are you, Darling?"

"Oh, Mommy, not good. Is Daddy there?"

"Yes, he is getting on the other phone."

"Hello, Sophia," she heard her Dad's voice chime in.

"Daddy," she replied, softly.

"Yes, Honey, how are you?"

"Mommy. Daddy. I need to come home . . . " Sophia's voice drifted and she automatically looked down at the floor shamefully as she said these words.

"Why, Honey?" her Dad asked.

"Something bad happened a couple of months ago . . . I am so sorry," Sophia's voice began to trail again then she added, "I never should have put myself in that situation." Tears streamed down Sophia's face starting slowly, then more quickly.

Everyone sat quietly waiting for Sophia to continue. Finally, she mustered up the courage, and out came, "I am so sorry, but I am pregnant." By this time tears streamed profusely as she wiped them with the back part of her hand that wasn't on the receiver.

Sophia's aunt firmly but gently hugged her and her uncle placed one hand lovingly on her back. There was silence on the line that lasted longer than any of them would have liked . . . then her dad's voice came back over the phone.

"Sophia, I don't know exactly what happened, but it is going to be OK . . . we love you. Nothing else matters but you knowing we love you. Let's get you home. Home is where you belong and we will handle the rest."

"Thank you, Daddy. I am so sorry I have let you both down."

Without explanation, Linn Sue had a deep knowing of what must have happened to Sophia. She knew her daughter, and even over the scrambled phone line she could detect and feel her daughter's pain, fear and sadness. Without reservation, Linn Sue responded, "There is no reason to be sorry. You are our child . . . just come home."

CHAPTER 33

The plane lifted off just after twelve noon, and the length of the flight gave Sophia plenty of time to think. Thinking was something she had done a lot of lately. As each hour passed, she felt herself getting more and more anxious about arriving back home, especially about being back at the village. Part of her was so happy that she was going to see her parents - they had always been there for her and she missed them terribly – but she was also saddened by the reason that had made it necessary for her to return now, without having attained her goal of a nursing degree. She thought back to how, for most of her life, things had been very easy as far as emotional stresses go. Yes, on occasion stray animals she had brought home would die and her parents had had to help her through the grief. But this grief only lasted a couple of days, and these were normal parent-child life issues. This was something totally different now. She was pregnant. The words echoed in her mind. In seven months she would be bringing a child into this world. A child she hadn't planned on. A child without a father. A child out of wedlock. She was also coming home to a village that had supported her with an education and had high hopes of her returning home to be a nurse. Now she was letting them down. Sophia's bottom lip quivered. The confusion of wanting to be home with and needing those who loved her, while knowing she was also returning home to those she felt she had let down was almost overwhelming. She was grateful and humiliated all at the same time.

The first leg of the trip completed, she caught her second flight without issue. Sophia attempted to rest as the plane ascended, however, she found it very hard to calm her mind enough to fall asleep as she shifted from side to side in her seat. She also frequently braced the middle of her stomach as she felt waves of low-grade nausea moving through, wondering if this was the beginning of what they called morning sickness, if it was from the pit of anxiety she felt deep inside her and was trying to fight, or a combination of both.

Sophia reflected now on how this plane ride was very different than the one on her way to the United States. There was no Graham Taylor sitting beside her. There was less excitement and exhilaration. Less hope. She had kept to herself throughout this flight, speaking to no one as she tried to process her situation and next steps. The only thing that was the same was Sophia's teddy bear stuffed in the open pouch on the side of her carry-on. Its head poked out from above the canvas, as it maintained its usual big smile.

****

When Sophia arrived at the airport, her parents welcomed her with hugs and kisses, embracing her long and hard. They were nothing but accepting of her and glad to have their daughter back where they could help her feel safe and not alone. Throughout the car ride home, as well as her acclimation back to the village, and throughout her whole pregnancy for that matter, they never once said anything to make her feel guilty or judged.

The same went for the villagers. They came to visit Sophia in a slow, calculated stream, bringing foods she liked and greeting her with loving arms. She appreciated their genuineness and sincere effort not to overwhelm her. Never once was anything said that would have made Sophia feel unaccepted or guilty for any reason. Despite this, it was Sophia, herself, that felt inadequate and shameful.

Much of Sophia's time over the next seven months was spent on the white sands of the beach, pondering life. She contemplated the past, the present and the future. She thought back to the times as a child when she combed this same beach, happily collecting shells to make things for the gift shop without a care in the world. Now she lay in the soft sand, looking out at the water over a swollen stomach creating a human life before her very eyes. Her skin was getting more and more taut by the day and the heartburn in her upper chest and throat were a constant reminder of what was happening. The thought amazed and scared her. The future, she had decided, was up to God. During this time, her faith deepened knowing that God had to have a reason for this. Whether it was trusting more in God or just her way of coping, she believed. And what she liked very much was that she would not have to see the likes of someone like Matt Chambers again. She was back in her village with people she trusted and made her feel safe.

Sophia's relationship with her mom deepened during this time. She needed her. Though Linn Sue had not been through what she was going through in the same manner, she knew what it was like to have a life within her, and she cared relentlessly for her daughter. She made sure she had fresh fruits and plenty of water each day. Even on the days when Sophia most felt like isolating herself with her thoughts and contemplations, she would go back to the house only to find that her mom had done something beautiful for her or the baby. She was able to find joy sitting with her mother, as she explained her own pregnancy and what it was like having Sophia as a baby. She always enjoyed the story about the little boy who gave her the gift of her favorite teddy bear when leaving the hospital. She looked forward to passing the bear on to her own child.

Sophia and her parents prepared the baby's area of the house. She and her mom spent the evenings making blankets, and they would occasionally giggle as her father tried to help determine names for the baby. Into the third trimester, Sophia felt her energy decreasing and discomfort set in. She found herself retiring earlier and earlier to bed as she prepared for what was ahead.

CHAPTER 34

Sophia's daughter, Destiny, was born early on a Sunday morning. Fortunately for Sophia, her pregnancy had gone fairly smoothly. Other than frequently being sick to her stomach around 3 o'clock in the afternoon during the first trimester, it was generally uneventful, as was the delivery. It took very little time at all and, except for the cries at birth, little Desi, as she would be nicknamed, was happy from the very start.

When Baby Destiny was brought up to Sophia's chest after birth, the new mom stared at the little being on top of her and felt engulfed with instant and overwhelming love along with a twinge of nervousness. The baby opened her eyes, and as Sophia peered down, she saw not the normal brown color of an Asian, but instead a unique shade of blue. "Mom, look at her eyes," she spoke in a stunned tone.

Linn Sue surveyed the newborn's face. "Oh, my, how beautiful she is. Sophia, she is truly a special child."

"Yes, she is amazing," replied Sophia. She then turned to her teary-eyed mom and asked innocently, "What do I do with her?"

"Just love her," replied Linn Sue.

"I can do that," was Sophia's reply as she looked back into the face of her newborn in awe and wonder.

Destiny was an easy-going baby with only a tiny, muffled cry even when she was upset or angry. She was petite and had distinct Asian features with thick, soft, black hair. All her features were Asian, except for her deep blue eyes that beamed as she smiled.

The bond between Sophia and Desi ran deep. They simply adored each other. Desi, of course, needed her mother. But Sophia needed her child too. She needed a reason to have had such a drastic change in her life and it helped to have a new focus and a way to be successful. She found this through being a mother. Sophia focused her energy on mothering and mothering alone, being as diligent a mom as she had been a student. She gave Desi her all, and didn't in the least bit allow herself to focus on how, or by whom, she had gotten such an amazing child.

Grandmother and Grandfather doted over Desi too. Though Desi wasn't planned, she was adored. And although the way in which she was conceived was so very harsh, she was easy to love. Each day, she was either being fed by Sophia, held by Grandmother or tickled and doted on by her grandfather throughout most of her waking time. Desi was loved; there was no doubt about it. She was a happy child with a perpetual smile and a contagious joy that spread easily to those around her.

Sophia shared her love of the beach with her daughter. By the age of four, Desi was used to the water. Many afternoons Desi, with her unique, blue eyes would be seen on the beach with her mother, wearing her little pink swimming suit and running up and down the shoreline collecting tiny shells. It wasn't uncommon for tourists to be mesmerized by the little girl's eyes, at times even asking to take a picture with her. Sometimes Sophia would let them, other times she would not want to interrupt her daughter's play. Desi would run down toward the water, spy the shells she wanted, then bring them back to her mom just a few feet away. Destiny, though curious and adventurous, never lost sight of her mom, who was easy to spot, donned with her large-brimmed white hat and flowing sarong tied around her waist. These little shells would then be strung into a bracelet or necklace, which would be sold to tourists in the family gift shop. Sophia enjoyed watching the life in Destiny and passing on her own heritage to the next generation.

At the end of these days outdoors, Destiny would cuddle up to her mom at bedtime, holding the well-loved teddy bear her mom had passed on to her, and the two would say a prayer, always followed by a little song Sophia had made up for her daughter. The song, translated, went something like this:

"You're the apple of my eye Little Desi . . .

You're the apple of my eye Little Desi . . .
You're the apple of my eye . . . you're the sun up in the sky . . .
You're the apple of my eye Little Desi . . ."

On one particular night, when both mom and daughter were fully content, Desi smiled her big smile and came back to her mother with a new verse of her own:

"You're the stars up in the sky Little Mommy . . .
You're the stars up in the sky Little Mommy . . .
You're the stars up in the sky . . . you're the birdies flying by . . .
You're the stars up in the sky Little Mommy . . ."

Sophia burst out laughing at her daughter's quick wit and creativity, and the two rolled around and laughed uproariously until their bellies hurt.

As Destiny got older, it didn't take long until she was joining her grandfather at the store. She would sit in the gift shop learning to string the little shells and ask question after question of her grandfather. Pae loved this time with his granddaughter. It brought back fond memories from when Sophia was little and he delighted in the one-on-one time with little Desi. It wasn't uncommon for her to strike up conversation with the tourists coming into the shop too. She would welcome them with her big, happy smile and show them some of her favorite things that she had helped make. Many of the visitors did a double take as they turned to look at the little girl and saw her mesmerizing blue eyes. They were fascinated by the depth of the aqua blue color in the eyes of this little Asian girl. They would often inquire about her blue eyes to Pae, who always had the same response. "They are a gift," he would reply.

As little Desi got older and was spending more and more time with Pae at the gift shop, it became apparent that Sophia had room for other endeavors in her life again. She decided to start working at the clinic. Although she wasn't a nurse, she enjoyed being involved with helping others in the community again. The villagers embraced her wholeheartedly, and although the fact that she hadn't finished nursing school still challenged her spirit on occasion, she worked diligently to provide the care she was able to do without a license. It wasn't too long until

Desi was old enough to go to the clinic with Sophia, just as she had done with her own mom as a child. Destiny would sit in the clinic playing with her little dolls, fetch items her mom and grandmother needed and interact with the staff and villagers that came in, providing an energy in the clinic that no one had seen since the days when Sophia was little and doing the same thing.

It felt as though mom and daughter, with the help of Grandma and Grandfather, had found their pace and their place in the village. They settled in and were at peace.

CHAPTER 35

The three months that Stephen wanted to himself was not exactly for a vacation. It was part of his structured strategy to continue connecting with his father. He had decided prior to even entering medical school at UCLA that he would, one day, travel back to the little Vietnamese village that he and his dad had visited to research the effects on others who may have suffered from the use of Agent Orange during the war - for surely his father was not the only one.

Stephen was set to fly out of the country within the next two weeks, and he had a lot to do in the meantime. He packed up all his belongings, rented a U-Haul and headed north on Interstate 5 toward his new home in Seattle. The long drive gave him hours to relax and ponder life. He thought of his father, his mom, his parent's love, and he began to wonder if he would ever understand and find the love his parents had once had. He did want that, and now, with school behind him, the thought of future companionship began to seep into his thoughts. How, when, and if he even had the capacity to love was another story, but perhaps a few boards of the fence that protected his heart had weakened and fallen to the ground, leaving the slightest opening for love to enter.

Stephen had found a small upper level two-bedroom apartment on the shores of Alki Beach in West Seattle. He would make the back room his bedroom and the front room, which looked over the shoreline, his office. It was a little more expensive than he would have liked, but Stephen wanted a view of Puget Sound, which he could see from his office, kitchen, dining room and deck. He also didn't mind paying a little extra for the luxury of walking along the shoreline or reading and writing while leaning against a log on the beach at sunset.

Once he was all moved in, Stephen slowly ventured out to the nearby restaurants and explored his surroundings. Within the week, he knew he had clearly made the right decision to accept the position at the hospital in Seattle. He enjoyed sitting in the small coffee shop just down the street, and happily took advantage of ordering take-out meals from several teriyaki restaurants, which he could then eat from the privacy of his deck as the late afternoon sun warmed his face. He felt a deep sense of peace, and a feeling that this was a very important part of his life. He was truly looking forward to his upcoming trip to Southeast Asia.

CHAPTER 36

The long flight to Vietnam may have been tough on many, but, except for the short layover in Tokyo, Stephen used every minute productively. He spent most of his time checking maps for the locations of hospitals in Vietnam where he would go regarding questions for his personal research project. When he arrived in Vietnam, he went to the same hotel that he and his father had gone to years before. He wouldn't be there long, as his travels would take him to one hotel after another. Before he started his journey, though, he made a point of going to the small, local gift shop to say hello to Pae, the gentleman who had helped his father so much while they were there. He wanted to share with him and thank him for the life-changing transformation he had helped his father with.

It was about 10 o'clock in the morning when Stephen walked into the gift shop. He was wearing khaki shorts with a loose, white, untucked button-up shirt. Sandals and his San Francisco Giants baseball cap completed his ensemble. He walked up to the counter where Pae sat on a tall stool. Stephen immediately noticed the white shell necklaces neatly hanging from a display on the counter. They were just as they'd been years back when he was with his father, and identical to the ones he was given by Pae's little girl.

"Pae?" spoke Stephen.

"Yes," Pae replied, a bit surprised that the man in front of him knew his name.

"Pae, I know you probably don't remember me but I am Stephen. My father and I came here about 15 years ago and you took us on a tour so my dad could find peace with the war. His name was Robert Nance."

As soon as Stephen said his father's name, a sincere smile came across Pae's face, and he stood up and reached out his hand. "Oh my. Oh, yes, I remember. Oh my goodness, young man, you have truly grown up."

"Yes. I was twelve then. A lot has happened over the years since then." Stephen paused, then continued, "Pae, your English is so good now."

Pae's smile beamed. He grabbed his canes and made his way to the front door putting up the "Sorry We're Closed" sign.

"My daughter went to school in America for a while. She's back now and we speak English most of the time." Pae waved for Stephen to sit down, then continued, "Well, Son, the store is closed now and I want to know all about what happened when you went back home."

With that, Stephen sat down on a high stool next to Pae. They sat across from each other at the checkout counter sharing, laughing, and on more than one occasion, tearing up as Stephen told Pae everything. He shared about his pain from the neglect of his father. He shared the special love between his parents and then about the hurt his mom had endured after the war from her husband's emotional distance. He then explained how his father had once again found his soul from the kind gesture and wise words Pae had provided so many years ago. Both had tears in their eyes when Stephen shared about his parents' embrace upon their return from Vietnam.

"Pae, it was like the man who had left on the trip found Mom's long lost husband and reintroduced them once again. I know it is hard to believe, but my father was finally right there in her arms. I saw it in her. I saw my mom's surprise, her astonishment, and then watched her heart fill up right before my eyes. It was amazing. Actually, it was a miracle. Without you, that moment would have never happened. From that day forward, we all grew closer and closer. Yes, my father was dying, but his heart was once again full and we had each other. That time meant everything to my mom and I. Pae, you did that. I don't know how I will ever make it up to you but I will find a way. My mom and I will always think of you as our angel . . . as part of our family," said Stephen earnestly.

A tear slowly ran down Pae's left cheek before it fell gently onto his shirt. "Thank you for your kind words, Stephen. It is a wonderful world if we let go of the things in our past that hinder us from the joys of the future. And you, Stephen, you surely have a wonderful wife back home."

"Oh, no. Never was good at the relationship thing. My heart is better left alone," replied Stephen.

"Why do you say that?"

"Pae, I just can't find a way to let love in. I am being sincere. I think I want it someday but the fear of getting hurt outweighs the need to find love. It means trusting another person with your heart. I just don't know if I can do that."

"Do you believe your dad loved you? Do you believe that you want to have love too?"

"I know he did, now. After he sincerely explained to me what he was going through. Those last six months opened my eyes to his love for my mom and me. I just don't have the answers to how I can find and accept love. It terrifies me, to be honest."

"So your father come to Vietnam with you and he has no answers but leaves with his soul. How did that happen? I tell you, Son. It happens at the appropriate time. I said the same words to your father. I said I do not believe you need all the answers. Just be part of bigger picture. Bigger plan. He may be just small part in story. Same with you, Stephen. Same thing I say to your father, I say to you. You do not have to have all the answers but you must be open yourself to love. You must find a way to let go of your past pain that holds you from love. You must find love, Stephen. Just like your father. He find love again. He endured so much misery and anguish here from wartime, but somehow he find love again. You must let go of your pain, Stephen. You must put it behind you. It does no good to carry pain as a burden. You must free yourself of it. Remember, Son, you don't need all the answers. You are only a small part of the story. But you must find love. You must." With that Pae winked, which caught Stephen by surprise.

"What was the last thing you said, Pae?"

"I say remember, Son, you don't need all the answers. You are only a small part of the story. But you must find love. You must."

Stephen smiled. At that moment he knew his father was close. "Thank you, Pae. Thank you so very much. I needed to hear those words."

For the next six weeks Stephen trekked across Vietnam. While going from village to village and to one hospital after another, he formulated his research and took in the beauty and culture of the country. He finally made it back to Pae's village, once again meeting him at the gift shop and sharing all he had seen, collected and learned. He also shared that he had thought a great deal about what Pae had told him about letting go of the past and trying to find love. He promised that he would take it all to heart once back in The States, as he was scheduled to go back home within the next couple of days.

The next day, Stephen decided to take a long walk on the beach. He went barefoot and was unshaven, wearing khakis, no shirt, and his now very seedy, well-travelled San Francisco baseball cap on his head. He looked scruffy, to say the least, but it was a mere walk on the water's edge before heading home. Once he reached the beach, he sat down and took in the scene of the bluish water and the gentle warm breeze blowing through his now longer and wavier sun bleached hair. Stephen closed his eyes and let his senses take it all in. He had not a care in the world as he sat silently by himself.

This was his time, so he, once again, pondered the words of his father that had been eloquently placed on Pae's tongue. *"Remember, Son, you don't need all the answers. You are only a small part of the story. But you must find love. You must."*

Stephen smiled. After about forty-five minutes of solitude and serenity, he decided to walk down the long, sandy beach that flanked the village. His feet gently splashed through the clear, warm water just near the shoreline. A ways ahead of him, he saw a small girl wading at the water's edge, while a lady in a big sun hat sat on a towel in the white sand just up the beach watching her attentively. The child seemed to be collecting something and putting it in a small, light-colored cloth bag. As he came closer, he could see her reaching into the water, looking at the prize and then putting it in the bag. As he walked forward and approached her, she looked up at him and he froze in his tracks. He didn't know how long he stood there staring, but he was transfixed on her eyes. They were a deep, translucent blue, enhanced by the natural darkness of the child's suntanned Asian skin. She was a beautiful child. In fact, more than beautiful. She was like a small goddess kneeling before him.

The little girl reached out toward Stephen, opened her hand, and in her tiny palm were a few white shells. He looked at them in silence and then gazed up the beach at the obvious mother of this amazing child. The mother had seen everything and shook her head approving that he could take the gifts offered by the young girl. He took the shells and said "thank you". The little girl smiled, and went back to her search for more treasures. Stephen walked about twenty feet and then looked back at the young child over his shoulder. She stared back at him softly, and then smiled again as if to say "perhaps we will meet again someday."

****

Once back in Seattle, Stephen settled into his new home overlooking the beach. One Saturday before starting his job, he took a few boxes into his office at the hospital, in order to give it a bit of character. He was never one for clutter, so he neatly put several books and a few souvenirs on the short bookcase along the wall behind his desk. On his desk was only a small, gold, upside down L-shaped lamp with a bright green glass covering encasing a 12-inch thin round bulb. Stephen liked the office dark, except for the small lamp illuminating his work area. The low lighting had always helped keep him focused on the tasks directly in front of him. On the lamp, he hung the necklace made of the white shells that he had received years ago from Pae's daughter, which reminded him of the wonderful trip with his father. With the rest of the afternoon, Stephen spent time filing the paperwork and notes he had put together from his trip to Vietnam. This would be an ongoing project close to his heart, as he owed it to his father, Carl, and the other veterans of all wars fought for our country. Now, however, it was time to start his career as an oncologist for one of the most prestigious cancer research hospitals in America. Stephen had thoroughly prepared himself for this moment, and he was ready to get started.

On his way home, he picked up some sushi and a bottle of wine to enjoy on his deck. It was early September, and the view from his apartment was stunning. As he sat on the deck, Stephen relaxed and took in another beautiful sunset that slowly dipped toward the peaks of the Olympic Mountains to the West across Puget Sound. He poured himself another glass of wine and watched the boats out on the bay cruise by as couples walked casually or sat together on the beach. He knew that Monday morning would come soon enough, so he was going to relax this evening and enjoy the tranquility of his new life. At that moment, he felt a very subtle sense of longing that he wished he could share this time with someone special. He really had never had the time or attitude that warranted any real deep thoughts of another person in his life. A commitment to a woman would have only distracted him from his goal of becoming a doctor. But now that he had reached that milestone, he felt something in him shifting. What would be next? Had his father's words spoken through Pae's beautiful statement finally started to penetrate and soften his heart?

The words echoed vividly in his mind, *"Remember, Son, you don't need all the answers. You are only a small part of the story. But you must find love. You must."*

This thought brought a smile to Stephen's face and in a whisper he said, "Yep, Dad. You're right. If, with everything you went through, you were able to let go and love again, then I need to do the same. I love you, Dad. I promise I will do this. It is time to let go of the past and look to the future."

Stephen then watched as the sun slowly lowered behind the mountains to the West, where it would start another day rising in the East for those on the other side of the world.

He raised his glass and spoke these words. "To destiny. I welcome you."

CHAPTER 37

Destiny had become quite the presence at the clinic. Patients and their families were delighted watching the little girl prance around the clinic with a mini clipboard in one hand and a teddy bear in the other, pretending she was doing the same procedures as the workers there.

In addition to her aqua blue eyes, Destiny had another easily identifiable quality. There was a breathiness in her voice, almost a slight wheeze that showed up especially when she got excited. Both Sophia and her grandmother noticed the little sound when it first started happening and quickly had a visiting doctor check it out at the clinic. When the doctor completed his examination and assured them nothing was wrong with the little girl, Sophia and her mom chalked the small sound up as another adoring and quirky trait their little sweetheart had. The slightly airy sound became part of little Desi's personality when she was most excited, buzzing around the clinic.

On one particular day when she was bustling around, Destiny stopped abruptly in the waiting room. "What are you here for?" she asked a patient sitting in the quaint, but sparse, small waiting area.

Though in pain, the patient, a middle-aged woman with a larger figure for a Vietnamese woman and a robust smile, turned to Destiny and said, "To see you."

This put a huge smile on little Desi's face as she pretended to write notes on her clipboard. Watching her in turn broadened the woman's smile as she continued, "See, I feel better already."

Desi ran exuberantly to the back to find her mom and report that she had a patient who had come to see her that day, and that she had already made her feel better. Sophia smiled at her daughter's enthusiasm and joy, as Desi then skipped down the hall telling tales to her teddy bear regarding whom they were going to heal next, as Sophia tended to the sweet lady in the waiting area.

A few days after that, when Sophia had already heard three different patients say little Desi would probably grow up to be a nurse, a new doctor, who had come from the city to work in the clinic, pulled Sophia aside and said he would like to talk to her in private. Sophia had no idea what the elder doctor was going to say, but stepped aside with him to listen.

The doctor told her he was concerned about the cough Destiny had and asked Sophia how long she had had it. He wanted to know if he could check it out. Although the doctor was kind with his words and mannerisms, he had deliberateness in his voice that alarmed Sophia.

"Cough?" thought Sophia. Sure, there was the little grunt sound and a wheeze that she made when she was excited or moving around, but the previous doctor said it was nothing to be concerned about. It was just part of Desi's developing personality and mannerisms. Besides, it hadn't been happening for very long. However, when she told the doctor that Destiny had been making the sound for a few months, he stated that it had been lingering too long. Respecting the doctor, Sophia allowed him to check it out.

As Sophia watched the doctor examine her young daughter, she became concerned by his expressions. She became even more concerned by his words that followed. The doctor explained that he did not like the respiratory sounds he heard when examining Desi. He assured Sophia that what he was hearing was something to be taken seriously and recommended they go to the city to see other doctors. These doctors, Sophia was told, would know more and have better equipment to examine Destiny. Sophia's heart pounded and her mind raced as she tried to grasp what the doctor was saying.

"Was he really saying that something was wrong with her sweet Destiny? Was this really happening?" thought Sophia, as she looked back at the doctor with a blank stare and tried to concentrate on what she was being told needed to happen next.

From there, everything seemed to be happening so fast, yet in slow motion at the same time. It was surreal. Instead of being the one comforting and providing guidance to others at the clinic, suddenly she was the recipient . . . the one needing the guidance and comfort . . . the one now labeled with a "sick" child. Sophia and her family were thrown into a whirlwind that she could barely believe was real.

Within a week, they had their first appointment with the city doctors. Sophia's parents insisted they accompany her and Desi, both for support and to be additional sets of ears regarding any information that would be given to them. Both Sophia and her mom were used to being nurturing yet methodical at the clinic in their village, but this was different. This was their little one, the baby in their family, and the highlight of their world. In an instant, their lives and emotions had been yanked into a place of alarmed confusion and distress.

The night before they were to leave for the city, as Sophia was packing Destiny's clothes in her suitcase, she noted how gently the moon cast light through the small window, accentuating her surroundings, the distant sound of waves and a cool draft that swept into the room. Sophia found these elements comforting, as she pondered the upheaval that was happening in her life just as she was feeling that everything had been coming together for her and her baby girl. She handled each article of clothing with care as she folded it and gently placed it in the overnight bag, feeling the soft fabrics and brushing away any trace of lint or wrinkles. She wasn't sure how long they would be there, and it gave her a sense of control and comfort to focus on preparing for the trip and packing her little girl's belongings. She knew it was a false sense of control, yet she appreciated it, nonetheless. She packed Destiny's hairbrush, her sandals, her sleepwear, and her favorite casual dresses. She stayed strong as she selected each item, choosing to focus on this rather than on what the doctors may or may not find, until she picked up a little dress she had bought for Desi. It was Desi's very favorite dress and the one she had worn just the day before the incident in the clinic that changed everything.

The afternoon when Desi had last worn that little yellow dress had been such a fabulous day. The two of them had taken an excursion down to the beach picking up shells and playing in the sand. Sophia thought back to how her daughter had used the skirt of the dress to carry the shells, bunching it up so the shells would not fall out, and then gently emptied the skirt's contents into a bigger bucket they were using that day. Sophia smiled as she remembered Desi's little waddle while carrying the shells in her dress, trying not to spill them. She then remembered how a gust of wind had picked up while they were there, throwing both of their hair into their faces and that they had been over-come with laughter watching each other try to gently spit the hair out of their mouths with the accompanying grainy sand. It was a moment only the two of them could appreciate, and despite her sadness it made Sophia giggle slightly thinking back to that day.

She looked at the dress, picked it up and pulled it in close to her, burying it into her face. She could smell the scent of her young child, mixed with laundry soap, as she took a deep breath in. As she exhaled, tears began to pour down her face. "Please, God, please, God, not my child," she sobbed.

Sophia's mom had been watching her daughter from the hallway at a distance, just as she had been lovingly watching her for the past few days, respectively giving her space but knowing that anytime the crash of emotion could hit, and that Sophia would need her. It was hard seeing her daughter go through this, knowing the bond between a mother and daughter. She had seen Sophia go through so much pain the last few years, and she had hoped things were going to get better for her. Detect-ing it was time for her to reach out, Linn Sue wandered over to Sophia, gently turned her around and rested her grown up daughter's head on her shoulder. No words were spoken. None were necessary. The time had come for her daughter's emotions to release, and she just needed to be consoled.

The two stayed like this for quite some time, until Sophia pulled away gently and muttered softly, "Thank you, Mom."

"You know I would take away any pain you feel if I could, Dear," remarked Linn Sue as she lightly swept Sophia's hair out of her face.

"Yes, Mom, I know," replied Sophia, as she wiped away tears that had fallen past her nose and into her mouth, tasting the saltiness as she swiped. The two women then reluctantly turned back to the overnight bag and finished the packing together.

CHAPTER 38

Early the next morning Sophia, Linn Sue, Pae and little Desi made the trek to the city. It was a somber ride for the adults, as they contemplated what was ahead of them. Sophia and Linn Sue occasionally found themselves silently staring out the window while Pae drove, only to be reeled back in by the undeniable excitement in Desi's voice. This road trip was anything but somber for her. The adventure generated intense excitement in her as they left their village, drove by various landscapes, passed other travelers and saw animals alongside the road. To Desi, going to the big city was like Disneyland, and she was ready for action. When her mom had told her they were going to the city, it sparked a curiosity in her and she had been counting down the days, continually asking her family how much longer it would be until they would leave. This excitement and anticipation continued while they were in route. The young child was a river of questions and statements, taking everything in like a sponge, wondering what it may be like in the big city.

"What are houses like there, Mom?" was one of her questions.

"A lot like ours, only more of them, more modern and some are much bigger," replied Sophia.

"Mom, why don't we live in the city?" was the next question.

"Because we live in our village," replied Sophia.

"Do they have gift shops in the city?" continued Destiny.

"Yes, but not as nice as your grandfather's," interjected Linn Sue, giving Sophia a break and managing to muster an authentic smile.

Destiny then turned to Pae and said, "Grandfather, did you ever live in the city?"

"No," he answered.

"Why?" probed Destiny.

"Because I like it in the village. And there I get to live with you," replied Pae, proud of his response.

And this is how a long portion of the ride continued, until little Desi wore herself out and fell asleep.

****

Desi woke up just as they were arriving at the hospital. She lifted her small head from her mother's shoulder, moved her teddy bear away from her face and stretched out her arms. With a big yawn and tussled hair, she looked around. She marveled at the size of the parking area and how many more vehicles there were compared to the clinic in their village. As they walked into the building, Desi was amazed by its size. This was the tallest building she had ever seen, and she believed it must be the biggest building that ever existed. As they walked through the corridor, she noted how much louder it was and how many more people they had working there compared to the clinic she was used to. As her mom got her checked in and her grandmother got everything else situated in the large, sterile waiting room, Destiny held tight to her grandfather's hand. There were signs on the walls with pictures she did not understand. There were a lot more people waiting to be seen than she could have ever expected, and many of them looked very, very sick, to the small child.

Just as she was starting to get a little nervous, a very pretty nurse came from around the corner and acknowledged her. At first, Destiny clutched her grandfather's hand in one of her own, and her teddy bear in the other. But once the nurse smiled and spoke, Destiny instantly liked her and was able to relax.

The nurse bent down near Desi and spoke sweetly, "What a nice bear you have with you. I get to spend the day with both of you."

Desi smiled back, proud of her teddy bear, and looked closely at the nurse. As Destiny told her about her mom giving her the teddy bear from when she was a little girl, she noted that she had shiny black hair pulled back tight and had a smell to her that, although Destiny could not name, she really liked. Desi found herself wondering if she would look and smell like this pretty woman someday.

Once settled in the exam room, she heard the adults discussing that the clinic in their village was not set up for what she needs, and that the people at the hospital were glad they came here. She also listened as the nurse asked a lot of questions about her. She asked how she was breathing, how she was eating, and if they had seen any changes in her. Destiny didn't understand these conversations which sent waves of confusion through her mind.

The nurse glanced at little Desi, recognizing her fears, and diligently went back to focusing on making her more comfortable with the situation. She kindly lifted Destiny up on the steel table, warning her that it may be cold and that the paper she would be sitting on would crinkle. She then pulled out a stethoscope much more elaborate than the one Desi had seen her grandmother use.

After explaining to Desi what she was going to do, she told her that her bear was going to get to go first. Destiny held onto the teddy bear while the nurse gently placed the stethoscope up against its chest.

"Well, what a big heart he has!" she proclaimed.

The other adults in the room followed with warm exclamations as Destiny giggled in response. Desi was examined after her bear was thoroughly looked over, and this is how things continued, with Thuong, the nurse, gently guiding the Nyugen family through the day. They saw doctor after doctor, went to the lab, and had several diagnostic procedures, with the teddy bear, each time, being poked and palpated ahead of Desi.

Then, as quickly as one tiring and overwhelming day came to a close, a second day started much the same way, with Destiny staying surprisingly tough for such a young child, and Thuong continuing to guide and care for Desi and the Nuygen family in the professional and nurturing manner they needed. Yet, at the end of the second day, when the Nuygen family was told they could go home, they still had no answers. They were told they would need to wait for test results and that follow up appointments would need to be made.

The car ride home was much quieter than the ride to the hospital. A fatigued Destiny settled in for a long rest. The little bit of conversation that did come from Desi right before she drifted to sleep was about how much she liked her nurse. Sophia smiled a weary, but genuine smile, and shared with her that the nurse's name, Thuong, meant "one who loves tenderly." Desi wasn't sure what "tenderly" meant, but she knew it had to be good.

CHAPTER 39

Linn Sue stood in the kitchen of her small but quaint home making chicken and vegetables. This had always been one of her family's favorite meals, and it gave her solace to be making it for them. As she cut the vegetables into long strands, she heard the sweet voice of Destiny's singing streaming in through the window. After listening to the child's melody for a minute, she peaked out to see the young child drawing stick figures in the dirt.

"She seems not to have a care in the world," thought Linn Sue as she paused from cutting to just watch her lovely granddaughter.

Linn Sue had been having more and more moments like this where she just wanted to stop, pay attention to those she loved, and keep time still. A lot had happened in her family, and she had stayed strong through it all. Despite her own emotions, she knew her family needed her, and this gave her the focus and strength she needed. She knew it was important that she keep her mind as clear as possible, so that she could stay sharp and be keenly aware of what was going on with those she loved. She wanted her instincts and intuition to be intact so that she would be ready to respond as Sophia, Destiny and her husband needed her throughout the family's struggles.

Though she realized that she was the glue that held her family together, Linn Sue had watched her family members struggle through many situations, and she, too, needed some space to allow herself to fall apart a little and let go of her own grief.

Years ago - almost immediately after their marriage - while fighting in the war, her adoring husband, Pae, was involved in a jeep accident.

Shortly thereafter, his friend stepped on a land mine, losing his life in the same explosion that took Pae's leg. To a proud, strong man like her husband, losing his leg was almost like losing life itself. For a long while, he grieved the loss of his friend, and for even longer he grieved the loss of his leg. Pae felt less of a man without his leg, and his stoic demeanor made him suffer in silence. It was hard watching the man she loved so much suffer in such a way and be so hard on himself. She had watched him rehabilitate and fight to regain his independence. Throughout this ordeal, she gave him the love and support he needed, nurturing him and staying strong when he was not. She also watched him overcome the loss and accept who he was. She witnessed him come through on the other side an even stronger man, with a huge amount of faith. He let the tragedy then lead him to greater purposes and doing more for other people. She marveled as her once stereotypically stoic Asian husband became more in touch with his emotions, more engaged and more loving than ever before. He had vowed to focus on their family, not let life's circumstances get in the way or pull him down, and to help others see that things could always get better. She was proud to have been part of Pae's recovery and even prouder to be his wife.

Linn Sue had, time and time again, watched her husband be a positive influence to other men in the community. She was also aware of how many lives he had touched as people passed through the gift shop. Some of these were even American men returning to fight their own demons. Her husband had particularly taken an interest in helping others overcome their limitations pertaining to the war, whether they be physical or emotional.

They had a good life, blessed with a beautiful little girl, Sophia, some years later. Linn Sue was amazed at what a hands-on father Pae was. He was very involved with Sophia, giving his attention and love to her generously and openly, which was unlike many other men, who seemed afraid to show how much they cared. Everything was going in Sophia's favor. She was such a light. She had so much potential. And as Sophia's mother, Linn Sue loved nurturing such a fabulous daughter.

She saw it as an honor and privilege. When her daughter left for school in California, she was sad, but she also couldn't have been prouder.

But then tragedy struck, and her daughter was treated in a way no woman should ever be treated by a man. When she and Pae got the phone call and the pieces came together shedding light on what had happened, her first reaction was disbelief. Then came rage toward the beast that would do such a thing, followed by anger directed at her brother-in-law and his wife, thinking they had not protected Sophia enough. But what settled in and stayed the longest was a mix of anger, disappointment and guilt toward herself, thinking she had not prepared her young, naïve daughter well enough for the realities of life in a large city.

She also witnessed how the events that happened in California impacted Pae. This normally upbeat, positive man, for a time, looked dragged down, heavy, and burdened beyond belief. She could see in his eyes what her husband was thinking. Without words she knew his thoughts. She knew he was thinking, "I am the man of the family, her father, her protector, and I let this happen."

Linn Sue knew he felt like there was nothing he could do. He wanted to change things but he couldn't. She knew he too felt responsible . . . as though he had failed his daughter. There was no doubt he felt as though he had no control over the events that happened to his very own daughter that night in California, leaving her devastated, scarred and pregnant.

Furthermore, Linn Sue knew that Sophia's not wanting to talk much about the event with her father, once she was back home, pained him. Previously, they had always talked about so much. It was evident that Pae never judged Sophia, nor did she, however, the conversation regarding their own daughter being hurt so brutally, and in such a devastating way, was difficult and lead to awkwardness. So instead, Pae and she focused on their love for Sophia, hoping that would help her heal.

Linn Sue also focused on the tangible task of helping Sophia through her pregnancy. She tried to guarantee she had the nutrition she needed and the support that any young woman needs, especially one that was going through this without a loving partner. But Linn Sue didn't have the personal experience of going through what her daughter was having to persevere. She didn't know what it was like to have been raped. Nor did she know what it was like not to have a loving husband by your side through a pregnancy. But she did the best she could each day to imagine what Sophia may be going through. She watched her pregnant daughter's expressions, her mannerisms, and her postures. She watched her daughter's growing belly and taught her everything she knew about pregnancy. She attempted to calculate what might be Sophia's next fear or concern. And she tried to provide her with an environment where she could process the tragedy, accept her situation and truly heal.

All of this led to beautiful little Destiny. Who could have thought that such a brilliant jewel could have come from such a horrific act? But it did. Desi came into their life, and nothing had ever been the same. The sweet bundle of energy brought them each new life, new love and a joy beyond belief. Pae's burdensome expression seemed to lift, Sophia's smile had come back, and Linn Sue was enjoying the role of grandmother. She didn't think that life could be much better than it was with her dear husband, her brilliant daughter, and this amazing granddaughter all close by.

But now anxiety has hit again and she watches her own daughter struggle with the fear that her baby girl is slipping away. She can feel Sophia's confusion and stress. She can sense her grief. And she is also feeling all of those same feelings of her own. When she stops and allows herself to think of the possibility of losing little Desi, or potentially what this sweet child may have to endure, it is too much.

As Linn Sue was paused looking out the window at little Desi playing, noting the sunshine casting a shine on her hair and listening to her playful melodies, it was one of those times for Linn Sue. At first the tears started streaming slowly, and then more rapidly they flowed, until Linn Sue finally buried her head into her apron and let it go.

As she cried, thoughts reeled through her head. She saw little Desi sitting in her lap as she read to her. She pictured Desi and Sophia walking away from the house toward the beach like they had so many times before. She thought of Desi at the gift shop helping Pae, and then her mind shifted to wondering what it would be like if she wasn't there anymore.

As the well of tears and personal grief sprung forward, Linn Sue tried to keep her tears and cries muffled in her apron so that Desi would not hear, but just as the last few tears were coming forth, and Linn Sue thought she was going to be able to regain her composure, Desi sprung through the door and stood facing her grandmother.

"Grandmother, are you OK?" she asked with a perplexed look on her face.

"Yes," replied Linn Sue, "I am all better now that you are here." With this she grabbed the small child into her arms and hugged her tight.

When Linn Sue was done hugging Destiny she looked at her, then cupped her little face in both of her hands and told her, "I wish I could take away any pain or problems you ever have to go through."

Not nearly understanding the magnitude of her grandmother's statement, but sensing her immense sincerity, Destiny reached up and slung both arms around her neck, hugging her close in return and whispered into her ear, "I know you would, Grandmother."

CHAPTER 40

Sophia, her parents, and little Destiny made multiple visits back and forth to various doctors in the city, who ran numerous tests and told them that she was very sick. They used the word cancer, yet no one could determine exactly what kind or what exactly to do for treatment.

Sophia could not believe this was happening. She and her daughter had been in such a good place, and she felt she was really getting her life back. After all she had been through, yet finding this child to be such a blessing to her and her family, how could this now be happening?

Meanwhile little Desi was, for the most part, her usual self. She wasn't fearful at the doctor visits anymore. Instead, her adventurous personality was full of inquisitiveness as she continued to watch what each health care professional did, and she explored each big, shiny gleaming piece of equipment – all very different from what she was used to at the small village clinic - with her beautiful, curious eyes. At each visit to the city, Sophia was told that Destiny was dropping in weight. Sophia also noticed Desi was sleeping more.

"But then again, isn't that what growing kids do?" Sophia would think as she contemplated any physical or behavioral changes in Destiny, and her mind would stop at the reality that she was requiring more sleep.

In many ways, it was hard for Sophia to believe her little girl was even sick. In fact, it would be hard for most anyone to believe it. She had so much zest for life. And her beautiful blue eyes, accompanied by her lovely smile, continued to sparkle. Yet, still, every doctor was both consistent and persistent that Destiny was just that . . . sick.

Days went by. Weeks went by. Yet Sophia was still no closer to getting answers as to what should be done for her sick child. She would hear the wheezing sound she once found endearing in her daughter's voice, and whether it was worse or just more pronounced because she now knew what it meant, the sound made her weep. She was living the life every mom prays will not happen to them, as she watched her young daughter's failing health, listened to doctors, and wondered what was going to happen next. Sophia wondered why this was happening to little Desi. She wondered how the doctors could not know what to do. And most of all she wondered how both she and her mom, familiar with being around sick people in the clinic, could have been so oblivious that Destiny's wheezing was a sign of something more, as they were around her every day. Sophia felt she was at fault. How could she have let her own daughter's health fail like this? Why had she not asked more questions of the first doctor at the clinic who said she was OK? Why hadn't she pushed for further examination when the sound did not go away? And even though nurses in the city explained to her that sometimes we don't recognize what is going on with people right in front of us because we are too close, that didn't matter to Sophia. She felt as though she was failing at what mattered most, and that was being Destiny's mother.

Nighttime was the hardest. During the day, they could go about their business, and there was plenty to tend to. But at night, when it was quiet and Desi was fast asleep, Sophia had time to think about what may be ahead for her young child. She spent many nights praying to God, thankful for the Christian faith that she and her family had adopted from the Americans passing through their village and the gift shop, their family that lived in the U.S., and the Bibles left in the clinic that she had spent hours studying as a young girl along side the medical books. Some nights, when she prayed by herself after tucking sweet Destiny in and after her parents had gone to bed, she was able to find gratitude within her struggles. She was able to be thankful for the kindness expressed by the healthcare clinicians they encountered, friends and local villagers. She was able to thank God for seeing her through struggles in the past and express confidence that He would get them through this too. She was able to be thankful for her parents and that her daughter seemed to be feeling pretty well, despite the situation. Other nights, she was tormented by anxiety, as worry and fear raised their ugly heads, and Sophia would find her prayers much more poignant, as she pleaded with God, begging for his help through her despair.

As difficult as it was for Sophia to think about the impact all of this was having on her daughter, it was also hard to watch the effects it was having on her parents. One evening she walked into Destiny's bedroom to find her father leaning over Destiny as she slept. He had his hand on her small stomach, gently patting it as he watched her chest rise with each breath. There was just enough light coming into the room for Sophia to see his face before Pae realized she was there. It was an expression she had never seen on her father's gentle face before. It was one of pain combined with deep devotion and fear. She could see her father struggling with what was happening to his grandchild, and it nearly devastated her to see the emotions so clearly on his face.

Over the next few weeks, Sophia and Desi continued to make long treks to see doctors in the city. Some days her dad was able to take them, other days they received rides from other villagers. The trips were getting expensive and taking a toll on the family financially. Still, Sophia wasn't getting anything clear from the doctors as far as exactly what was going on or how to proceed. Her family had reached out to any contacts they could think of who may possibly have influence, even Sophia's uncle and aunt in the U.S. and any connections they had there, yet nothing was leading to any tangible information regarding Desi's treatment. Sophia was willing to do anything to save her little girl, however, she felt she was at a complete loss of control and was barely hanging on by a thread.

One evening, while sitting bedside with her sleeping daughter, Sophia said aloud, "I don't know what to do. I don't want to lose my daughter."

As she sat there sobbing and crying, she prayed fervently. "Please, Dear Lord, help me. What is your will? Talk to me. Please."

As she cried this out, the verse Jeremiah 29:11 immediately came into her mind. Crisply from a voice within she heard *"I know the plans I have for you,"* declares the Lord, *"plans to prosper you and not to harm you, plans to give you hope and a future."*

In despair, Sophia cried out again to God pleading, "I don't understand, I don't know what that means."

She picked up her Bible, hoping for more signs or guidance. Right then, a business card fell out from within the pages and landed on the floor. She picked it up and saw the name Graham Taylor on the front side. On the back it read, *"Call me if you need anything. Graham."*

Sophia thought back to the kind businessman she had met on the airplane when going to the United States to study. She remembered back to how naïve she had been at this time and how Graham had done so much, while they were traveling the same route, to help her feel at ease and teach her what he could about life in the United States. Meeting him at that time had been so valuable, though she wished she had heeded his warning, and she knew that he had been sincere in his words for her to reach out to him if she needed anything.

She began to wonder if she should reach out to him now. But as quickly as she got a spark of hope, doubt set in. So much time had passed. She began to wonder, "Would he remember me?"

Her self talk continued, "I can't ask him for help. It has been too long since he gave me this card."

Right then, however she flipped the card from one side to the other in her hands again and noticed something she did not notice the first time. Embossed in gold on the card was *"Philippians 4:6-7."*

Sophia tried to remember what that verse may be, and when it did not come to her, she looked it up in her Bible. There she read, *"Do not be anxious about anything, but in every situation, by prayer and petition, with thanksgiving, present your requests to God. And the peace of God, which transcends all understanding, will guard your hearts and your minds in Christ Jesus."*

She sat at the edge of the bed for a moment. A sense of peace came over her, and as she put her Bible back on the nightstand she had a feeling of letting go.

As she fell asleep, she felt a "knowing." It was as though God was saying, "You pleaded with me and I answered. Now it is up to you to follow through."

The next day Sophia made the call. She found out from the receptionist that Graham was away for two days on a business trip, but she was advised to leave a message. In the message Sophia spoke genuinely, "Hi, Graham, this is Sophia Nyugen. I hope you remember me. We were on the same plane from Vietnam when I was going to LA to go to school . . .

CHAPTER 41

Sophia looked out the window of the 25th floor of their hotel as the beautiful view of the Puget Sound lay out before her. The cool, early autumn morning air had brought with it a patchy thin layer of fog that adorned the bluish green expanse of water. A large white ferry with green trim was slowly coming into the landing at the pier near Madison Street. She sipped on her tea and took in the view. It amazed her how much had changed in the last week. On Monday night she had laid in her bed, hopeless, crying and pleading with God for his mercy to save her sick daughter. Tuesday she had left the message at Graham Taylor's office in Arizona. Thursday he had returned her call, and with his international contacts he was able to get the right people involved to approve Sophia and Desi for emergency travel to the USA. On Saturday the tickets were waiting for them at the airport in Vietnam. Now in Seattle, on this beautiful Monday morning she stood in a Five Star downtown hotel eating breakfast sent up by room service, taking in this view and watching her daughter sleeping soundly in the big bed behind her. She was back in the United States, and just as she had vowed, she would do anything to help her daughter following God's guidance, including coming back to the U.S. Fortunately for her, she had an angel of a man helping her. She gave God credit for each of these things.

It was 6:30 a.m. and at 8:00 a.m. a taxi was scheduled to take them to The Fred Hutchinson Cancer Research Hospital, about a mile away, where they would check in for an eventual appointment with Dr. Nance at 10:30 a.m. Graham had thought of everything. It should not have surprised her with all his traveling around the world, but at this moment, everything seemed a bit surreal. They had talked late last night after Desi had gone to sleep. He had explained his unique relationship with her doctor, Stephen Nance, a 32-year-old respected oncologist. He explained how Stephen's father, Robert, had saved his life in Vietnam. He also told her of Robert's passing and how he had subtly looked out for Stephen and his mom from afar over the years. Sophia's appreciation was so very deep and sincere for all he had done for her and Desi. Graham was well aware of this, and it touched his soul to be helping the sweet, naïve girl he had met on the plane seven years earlier. It was as if she was the daughter he had never had.

At 7:00 a.m., Sophia gently woke her daughter. Her eyes opened slowly, but when she saw her mom, a smile broke across her face. She looked around the huge room and began to giggle. Sophia leaned over and wrapped her arms around Desi.

"Mommy, this is amazing. Everything is so amazing, Mommy. Look, Mommy, at all the food. Amazing! Mommy, look at the ocean. It's beautiful. Look how high we are. Look at the big city, Mommy. Mommy, where are we?"

"Seattle, Honey. Mr. Taylor got us here."

"Who is Mr. Taylor? Is he a relative?"

"In a way he is, now. He is someone I met several years ago, and we became friends. Someone very special who looked after me like my daddy does. But he has become much more than a friend, now. I prayed to God and God put Mr. Taylor into our lives. He did all this for us."

"I like him, Mommy. He helped us a lot. I hope I get to meet him someday so my teddy bear can give him a hug." Desi pulled her teddy bear in close to her little body, as she had down thousands of times before.

By 10:00 a.m., Desi was sitting in her hospital bed wearing her small pink gown. She had her worn teddy bear in the blankets under her arm. Registration, instructions by the nurse as to today's agenda and the preliminary blood tests were already done.

Just after 10:30 a.m. the door quickly swung open and a tall, young doctor appeared in dark slacks and a white lab coat. Slightly rushed and holding a medical chart in his hand, he introduced himself to Sophia who was standing near the 4th floor window wearing her white sweater and a long dark skirt. He reached out and shook Sophia's hand noticing her subtle, natural beauty.

"Sorry I am a few minutes late. A busy morning. My name is Dr. Stephen Nance. I will be your daughter's doctor. We will be getting results from the blood tests later. Let me assure you that this is one of the finest hospitals in the world for your daughter's case."

"Thank you, Dr. Nance. Mr. Taylor has shared a great deal about the hospital and about you. We feel very comfortable and extremely blessed that you were able to get us in so quickly," replied Sophia with a sudden recollection that she had seen this man before. This handsome doctor looked familiar.

"Well, Miss Nguyen, Graham is someone very important in my life and when he explained your case and how important you were to him, we simply had to make this happen for your little girl."

"Thank you very much. This is my daughter, Desi."

Sophia walked toward the bed and Stephen followed behind her thumbing through the chart. "Desi, say hi to Dr. Nance."

With that Stephen looked up from the chart at the little girl sitting in the bed with the covers pulled up to her waist. He stopped in his tracks, stunned.

Stephen's eyes were glued to hers, unable to look away. The tanned features and the sun coming in the window enhanced the beauty and depth of Desi's mesmerizing blue eyes. He stood in a moment of Déjà vu. Stephen had seen these eyes before. He was not positive but one does not forget those eyes. Finally he reclaimed his senses and walked up closer to the beautiful child.

"Hello, Dr. Nance. Are you going to make me better? Mommy said you and Mr. Taylor are a gift from God."

Stephen smiled at her openness and kind words. " Well I am going to really try to make you better, Desi."

"Good. Can my teddy bear give you a hug?" With that, Desi took the tattered stuffed toy from under the blankets and held it out to him.

Again, Stephen was caught off guard, frozen in the moment. The teddy bear only a foot from his face revealed small dog tags with the initials SN engraved on them around its neck. He stared at the toy for what seemed like minutes, taking it all in, yet not being able to clearly comprehend it all. He finally stepped back and slowly turned his head in Sophia's direction. She was looking back at him, confused by his shocked demeanor.

"Are you ok, Dr. Nance? Dr. Nance. Are you ok?"

"What? I mean yes. Yes, I'm fine."

Stephen paused to gather his thoughts. He then looked back at Desi holding the bear. Next he looked back at Sophia. "May I ask you a question?"

"Of course." Sophia replied.

"May I ask where your daughter got that teddy bear?"

"Oh. That's very, very old. I got it from a little boy in California when I was born 26 years ago."

The answer was surreal. He knew it was his teddy bear that he'd given away years ago, but how did it get here today and why? So much was going through Stephen's mind. He felt that he needed to step outside and regroup.

"Excuse me, Miss Nguyen. Would you mind if I stepped out for a moment to review some things?"

"Of course not. We're just right here. We'll wait."

Stephen exited the room and leaned against the hallway wall, deeply exhaling, releasing the air that had been unconsciously held in his lungs for the last several minutes. After about half a minute he began to briskly walk toward the elevator and press the 7th floor button, which is where his office was. As he entered his office, only the small, green glass covered desk lamp lit the room. He walked to his desk and sat in his chair. For a moment, he just sat there in the darkness looking in front of him. He then looked at the desk lamp. He was not actually looking at the light, but the necklace made of white shells that hung from it. This was the necklace that Pae's daughter had given him when he and his dad were in Vietnam. For a long time now it had served as a remembrance to him of that time with his father. Stephen's mind then shifted to thoughts of his childhood teddy bear that he had given a newborn baby when meeting her mother at the hospital years ago. This same teddy bear now rested under the arm of the little girl downstairs with the mesmerizing blue eyes, which he was figuring out was the same little girl he saw on the beach during his second venture to Vietnam. Stephen sat stoically in his chair, yet his head swirled, as he speculated that the newborn baby he encountered years ago had grown up into a beautiful woman. And now it was his job to save this beautiful woman's daughter's life from the grips of cancer. It was too much. It made his head spin. Stephen put his fingers on the necklace still hanging from the lamp. He let the shells run through his fingers like rosary beads. Confused, he began to talk. Not to himself, but to someone he needed guidance from.

"Dad? Dad, I know you are here. This is too much for me to comprehend. I'm confused. I feel lost. Please. If you can hear me, please talk to me. Tell me what is happening. I feel like this is one of those moments in life that is so very important, so pivotal that I must get it right. Please tell me what I need to do. Dad, please, I truly need you. Please."

He sat in silence for a couple of minutes, the necklace still running through his fingers. He then thought to himself, "Ok. Time to go back to work." Stephen stood, and as he took his first step, the phone rang. He sat back down and grabbed the receiver.

"Hello. Dr. Nance speaking."

"Stephen. It's Graham. Just checking in. Did Sophia and her daughter get there ok?"

"Yes," Stephen responded, "They are in their room right now. I was just heading back down there."

"Good. Good, Stephen. How are you, Stephen? Is your mom doing ok? You still single? Still just trying to be the best doctor in the world?"

"I don't know about the best doctor in the world but, yes, single. I just don't have the time to be with someone."

"Son, let me tell you something. Listen really well. I have all the money a man could ever need. Financially I am a true success. On paper I am what businessmen aspire to be. I am wealthy and free. But let me tell you something. I'd give that all away to have found the right woman and gotten married. Work was always the priority. Now I have this huge house with six bedrooms, three garages, a swimming pool and a view of the Arizona desert with some beautiful mountains in the distance. But it is just a house. That's all it is. A house. Lumber, nails, cement and a lot of material items that I call personal necessities. But, Stephen, it isn't a home. You can't call a house a home if you are lonely within it. I don't want you to do the same thing I did. I don't want you to have everything except the most important thing . . . love. That Sophia is a wonderful and unique woman. I knew that when I first met her seven years ago. Her spirit. How she carried herself. How sweet she was and, yes, her innocent naïve demeanor too. She is special. My advice, Son, is don't let that woman get away. I will talk to you later today. Good day, Stephen."

"*Son!*" That word was clearly directed at him. It was the answer that his father put on the lips of Graham. He stared at the hanging necklace in his hand, held it tighter, smiled, then got up and walked to the door to leave. As he stepped through, he looked back at the green lamp on the desk aglow in the darkness. He paused and before he closed the door he spoke these words, "*Thanks, Dad.*"

CHAPTER 42

"It was forced," she said in a soft, trite voice.

"Oh," was all he could stammer as a response.

Stephen had spent the last week fervently ordering tests, examining and re-examining Destiny, looking at her lab values and combing through case studies showing any similarity while caring for his other patients. He now sat in the dim light of his office surrounded by patient charts and medical records, thinking back to the conversation he'd had earlier that day with the beautiful mother of his patient, Destiny Nugyen. When discussing the possibilities of what could be going on with the little girl, the need for further tests and the importance of family history, he inquired about the little girl's father. Stephen was pretty confident the father was not directly in the picture, but figured there was possibly contact between him and Sophia, and therefore, a way to obtain any necessary medical information. When he explained this to Sophia, she gave him an empty look at first, followed by her statement that the pregnancy was "forced." It didn't require his scholarly, analytical mind to realize what Sophia was trying to tell him. Stephen was embarrassed by his lack of considering all possibilities before opening this conversation; he was also floored that such a beautiful little girl came from such a horrific act. But most of all, he felt a pit swell up in his stomach and a sense of anger that was unusual to him. He did not want to picture what this lovely Asian woman, who he was so fond of, had endured.

Stephen's mind played tricks on him, and at times he was in denial, telling himself he wasn't sure what it was about this case that caught his attention and captured him so much. After all, he was a professional and had seen many things in his career as an oncologist already. Each cancer had its own story and was attached to a person with his or her own story, as well. As a researcher, he had always chosen to focus on the pathology, yet there was something about this situation, this set of people, which made him want to do more. As he sat and thought about this undeniable fact, he wondered about the little girl's captivating blue eyes? Her shockingly blue eyes against her naturally darker skin had definitely caught his attention, as it did most people. The researcher in him had even looked up how an Asian child could genetically have blue eyes, scribbling Punnett squares on notebook paper as he considered all the potential scenarios in which the two recessive genes could have matched up. Or was it the mother's beauty and the way he watched her so kindly address and attempt to nurture the patients and their families in the waiting areas, despite what she was going through with her own daughter? Destiny's mother was definitely a very special lady herself, as the nurses, front staff and everyone else at the facility had noticed and mentioned to him, too. Or was it that they were from the area of Vietnam he had visited with his father and were referred to him by his dad's dear friend from the war, Graham Taylor? Stephen was definitely drawn to any area is his life that got him closer to that of his father's, but there was no denying synchronicities taking place with his teddy bear and the little girl with blue eyes. Any outsider looking in would be able to point out his attraction to Sophia and his fondness of little Destiny, and it would be nearly impossible to deny that all of these factors played a role. The number of times their lives had passed and encircled each other was astonishing, almost too much for Stephen to believe.

Regardless of the motivation, it occurred to Stephen that in order to best determine the course of action for this little girl, he needed to know the medical history of her biological father. And he could not expect Sophia, under the circumstances, to do this, so he took it upon himself to be the one to take action. Following another soft-spoken conversation with Sophia, he was able to get the assailant's name. It took less time for him to find the guy's phone number via the phonebook, than it did for him to persuade Sophia to let him contact him. He had to guarantee her that it was only to help with Desi's condition, and explain thoroughly the link between varying cancers, their treatment, and genetics. Nonetheless, within 24 hours he was placing the call.

"Hello," answered a male voice.

"Hello, is this Matt Chambers?" Stephen spoke through the phone.

"Yes," he replied.

"This is Dr. Stephen Nance from The Fred Hutchinson Cancer Research Hospital in Seattle, Washington," Stephen spoke professionally and authoritatively, "I have a very sick child I am working with at the hospital. It is believed that you are the child's father. The mother's name is Sophia Nyugen."

There was a little bit of rustling on the other end of the phone and then silence. For a few seconds, Stephen thought maybe Matt Chambers had just walked away from the phone. Then came back slowly, "You've got to be kidding." It wasn't spoken as though he really thought it was a joke, but rather in absolute surprise.

Stephen could feel his professionalism start to waiver - there were things he would like to say to this man - but he knew that he needed to choose his words carefully in order to achieve what was best for little Destiny. Stephen went on to explain the importance of finding the little girl's blood relatives on her father's side in order to better determine what type of cancer she had, as well as what treatment options would be most effective. Matt still lived in the Los Angeles area, the Inland Empire outside of LA to be exact, and by the end of the phone conversation he had agreed to meet Stephen at a quiet, but public, café in Ranchos Cucamonga in a few days.

****

Stephen didn't mind the traffic taking him out of Los Angeles on I-10, referred to by locals as "the 10". It gave him time to think. He had caught an early flight out of Seattle to LAX and now he was heading to meet Sophia's assailant. What he was doing was so outside his box, so different from his usual realm. He was a doctor for Heaven's sake, not a private investigator. Of course, right now he thought a police officer would be the appropriate person meeting with Matt Chambers. He told himself he would accomplish his goal by being professional. That he would stick to the medical facts. His plan was to get the information he needed to help Destiny in her current situation, not go into the circumstances surrounding her conception. If Stephen could stick to this plan, he felt it would be worth stepping out of his comfort zone. Besides that, his desire to help this child outweighed the temporary discomfort he was going to have to face.

When Stephen arrived at the café, he saw a man of medium build dressed in a t-shirt and blue jeans sitting on the patio exactly where Matt Chambers described he would be. Stephen guessed him to be about five years younger than he was, although his skin looked weathered and his eyes more worn.

He had thought about what Matt would be like. How could anyone do such a horrible, evil act to a lovely lady like Sophia? Stephen expected to find someone crass, full of hatred and almost demonic sitting at the table. Instead, what he found was someone immediately remorseful and overwhelmed with humility. Within seconds of sitting down, Matt began speaking with redemption. He took responsibility for his actions and gave no sign that he didn't believe Destiny was his biological daughter.

"I was in a very dark place," said Matt. "I was angry. Angry with my father for divorcing my mother, then for not handing me the family business but insisting I go to college."

Matt looked away briefly then continued, "I was drinking a lot and then started messing with drugs. That night I was so horrible to Sophia; I was high as a kite. I remember going back to the party afterwards and bragging how I conquered the Asian Virgin. It was awful of me. Just awful."

Stephen just sat there listening. His first response was "Oh, no, this was not where I wanted this to go." But then he found himself surprisingly interested in knowing what had happened. He did, however, maintain his stoic posture and professionalism while the man sitting across from him continued.

"I never should have put her through that," Matt's voice slightly quivered, "She didn't deserve it. Since I have been clean, there has not been a day that has gone by that I didn't feel terrible for what I did to her. I have forgiven myself for a lot of things including the anguish I put my family through, but that night and what I put Sophia through is the one thing I have not been able to forgive myself for. And I had no idea there was a child involved." Matt laid his forehead in his hands for a minute then looked back up.

Stephen managed to provide an understanding gesture and squeak out a "We all make mistakes." Then he let Matt continue.

"Sophia left school at the end of that semester. Half way through the next semester I left, too." Matt went on, slowly looking away.

Stephen then learned that Matt had spent the next couple of years in the mountains near Crestline with a handful of other people, occasionally breaking into homes and cars to help fund their drug and alcohol habits. He even had a stretch of homelessness in downtown LA until his sister came looking for him.

Matt continued, "It was my sister who helped me, though I didn't give her the credit she deserved. Our father had died, and that must have made her want to bring the family she had left back together. Regardless the reason, she came looking for me. And she found me. She found me right there in all of my stupid drama. She gave me a place to stay and tried to get me the help I needed. Yet I still did so many things under her roof I am not proud of, so many things that I shouldn't have done. It wasn't until she was diagnosed with cancer, that I changed my ways."

This caught Stephen's attention as Matt went on to tell him about how his sister had died of cancer about a year and a half ago. Stephen continued to listen as Matt described his sister's battle and how her death had led him to such a profound change. As they closed their meeting at the café, Matt agreed that although he expected Sophia to want nothing to do with him, that he would do whatever was needed to help young Destiny.

Stephen left this encounter with such mixed emotions. He was told so much about the personal side of things that it could have made his head spin. What he chose to focus on though, was the very important piece of medical information he found out during his discussion with Matt, that Matt's sister had Chronic Lymphocytic Leukemia (CLL). This diagnosis had crossed Stephen's mind for Destiny. Though almost unheard of in children, some of her symptoms, or rather lack of initial symptoms, pointed toward this as a possible diagnosis. More tests would need to be run. However, the thought of this young child having CLL was disturbing. Though in adults often times the cancer was slow growing, the impact on a child seemed bleak.

CHAPTER 43

When Stephen got back to Seattle, all Sophia wanted was the facts in regard to how they affected Destiny. He tried to relay to her Matt's remorse, and describe some of what was going on in his life leading up to his behaviors, but Sophia wanted nothing to do with any of this information. She had buried what Matt Chambers had done to her very deep and stayed strong, focusing only on raising her daughter. There was no way she wanted to dive back into the pain of that horrible night and the events that followed, especially while also dealing with her daughter's illness.

Yet it wasn't until Matt contacted Stephen at the office, saying again that he wanted to do whatever was needed to make things right, and shared with Stephen that he had inheritance money from his dad and sister that he wanted to put toward Destiny's medical needs, that it became more apparent that Stephen needed to talk to Sophia about the deeper topic. Matt specifically ended this conversation asking Stephen to tell Sophia he was very sorry.

A few days later, Stephen received a letter in the mail handwritten by Matt and asking that it please be given to Sophia. Though in some ways he wanted to protect her from pain, not give it to her, and pretend he never received it, he knew this would not do anyone any justice - and would definitely not best serve little Desi.

So with a knot in his stomach, he reluctantly approached Sophia. He didn't want to push too hard, but he hoped she would at least listen to him, read the letter and hear what he had to say.

It was about 8:00 on a Wednesday evening and not unusual for Stephen to still be at the hospital, when he decided to pull Sophia aside. She had been sitting bedside with Desi all day and he told her he thought a little fresh air would do her some good while Destiny slept. Sophia agreed to take a walk outside with him. Stephen began the walk pointing out some architecture and other random information outside of the hospital. Then he started in with his task at hand.

"Sophia," Stephen spoke gently, "I really need to talk to you."

"Yes," she replied assuming it was going to be about Desi.

He chose to get straight to the point. "When I met with Matt Chambers I wanted to hate him, but he was so sincerely remorseful for what he had done to you. He knew he had been a very stupid kid. And of all the things he had done; drinking, partying and taking drugs, what he did to you was the one thing he could not forgive himself for."

Sophia at first looked at him confused, then tensed up and turned her head down and to the side.

He continued, "This does not in any way lessen what he did to you. You in no way deserved that and it was a vile, horrendous act, but you need to know he realizes that and is remorseful."

Stephen could barely believe how he was speaking. He was a man who usually felt awkward having these types of emotional conversations, but this time he felt strangely at peace being the one bringing up this topic. He felt as though it was necessary, and was his place to do so. He wanted what was best for Sophia and her daughter, and he was beginning to realize just how much he really cared.

As they continued walking along the sidewalk. Sophia remained quiet. He couldn't directly see her eyes to tell how she was responding, so he decided to continue. They had walked a little way now and were close to a light projecting from one of the main buildings. Stephen gently pulled Sophia by the elbow to under the light, reached into his pocket and pulled out the note from Matt.

"Matt wanted me to give you this." He handed her an envelope. "He mailed it to me after we met in Los Angeles."

Sophia was confused for a minute. She looked at Stephen, then at the envelope. Her instinct said to cram it into her purse and then maybe, just maybe, read it later when she was alone. But for some reason she chose instead to open it, and began reading it there with Stephen.

Sophia's hands shook, and she started sobbing even before she unfolded the letter. Written in very legible handwriting on simple, lined paper were these words:

"Sophia, I cannot even begin to expect your forgiveness for what I did to you. I am so, so sorry for what I did as a stupid, arrogant kid. I robbed you of so much and I am so, so sorry. My own pain and inability to deal with how my life had been altered gave me no right to steal your joy and alter yours. I am very, very sorry and there is not a day that goes by that I do not regret what I did to you. You do not have to have anything to do with me, but I promise you I am no longer drinking and doing drugs and I want to do whatever is needed to help Destiny's situation. I know it doesn't change what I did to you, but please let me do what I can to make this situation better. Sincerely, Matt"

Sophia drifted to a bench nearby and sat down. She sat for several minutes not saying a word. Stephen sat down next to her. He could not believe how emotionally involved he was letting himself be with Sophia and Destiny. For so long, he had been so removed emotionally from those around him. He loved his mom and displayed love toward her when he saw or talked to her. But as for those immediately around him, his colleagues, co-workers, patients and their families, he kept an emotional distance. With Sophia and Destiny, things were different. He could feel his emotional barriers being lowered. He wanted to be involved. He wanted to be let in and let himself experience what they were going through. He did not know, however, if he would have the right words when the time finally came to speak, but he did know the silence right now was beginning to feel overwhelming. He began to worry about what Sophia's response was going to be when she finally did say something.

People process information and emotions differently and on different timelines. In this case, Sophia's first instinct was rage. "How dare he!" she thought. "Matt Chambers is filth!" her mind went on. He had pushed himself into her life, taken from her in a nightmarish fashion and robbed her of her dreams! "He isn't worth the time it took to scribble words on a piece of paper! He doesn't deserve a second thought from her and he doesn't deserve forgiveness! He is absolutely NOT going to have any involvement in ANYTHING concerning Destiny. And there is NO way a little letter is going to change anything!!" the anger imploded deep inside her. Yet still she said nothing out loud.

Through the thoughts, through the confusion, and through the rage, Sophia allowed herself to keep breathing, until slowly she was able to look over at Stephen still sitting there with her.

Stephen spoke softly and kindly, but as though he was tapped into her, "Sometimes we have to forgive purely for ourselves. To save us from emotional cancer. You need to forgive to help save Desi. But also for yourself. Graham has been an absolute angel. He has covered many of the bills, but why let your anger cost Graham more and more financially when Matt is willing to help with the cost of Desi's medical bills?"

Stephen embraced her, giving her a supportive hug, while they sat there for a long time. Sophia nestled her face into the space above his collarbone and sobbed. She sobbed long, hard and steady until she thought there could not be another drop left, then she cried some more.

CHAPTER 44

In the week that followed, little was said about the letter or Matt Chambers. Although one day when Stephen and Sophia were alone with Desi in the hospital room, one on each side, Sophia did mouth the words "thank you for the other night" to Stephen. Her eyes were warm and the way her mouth curled up as she looked at him with such appreciation made Stephen's heart almost beat out of his chest. She was sincere in her gratitude and her fondness for him was evident as she looked into his face.

Much time was consumed talking about Desi's symptoms and possible treatments. However, Stephen had persuaded Sophia to take short breaks away from Desi's bedside to walk with him each evening. This gave her the much needed break and fresh air she needed to rejuvenate herself. They each found themselves looking forward to this part of the day when they could escape from the chaos inside the hospital. During this time, they would chat about Vietnam, what it was like growing up, or any other topics that came to mind. They learned more and more about each other and often went back to discussing the times their paths had crossed. Both loved their fathers deeply and had utmost respect for their mothers. Both had deep desires to help others and valued education. And both had their fair share of emotional pain.

Destiny's tests and biopsies came back conclusive and it was determined that she had Non-Hodgkin Lymphoma. Though not a diagnosis any parent wants to hear, the entire medical staff agreed it was much better than the diagnosis of CLL as they had once feared it could be. Discovering it was Non-Hodgkin Lymphoma explained why little

Desi had the fatigue and weight loss, and especially explained how she could have the swollen lymph nodes around her collarbone and neck, yet without pain. Fortunately, her cancer was at an early stage, and due to both Sophia and Matt Chambers going through tests, it was determined that she did not also have an inherited autoimmune disease that genetically predisposed her to this cancer. The down side was that she was going to have to go through a vigorous regimen of chemotherapy and, because the cancer was in her neck and head region, she was going to have to have chemotherapy in her spinal fluid.

Sophia found herself very concerned over what her daughter was going to have to endure. She was concerned about how to explain things to Desi and all that comes with being a parent to a little girl with a childhood cancer. She thought about side effects. She thought about how treatment would affect Desi long term. She thought about her own fears surrounding the word "cancer" itself. But there was one other fear that kept lurking as treatment was discussed, and that was how much it was going to cost. They were visiting here from another country and were not a family of means. Surely these treatments and hospital stays were not cheap. And she couldn't expect all of this from Graham. How on earth were they ever going to pay for it? Of course she would do anything necessary to save her little girl, but the thought of mounting expenses scared her very much.

Sophia was sitting in a straight back chair in Destiny's room when Stephen rounded the corner. Her posture was different than he had ever seen. She sat tensely with her legs awry, kind of twisted around each other to one side. Her arms were mimicking the same position and she was biting on her lower lip. What seemed even more out of place was that Destiny was awake, and although quietly playing with her teddy bear, it wasn't like Sophia to not be interacting with her.

"Knock, knock," said Stephen as he gestured a knock on the open door.

Destiny looked up and said, "Hi, Dr. Nance," with a smile and her big blue eyes shining at him.

"Wow, for a sick little girl, she sure is positive," he thought to himself. Then he replied aloud to her, "How's my favorite little girl today?"

"Good," Destiny replied and then waved the teddy bear's hand at him.

"And how is he?" asked Stephen, gesturing toward the bear.

"Grrrrreat!" said Destiny, with a playful growl.

Still not a sound or acknowledgement came from Sophia. She sat there deep in thought and with such a perplexed expression, that Stephen could not let it slide. "Destiny, your mom and I are going to run to the cafeteria for a few minutes. Is there anything we could bring back for you?"

"Ice cream! Chocolate for me and strawberry for him," replied Destiny as she pointed to the bear. Stephen swore his fuzzy childhood friend was smiling as he sat propped up in little Desi's bed.

"OK, you got it!" replied Stephen as he stood up and gently guided Sophia by the elbow.

Sophia had shown signs of paying attention to the conversation when Stephen mentioned the two of them going to the cafeteria. And she managed a smile when Destiny mentioned ice cream; however, she was definitely concerned about something. Once out in the hallway and walking to the cafeteria, Stephen asked her, "What is bothering you?"

Sophia hesitated to tell him. She didn't want to bother him with this, too. Stephen was already doing so much for them. But she found herself wanting to be honest with him. Besides Graham, he was truly her only friend here, and although it was her parents she would usually talk to about things like this, she could not call them across the world and bother them with this problem, when they were already heartbroken that their granddaughter had cancer. It would put too much pressure on her parents to want to help, and she knew they did not have that kind of money.

"I don't know how I will ever pay for Destiny's treatments and this hospital stay," Sophia said humbly, "I honestly have no idea how I will cover these expenses."

Stephen took a deep breath and looked at her earnestly, "Look, what you need to focus on right now is Desi and her recovery. That is where your thoughts need to be. Let the rest work itself out."

"I know," replied Sophia, "But it is a big concern and not one to be ignored."

"Remember you have Graham Taylor to help you."

"I know that, and am so appreciative of him and all he has done. After all, he got us here. He got us to you." With that Sophia gave Stephen a big smile. The she went on, "and he is paying for me to have a hotel room that I am really only going to when I shower. I cannot expect anymore from him. He has already done so much."

"I know," replied Stephen, "But Graham does these things because he wants to. It is who he is. And he cares about you and Destiny."

Stephen paused, thought about his words and then continued, "Also Matt Chambers has the financial ability to help and he wants to. He hopes you will let him." Stephen saw the look swelling up on Sophia's face yet continued, "Before you say "no", please listen to me. I know you don't want to hear this, but he is a changed man. Nothing makes the act of what he did to you acceptable in any way. You should never have to have anything to do with him, yourself. But he received a large sum of money through the death of his father and his sister, and he wants to use it for Desi's medical care. This is a way he can make things at least a little better, and I think you need to do it for Desi's sake.

By now they were in the cafeteria, but the room seemed to be whirling around Sophia. She could barely think straight. How could a man who was so awful to her, now want to do something nice? How could she accept his financial help for Desi without it seeming as though she was accepting or condoning what he did to her? Right now this was all just too much. She needed to get away from this conversation.

She politely excused herself from Stephen saying, "I just need a few minutes to gather my thoughts," as she gingerly exited the cafeteria and walked down the hall.

Sophia walked into the women's restroom and straight into a stall. She sat down and lowered her head into her cupped hands. After a couple of deep breaths, she looked up and saw a pamphlet posted by a local church on the stall door with these words:

"Choosing Forgiveness is not forgetting.
Choosing Forgiveness is not condoning.
Choosing Forgiveness is not reconciling.
Choosing Forgiveness is not a one-time event.
Forgiving is living as Jesus."

"Be kind and compassionate to one another, forgiving each other, just as in Christ God forgave you." Ephesians 4:32

"God is the only fuel strong enough to make life-long forgiveness feasible."

Sophia shook her head ever so slightly back and forth then started to sob. She cried long, healing sobs and right there in the bathroom stall; the delicate, small-framed Asian woman, who was no longer a naïve girl, dropped to her knees on the floor.

Sophia cried out, "God, please help me to forgive!" And then she continued to cry uncontrollably.

After quite some time, Sophia pulled herself together, stood up, and straightened her pants and blouse. She then went to the sink and washed her hands and face. It was almost ceremonial, as she cleansed each side of her hands methodically with soap and then turned her attention to her face in the mirror. She looked deep into the eyes peering back at her and allowed herself to have complete compassion. Compassion for herself, what she felt she had let happen, and for all the ways she had told her younger, more naïve self, the incident could have been prevented. She gave herself the same compassion she had given animals and the people at the clinic in her home village during her teenage years.

Once back in the cafeteria, Sophia looked for Stephen but he was not to be found. She had scanned the room and walked around a lap or two when she decided it best to head back to Destiny's room. As she opened the cafeteria doors to exit, Stephen came from around the corner of the hallway.

"So, sorry," said Stephen "I had to respond to a call."

"That's OK," replied Sophia, "I sort of needed the time to myself."

Stephen could tell she had been crying, and smelled the scent of fresh soap, as he got closer. He gave her a look of question, wondering if she was all right. Without hesitation Sophia said in a smooth, gentle but strong voice, "I will no longer let unforgiveness poison me."

With this, her hands reached out and touched Stephen's. Right there in the middle of the hospital hallway Stephen grabbed her and held her closely in a warm embrace. He was so proud of her and thought he would always remember the clean, gentle scent of soap that day as his lowered nose brushed across her face.

The next day, Sophia gave Stephen the go ahead to accept the financial help offered by Matt Chambers for Destiny's hospital bills. She was doing it for Destiny and also as a step toward her own forgiveness.

CHAPTER 45

The following weeks and months of chemotherapy treatments were hard on little Desi's body and even more grueling for her mother to watch. The nurses were so good and tender with her, though. They would sweetly describe what they were doing each time they administered a chemotherapy dose. And Desi, who seemed wise beyond her years, would reply with a sweet "thank you." Through each and every treatment, Desi's teddy bear, or "gau bong" in Vietnamese, was present to comfort her. Desi found security in the worn, tattered friend that had once been her mother's. A younger nurse, Jan, had even made a small hospital gown for Teddy, the name Destiny had fondly given him years ago. On the shifts when Jan was working, she would first pretend to administer the medication to Teddy and then gently give Desi her dose.

Each time Teddy received his dose, Destiny would gently pat him as her mom did her and say, "You are going to be OK. Just 7 more doses after today." She always managed to cheerfully recite whichever number of treatments were left that her mom had told her that day.

On one particular day, however, Destiny wasn't feeling so cheerful and was getting tired of being messed with in the hospital. She was tired of being poked and prodded, tired of sounds and monitors, and tired of being sick. The accumulation of the chemotherapy in her system was taking a toll and both daughter and mother were exhausted. When the nurse came in and it wasn't the one that also gives it to Teddy, Desi became unnerved. She held Teddy up directly in front of the nurse and demanded, "Teddy, don't let her come near me!"

The nurse had worked with many children but had never seen Desi behave like this so was taken by surprise. "Why Destiny, you know we have to do this," she replied.

Desi then turned to her mom with big tears and said, "Mommy don't let them do this today."

It took everything Sophia had, to remain calm while seeing her young daughter pleading with her. She had stayed there day and night with her little girl, getting very little sleep as the nurses came in hourly to check vitals, and she knew that Destiny had been in and out of sleep herself. Sophia's primary focus, besides consoling her daughter, had been to make sure Desi kept taking in lots of fluids in an attempt to try to decrease some of the side effects of the chemotherapy. But Sophia knew, too, that she had to stay strong, because it was important for Desi's sake that they stay on schedule with the treatments.

"We must," responded Sophia.

The nurse moved forward to take Destiny's temperature. But Destiny pursed her lips together and refused to open them. The nurse then tried to distract Sophia by asking her about Teddy. This worked for a second, but when the nurse came forward with the thermometer Desi became obstinate again and insisted that she didn't want any part of it.

The nurse remained patient but Sophia could feel her own frustration rising. She didn't want to have to be forceful with Desi knowing that she was going through so much, but she also wanted treatment to get underway. She carefully crawled onto her bed, trying not to disturb any of the lines or tubes attached to Desi. Then she slid her fingers between her daughter's right hand and squeezed her cheeks lovingly till they opened up like a fish. Defeated, Desi let the nurse take her temperature.

Next came time for a blood pressure reading, and Desi went back into resistance mode, arms stiff against her sides. Before either Sophia or the nurse had time to respond, Stephen responded from the doorway. He had been watching from the nurse's station and was actually amused that sweet little Destiny could be a little fiery. He had been practicing his Vietnamese, waiting for the opportunity to use it to bond with Desi.

"Gau bong," said Stephen's voice in almost perfect dialect, as he motioned toward Teddy.

Destiny looked at him shocked, then smiled.

Stephen then attempted to ask, "Is Teddy getting his medication first?" in the most broken Vietnamese Destiny had ever heard.

She broke out into giggles. She looked at her mom, who was smiling as well, then at the nurse and back at Stephen as she said, "Teddy first." Within seconds, Teddy was getting his blood pressure taken, then Destiny allowed the nurse to continue taking her vitals, as well as dispensing their medication. Teddy continued to get every procedure prior to Desi getting hers, and amid the tension-relieving attempt at a new language, Stephen and Destiny's bond had become greater.

CHAPTER 46

Since Stephen had moved to Seattle, his mom had come to visit only a couple of times, flying in for a few days at a time. She liked the city and the change of pace and always welcomed time with her son, so when Stephen called her saying that Graham was going to be in town and he would like it if she would come as well, Abby welcomed the opportunity. She knew that Graham had been helping a young woman from Vietnam with a sick little girl and that he had brought them to Stephen at the cancer hospital. What she didn't expect was how openly her son talked about this young woman and her daughter, Destiny, on the phone.

"Mom, Destiny, will be getting out of the hospital and Graham and I will be there. I would like you there too," announced Stephen.

"Ok," replied Abby. "Let me know the dates and I can look at flights unless you have already done that."

"Yes, I have already looked at flights and it will work out for you to come early on that Tuesday morning. This way you can get to know Sophia and Desi a little bit beforehand." Stephen paused briefly, and then kept talking. "It is important to me that Sophia feels supported, and her own family cannot be here. Thanks, Mom, I am so glad you are coming."

As they hung up the phone, Abby thought to herself about the difference in her son's tone. Not only had he never called his patients by name when talking to her, but never had she heard him express concern over a family member of that patient being supported as well. His conversation regarding work usually consisted of the pathology of cases, new pharmaceuticals that had been developed, or how the hospital was implementing new procedures. Only when she asked about the patients themselves had he ever shared any of their stories, and even then, it was usually just general demographics like where they were from, their age, or how their cancer may have originated. On very few occasions she had been able to draw out information like that they were the mother of three kids, had been a farmer in Nebraska, or had once performed in the New York Philharmonic. But these scattered insights pertaining to the actual people were rare, and never had she been asked to meet them!

****

The morning Abby arrived in Seattle, Stephen was ready and waiting when the airplane landed. As she got off the plane and scanned the immediate area, it didn't take long at all to spot her very punctual son. When he saw his mom, he smiled, and it reminded her how much he looked like his father. As the two embraced, Abby took in the moment getting to be with her son that she missed so much. Once they had retrieved her baggage, they walked to the parking lot and settled into Stephen's car.

"Ok, Mom, if you are hungry we can stop and grab something, but I want to get to the hospital as soon as we can so you can meet Sophia and Desi. I think you will like them and I know they will like you," said Stephen with a twinkle in his eye unlike anything Abby had ever seen before.

"OK, Son, whatever you would like sounds good to me," replied Abby.

"They are from the area that Dad and I went to visit in Vietnam. And I can't believe that she knew Graham. And then Graham connected us to see if I could help Desi. Mom, so much has matched up in my life recently that I can't even describe. Dad and I even went to Sophia's parent's gift shop. Remember Pae? He owns the gift shop. He was the one who helped Dad heal and alter his perspective on life. They make the shell necklaces and sell them. The one I have, Sophia actually gave me as a little girl when I was there with Dad. It is the one I have carried around ever since Dad's and my trip. Everything is so unbelievable . . . ."

"Son, you mean serendipitous."

Stephen paused as if taking in what his mom had said, nodded and went on to tell her about the surreal conversation he had with Graham immediately after he had met Sophia and Destiny in her room at the hospital.

Abby smiled and Stephen continued, "Then there was the teddy bear! You know the one that Dad gave me with his dog tags and I ended up giving it to the baby at the hospital that time after my accident at Disneyland?"

"Oh, yes, how could I ever forget that teddy bear?" replied Abby. "Did you realize that your father had given that to me on our first date?"

"He did?" responded Stephen in surprise. He was caught off guard that he had never known this fact.

"But wait, let's get back to what you were saying, Stephen. What is it about the teddy bear?"

"Desi has it! The same one, with the dog tags and everything!"

"She does?"

"Yes, apparently Sophia was the baby I gave it to," Stephen smiled and shook his head as he continued to barely believe it himself. "Mom, the initials on the dog tags . . . SN . . . Stephen Nance? . . . well it could also stand for Sophia Nyugen."

At first Abby opened her eyes wide with shock, but it didn't take more than a few seconds for her to assimilate what she was hearing and settle into the peace and knowing that she had become familiar with. She shook her head quietly as she marveled to herself how amazingly God works and brings life experiences back around. "And He even has a sense of humor!" she thought to herself, "Bringing that teddy bear back into the picture!" She thought of Robert, wondering if he was smiling down on them. She wondered if he had any idea that the teddy bear would have such an impact on so many when he bought it that day for her on the boardwalk.

This day was a very different experience from Stephen usually picking her up from the airport. Up to this point, plans had never included another person and usually involved either going out to dinner or cooking together at Stephen's place that night. Abby smiled from the warmth and joy she felt within, realizing some things might be changing in her son's world. She had been concerned through the years regarding his personal life, or lack of, thinking he worked too hard and hadn't given relationships a chance. It appeared this could be different now. She smiled again to herself, happy that her son may be growing in this way. However, she kept her thoughts to herself, so as not to pressure Stephen in any way.

The rest of the way to the hospital, Abby listened intently to Stephen as he detailed everything that had transpired over the last couple of months, including his thoughts and his emotions. Abbey enjoyed this new side of Stephen that was opening up. She delighted in the thought of her serious, ever so professional son giving such thought and energy to faith and events happening beyond what can be rationally explained. The awe in her son's tone was obvious and Abby was excited to meet this special woman and little girl who drew this out of him.

Once at the hospital, Stephen and Abby ascended to Desi and Sophia's floor. Graham was standing there in the hallway when the elevator door opened. He was deep in conversation on the telephone, yet looked up at just the right moment to give Stephen and Abby a sincere smile. He paused from his conversation to give Abby a gentle hug then gestured them toward Desi's room, saying he would be in soon. The two proceeded down the hallway, leaving Graham to finish his call. Upon entering the room, Abby immediately felt the brilliance of this special little girl and her beautiful, poised mom.

Sophia extended her hand to Abby, saying, "Hello, we have heard so much about you and are so glad you came."

As Abby reached out, she couldn't help but notice how petite Sophia's hand was; yet she had such a strong but gentle grip. Abby smiled warmly, causing Sophia to immediately relax as everyone settled into the room. Sophia had been a bit nervous prior to meeting Stephen's mom, but now felt a sense of peace and comfort, which was evident in her body language as her face and shoulders softened.

Destiny quickly became the center of attention. She reached out, giving Abby the paper dolls she had cut and colored. Then she began telling her about all of her experiences in the hospital, followed by everything she wanted to do when she was out. Graham had soon joined them and the room became full of adult laughter inspired by the light of this young child. Abby liked watching how Sophia looked adoringly and proudly at her daughter, listening to her every word. She enjoyed hearing her deep appreciation for both Graham and Stephen regarding all that they had done for them. Abby especially liked observing how Sophia and Stephen would exchange looks of knowing and agreement as they recapped events from the past several months. Stephen's demeanor had become lighter and the way he and Sophia conversed gave Abby an impression of mutual respect and adoration.

CHAPTER 47

While Graham and Abby were available to stay with Desi for an evening, it was decided that Stephen and Sophia would have a night to themselves. Stephen invited Sophia to shower and get ready for their evening at his place, and she took him up on it. She surprisingly felt comfortable with the situation and, besides, she was interested in seeing where Dr. Stephen Nance lived. She had given up the hotel room Graham had arranged for her since she had only been going there to shower, spending the rest of her time with Destiny in her hospital room. For weeks now she had been using a shower at the hospital, so the thought of a long, more private shower was appealing.

When arriving at his apartment building, the two politely greeted another tenant who was leaving, then went up the stairs to the second floor. As they entered the apartment, Sophia was immediately impressed by how orderly and clean it was. What did surprise her, though, was how cozy and warm it felt. It definitely was nothing like the sterile hospital she had spent all of her time in over the last few months. Stephen's living room had a nice, contemporary-looking couch on one side. Above it was a large, beautifully framed photograph of the Golden Gate Bridge. There were even three decorative throw pillows on the couch and one on the matching chair. In the dining area sat an elegant but simple glass table with metal, padded chairs. Three bluish-colored candles sat on a metal tray in the middle of the table. She smiled at Stephen's attention to detail and decorative skills despite having an analytical mind and being a workaholic who probably spent very little time at his apartment.

The kitchen had a large countertop with two solid barstools. Sophia noticed immediately that there was a gas stove and very nice pots and pans hanging from an overhead rack. The other thing that caught Sophia's attention was how many cookbooks this man, Stephen Nance, had lined up library-style on one of the counters.

"Wow, you must really like to cook," said Sophia.

"Oh, yes, did you notice the cookbooks?" replied Stephen.

"Yes, I have never seen so many in one place. And it looks like you actually use them!" said Sophia as she casually navigated through one of the books, noting that some of the pages had been curled over to mark certain recipes.

"Well, cooking is kind of therapy for me and probably my only real pastime outside of practicing medicine." He paused, and then went on to explain how cooking was something his mom and he did together after his dad passed away. "It gives me peace and a sense of completion. Plus, it doesn't hurt that I like to eat."

Sophia knew that Stephen's dad had passed away but it suddenly occurred to her that she did not know how. They had spent so much time and energy focused on Desi and her illness that she had not even asked. She thought about this and felt a slight twinge of guilt. This wonderful man had been so kind to her yet she had been so focused on her own problems that she hadn't even asked him how he lost his father.

"How did your dad pass?" asked Sophia aloud.

"Cancer," replied Stephen, "from the war in Vietnam."

"Stephen, did you speak at a community college in Los Angeles about seven years ago?"

"Yes, I did. All of us fellows had to. It was part of the program."

"Stephen, I remember you. You spoke about losing your father in Vietnam. I sat in the front row. Our eyes met."

"Oh, my gosh, I remember you. I waited in the hallway hoping to meet you, but then I got a page and had to leave."

They both shook their heads smiling.

Stephen went on to explain the specific cancer that took his father's life, how it was related to combat in Vietnam, and he even detailed to her about his father's PTSD. He told her how different things became for he and his mom upon his father's return, including the stark difference in his father after his diagnosis and up to his death. Stephen told Sophia all that he learned about his father during their pilgrimage to Vietnam, where he met her and her family. He also shared how her father, Pae's, wisdom and perspective on life had helped heal his father by coming to grips with the Vietnam War. The two discussed how Pae lost his leg and how different his response to the war experience had been. Sophia felt a huge amount of compassion for what Stephen must have felt like growing up with his father so distant and emotionally absent. She thought back to her own father who was so involved and loving, recognizing it could have so easily been the other way around.

An hour had passed, and Stephen realized Sophia had not yet showered. He led her to the bathroom and handed her some towels. They had decided that staying in and having Stephen cook a meal at home would be a great way to spend the rest of the evening. He had asked Sophia what her favorite dish was to make and she told him it was rice, chicken and vegetables because she used to prepare this meal for her parents. He decided he wanted to make something very different for her. Once Sophia was in the shower, he looked in his cabinets to assess what he needed, made a quick list, grabbed his keys and headed out the door. He had decided on beef medallions in a mushroom sauce, baked potatoes and a salad. He hoped she wouldn't be disappointed, and felt a rush of adrenaline at the thought of cooking for Sophia, this special woman he was finding himself falling for.

Once Sophia was out of the shower, she dried herself off, got dressed and walked out of the bathroom. Her mind was full of thoughts regarding what the rest of the evening might hold. It was nice that Stephen wanted to cook for her. And she really did mean it when she told him to surprise her. Her stomach was turning slightly. She knew part of it was that she was hungry, but she also acknowledged that she was a little nervous too. This was the first time she and Stephen had been together away from the hospital. Sure, the two of them had spent quite a bit of time talking and getting to know each other, but this was the first time in his personal environment. It made Sophia slightly nervous, but she was happy to be here and was looking forward to the evening.

Suddenly, out of the corner of her eye, she saw a glimpse of something scurrying across the room. She wasn't sure what it was, but it was fast and out of sight as quickly as it appeared. Then there it was again, something darting across the room! Slowly, from behind the couch, a cat came walking toward her. She chuckled out loud as she thought, "Stephen Nance has a cat!" One more thing to add to the list of all she had learned today about this amazing man.

When Stephen got back from the store, he unlocked the door humming. Traffic had been light and he was able to quickly get everything he needed at the store. His smile broadened when he entered the door to his apartment and saw Sophia standing there, her hair still wet. He laughed out loud when he realized she was holding Fastball, his cat!

"How did you catch him?" asked Stephen.

"I didn't," replied Sophia, "He just came to me."

"That cat doesn't come to anyone," said Stephen back, "Not even me. And I am the one who feeds him. He usually hides in my closet and sleeps. When he isn't sleeping he's darting around, running all over the place. That's why I named him Fastball. After the baseball pitch."

Not totally understanding the name or his reference to baseball, Sophia was still able to get the gist of what Stephen was saying. She explained how, after a minute or so, the cat had just stopped calmly in front of her and let her pick him up. The two had been nestling together ever since, waiting for Stephen to get back from the store.

Stephen shook his head, amazed. His mom had gotten him Fastball as a kitten during his last year of fellowship. She had been concerned that he needed company and something else in his life besides medicine. He had reluctantly accepted the kitten and actually found him the perfect roommate, except for his leaping across his books in the evening when he was trying to study. Now the self-sufficient cat that never wanted to be handled, was nestled warmly and contently in Sophia's arms, purring.

"Go figure," said Stephen, "Do you always have this impact on animals?"

"They were actually some of my first patients when I was a little girl," replied Sophia. She explained about how she would hang out at the clinic where her mother worked and how much she aspired to be a nurse, and how her dad had let her use the chicken coop behind their house when people from the village would bring their sick or injured pets for her to care for. Stephen smiled as he pictured a little Sophia optimistically treating all the local animals.

Over dinner, they discussed more and more about their childhoods, dreams, aspirations, what had gone right in their lives, and what had gone wrong. Sophia asked him to explain more what "fastball" meant, so Stephen ended up sharing with her about his baseball days. Sophia described what it was like parenting Desi on her own. He admitted he never saw himself as the fatherly type, but if he were ever blessed to have a daughter as special as Destiny, he would be pleased. The couple mused over the times their paths had crossed throughout their lives, across oceans and time; in the hospital when Sophia was born, in Vietnam as children, at the community college, on the beach when he first saw Destiny's mesmerizing eyes, and finally at the hospital where he was giving treatment that they hoped would heal Destiny.

"Heal Destiny," Stephen reiterated aloud, "There is more than one meaning in those words." Sophia smiled softly and came around the table, gently leaning her head into Stephen's shoulder.

His mind went back to the moment he saw Destiny in Vietnam before starting this job in Seattle. Little Destiny had been playing along the water's edge, collecting shells. He admitted he could not make out Sophia with the large brimmed hat that she had been wearing. He also confessed that he was surely unrecognizable because of his scruffy facial hair, khaki shorts, flip-flops and very worn San Francisco Giants baseball cap. Sophia blushed at the image of Stephen walking along the beach, unkempt and straggly, but still handsome. He had been right there within steps of her, yet still unseen.

"It was her blue eyes," said Stephen, "I was mesmerized. Then when I saw those same blue eyes the day I met you in the hospital . . . then the bear, and my white shell necklace hanging in my office that came from your family's gift shop . . . and you being Pae's daughter was the final piece. I knew this was a pivotal moment in time that would change my life when Graham called and told me 'Son, don't let this girl get away.' It was the words of my father."

Sophia moved her head to one side marveling over all the synchronicities and how much thought she could see in Stephen's eyes. Stephen smiled, grateful that she had come around the table to get closer to him. The citrus fragrance of her freshly washed hair filled his senses, and he could feel her breath against him. Everything about this woman felt right.

Stephen took a deep breath in, slowly exhaled, and gently whispered, "It is the blue-eyed girl's mom who has me mesmerized at this moment. I am so happy that our paths have come together again." With this, he gently tilted Sophia's head back and looked into her eyes. He leaned in and gave her the kiss he had wanted to give her for quite some time.

CHAPTER 48

While Stephen and Sophia were enjoying the evening alone, Abby and Graham stayed with Destiny, having a nice time of their own. Destiny, now feeling better though still a little weak, had the stamina to do at least some things little girls her age like to do. They started out the evening drawing in coloring books. Even Graham, dressed dapperly in his usual suit jacket and button up shirt, rolled up his sleeves and sweetly colored with little Desi. They played games of Old Maid and Go Fish, the two adults letting Desi win two out of three times. Abby got tickled as she watched young Desi slightly bend the corner of the Old Maid card when she thought the adults were not looking. She watched Destiny scan the cards in each of their hands methodically and seriously as she looked for the slight crease she had made to alert her not to pull that card. Abby nudged Graham the third time she saw Desi doing this so he could join in the fun she was having. She carefully signaled her eyes toward Destiny, and once Graham realized what was going on the two adults could not help but roll in a fit of laughter. Little Destiny looked back at them somewhat puzzled and went right back to scanning their cards, taking the game very seriously.

Abby took in every moment of the evening. She was enjoying spending time with this very special little girl. Several times throughout the night, she found herself marveling at little Desi's features. Her skin. Her smile. Her little hands. And most of all her beautifully captivating blue eyes. Abby loved how the little girl immediately tried to engage her when they first met, and she loved how she laughed in a way that made her whole body move with excitement. Abby was also enjoying

the evening with Graham. Through the years, the two talked occasionally on the phone when Graham would check in on her and Stephen.
Graham had been available for Stephen as a father figure, both fielding
difficult questions and attending major events in Stephen's life such as
graduations. And, of course, he had been there at Robert's funeral, staying a few days after to help them put the pieces back together. But aside
from a couple of dinners when Graham was passing through town, it
was rare for Graham and Abby to spend time one-on-one together
without Stephen there, too.

As the evening lingered on and Destiny's eyes started growing heavy,
Abby decided to crawl right up in bed with her. Destiny smiled as Abby
stroked her head and held the little girl's hand, caressing each finger
gently one at a time. Abby remembered something she used to do teasingly to Stephen when he was a little boy and decided to give it a try.

"Destiny, do you like bedtime stories?" she asked.

"Oh, yes!"

"Well, I have one for you."

"I want to hear it," proclaimed Destiny.

"Well, OK, but you have to listen closely," remarked Abby and she
then went into her version of a bedtime story, *"Once upon a time . . . in a
land far away . . . there was a land far, far away . . . once upon a time."*

Destiny looked up at Abby, giggled and said, "That is silly." She then
recited back, *"Once upon a time . . . in a land far away . . . there was
a land far, far away . . ."* Destiny stopped herself, giggled again, then
turned to Abby's face and said, "Keep going . . ."

Abby started back up, *"Once upon a time . . . in a land far away . . .
there was a land far, far away . . . far, far, far away . . . a long time ago . .
. a long, long time ago . . . a long, long, long time ago . . . once upon a time
. . . in a land far away . . . far, far away . . . far, far, far away . . . once
upon a time."*

Abby felt little Desi's head settle in deeper and looked down to see
her eyes closed. She watched the little angel's chest go up and down
as she gently breathed and peacefully fell into a deep sleep. Abby then

looked over at Graham who had been watching Abby with admiration as she interacted with the sweet little girl.

"Works every time," Abby softly said as she gently moved herself out from under Desi's head, tucking her in tightly and patting her head one last time. Abby then moved over to the other chair at the small table with Graham.

"You were so warm and gentle with her, Abby. Is that something you used to do with Stephen?"

"Yes," answered Abby, thinking back to those special moments. "You know we really did have some good times. It wasn't always so rough, even though we did go through a lot with Robert before and after losing him."

"Oh, I know. I am sure of that. And it is those memories we want to hold onto most," said Graham kindly.

"Absolutely," agreed Abby as she studied his features. She noticed, though he was aging, how gentle the wrinkles were around his mouth and how his eyes still had the same brightness that they always had. She thought back to Robert's eyes and how saddened they had become after the war. She wondered how one person could respond one way to life's events and how another could respond entirely differently. She then thought of how wonderful and supportive Graham had been to her and Stephen. Graham had always managed to maintain a connection over time. She thought how fortunate they were to have him in their lives. She also thought about how much Graham was now doing for this little girl, how much he did for all those he encountered, and how much, in general, he enriched other's lives.

At the same time, Graham was looking at how the light was hitting Abby's soft features. He had always seen her as so gentle, yet strong. He had admired her loyalty to Robert and her perseverance in raising her son alone. He had always found conversation with Abby to be easy and engaging, and he liked to hear her laughter. She was the kind of person who brought warmth to any room.

As Abby's mind shifted back to how often Graham had been involved in their lives throughout the years, especially Stephen's, she asked Graham aloud and for the first time, "Why have you been so good to us?"

At first Graham was a little surprised, then he looked at Abby and responded, "Well, at first I felt I owed Robert. For Heaven's sake, he literally saved me on the battlefield. My gratitude was immense. Then it became hard seeing him in such a dark place after the war. It was tough seeing such an amazing man, who I had so much respect for, not see it in himself. And there was nothing I could do to change that. Then came the cancer. I couldn't do anything about that either. But there was you and Stephen. I could do something about that. Robert didn't ask me to. It was something I decided. Something I wanted to do. I wanted to be there for you and Stephen. You know, make sure you two were always doing OK."

Graham paused, looked at his hands for a second then continued, "I never had a family of my own. I have always been busy traveling, running my business, and never met anyone I wanted to settle down with. Or maybe I met them but didn't give them a chance. I love kids. Wouldn't have minded having some of my own. But having you and Stephen in my life gave me a sense of family. I always kind of saw you and Stephen in that way."

Graham's eyes drew even softer and he felt a slight lump in his throat as he continued, "I always looked forward to seeing or talking with Stephen and to hearing about you. No disrespect to Robert, of course. It's just that, as I got to know each of you, I felt more and more of a personal connection and enjoyed you both in my life. My gosh, I am so proud of Stephen. And I always admired you. Your gentle nature and strength are unlike any woman I have ever known. Watching you tonight with Desi just reinforced that. I am so happy to be part of your life."

Abby blushed slightly and replied, "Thank you. The pleasure is surely mine."

The two went on to discuss much of what had happened in their individual lives. They spoke about Graham's travels and places Abby would love to visit. They also shared what their hopes were for Stephen.

For little Desi. And for Sophia. They reminisced what it was like after the war and what it is like at their age now. They discussed the weather, music they liked, a little bit about politics and quite a bit about Seattle. The conversation was so natural, it made Abby think about how comfortable it was to be around Graham. He had a personality that was just easy to be around. He was real and he could be serious, yet he kept things in perspective and was able to maintain a light-heartedness very different from what she had been used to in a man.

Leaning her head to one side, Abby asked Graham, "How do you do it? How can one person have certain experiences in life and come out striving and another slip into a world of depression?"

Graham took this question seriously and responded with exactly what he had concluded when wondering the same question years ago, "Well, a lot of people say it has to do with personality. How we view the world and process things. But for me it is my Faith. I don't know how anyone can make it through the troubles in this world without a solid foundation and something to believe in that is bigger than ourselves."

He paused, looking at Abby, who was listening intently, then continued, "When my life was spared during the war and I came back, I thanked God and vowed to keep thanking him each and every day of my life. Even when we were treated so poorly by people who were against the war, I focused on God and staying grateful. I vowed to have positive impact each and every day. It isn't a matter of striving and proving myself worthy to have been saved. It is out of gratitude and because it is the right thing to do. Paying it forward in a way."

"Also remember what I told Stephen after the funeral. I wasn't in Vietnam as long as Robert. I didn't experience or see as much as he did. He was stronger than me. That may have been his downfall. He tried to fight the demons. I did not. I knew I could not beat them on my own, so I sought counseling. God and good therapy healed me for the most part. I still have emotional wounds; I simply learned how to keep things in perspective. I thank God for that."

Abby could not think Graham a man of any more integrity than she did right now. She smiled and spoke softly, "So beautifully said."

Right then, Sophia gently opened the door. She and Stephen peeped their heads in. Seeing that Destiny was asleep, they quietly slid into the room.

"How was everything tonight?" asked Sophia.

"Couldn't have been better," agreed both Graham and Abby, with smiles on their faces, nodding first at each other then both toward Destiny, still soundly sleeping in her bed.

CHAPTER 49

Thanks to the medical staff keeping Destiny's risk of contracting secondary infections low during treatment, and dedicated physical therapists who helped Destiny gain her strength back quickly, she was able to leave the hospital relatively soon once treatment was complete. Her prognosis and future were still unsure and she was feeble compared to other children her age, but it felt good to Sophia knowing her little girl was past the treatment that had made her so frail. And although the unknown was still a bit scary, it was going to be nice not to feel so confined to the hospital's walls.

The day Destiny was to be discharged was rather surreal. One by one, various staff members she had encountered throughout her stay came in to see her. They gave her cards, hugs, and wished her well. Everyone - from the lady who brought her the noon meal each day to the volunteer that dropped by mid-afternoon with activities to occupy the time – stopped in to give their good-byes. Destiny was particularly fond of and Sophia equally touched by a figurine one of the housekeepers, Pedro, had carved for her. It was a small wooden replica of Teddy, dog tags and all. The lab team had even come together and made a large banner that read "Congratulations and Best Wishes to Our Little Angel." Her room was full of balloons and kind notes. As Destiny and Sophia looked around they noted how festive the room had become.

"Mommy, I am going to miss all these people. They have been so good to us," said Destiny with her lip slightly quivering.

"I am too," replied Sophia as she thought to herself how bitter sweet it was that they would actually miss this place considering what her young daughter had been through here. She also wished her parents could have been here to celebrate Destiny leaving the hospital with them. Though she had kept them informed of each event along the way, amidst the chaos it had seemed like a lot to try to get her parents to the U.S. in time for Destiny's discharge. In retrospect she wished she had, so everyone could have met each other.

Stephen came to the door and Destiny hollered out, "Dr. Nance!!" as she ran and threw her arms around him, eliciting a smile and a blush from Sophia.

Before any of them had the chance to say anything further, Abby and Graham walked in followed by two of Sophia's favorite nurses, the young nurse, Jan, who had always given Teddy his treatment first, and the seasoned nurse, Connie, who Destiny had gotten so upset with until Connie became aware of their routine. Destiny and Connie made eye contact endearingly, with the nurse giving her a playful, toothy grin. Sophia, knowing Connie worked nights, was touched realizing that she must have come in on her time off just to say good-bye to her daughter.

The two nurses carried a cake, plates, utensils and napkins. Behind them was a congregation of staff from the unit, all of whom were smiling and cheering as Destiny beamed with appreciation and excitement. She had no idea they threw parties here and was ecstatic to be celebrated in such a way.

Once the cake had been served and everyone had given their favorite little patient final hugs and warm words, often accompanied by a sniffle or tears, the room started to clear out. It was now only Destiny, Sophia, Stephen, Abby, Graham and nurse Jan, who had been with Destiny throughout her entire treatment. Jan, with her bottom lip slightly quivering, gave Desi a big hug and asked if she was all packed up and ready to go.

"Yep," replied Desi, hugging Teddy tight for comfort, but her eyes also wide open with excitement.

Jan went over the discharge paperwork with Sophia, at which time Sophia also took the opportunity to let her know just how thankful she was and how much she appreciated all the staff had done for them.

"Without all of you, I don't know how we would have made it through all of this," said Sophia, "and to see my little girl with some energy again and full of life means the world. Thank you. Thank you." With these words she hugged Jan extra tight.

"It has been an honor and a privilege," replied Jan, "It is our job, yet there is something extra special about Desi. And there is something extra special about you." With this she lowered her voice to a softer tone so only Sophia could hear and said, "Dr. Nance obviously sees it too." The two ladies gave each other a knowing smile.

Jan then asked Destiny get into a wheelchair, which she literally hopped into. Her belongings were loaded up on a cart and taken as well. As they left the room, Destiny and Sophia both took one last look around. They had spent a lot of time here, Destiny completely confined to these walls. They knew exactly how the room was set up by heart, the way the large fir tree outside the window branched out to block the sun, where the machines with all their bells and whistles were kept lined up against the wall, and exactly what time of day the nurses would come through to check vitals. They had also committed to memory every shift change, every speckle they had counted on the ceiling, and the elaborate bedtime stories they had made up to distract from the pain right there in this room.

As they wheeled through the hallway, and past the nurse's station on their way to the elevator, Destiny explored all that she could with her eyes. These were the areas she had gotten to see very little of as they kept her safely tucked in her room to decrease the risk of other germs affecting her. Now she noted where the nurses gathered around, she saw the med carts and wondered what they were for, she noticed a half open door with a mop cart in it and then another door that a nurse was propping open with her foot as she reached for fresh linens. Destiny noted stronger smells of what she had faintly smelled from her room. Some weren't so pleasant; others were of rubbing alcohol and cleaners. Destiny heard the familiar equipment noises coming from each room. Midway down the hall she heard a high-pitched gasp that scared her. It was the sound of someone in pain. Immediately she reached out for her mom who, watching her daughter's reactions, was already intuitively reaching out to rub her shoulder, letting her know she was OK.

What Destiny kept her eyes on most as they passed by were the patients in the other rooms. She saw people of all ages. Some had hair; others did not. She saw some sitting up in chairs, while others were lying down. Some had visitors gathered around; others were alone. A few of the patients waved and gave them a smile as they passed by. Others faced straight ahead toward the wall, possibly asleep, or maybe not. Destiny saw one other child, probably slightly older than she was, in a room close to the elevator. They made eye contact just as Destiny was passing. Each held up their stuffed bears as a "hello." Destiny thought to herself that this little girl looked even sicker than she had and hoped she and her bear would eventually leave the hospital just like she was doing now.

Once down the elevator and out the front door of the hospital, Destiny experienced the first brush of fresh air that she had felt in a long time. The breeze and the warmth of the sunshine swept across her face. She lifted her head toward the sky and took it in. Nothing had ever felt so good. All the adults stopped, lovingly admiring the young girl's pleasure at being reintroduced to life's finer things.

Once satisfied by the pleasure of being outdoors, she and Teddy turned back toward the building, giving it one last look before they were loaded into the car.

As they began to pull away from the curb, Sophia took one more look at the building herself. She couldn't help but think of all that had happened there. She thought of all her young daughter had been through physically and emotionally. She then thought how much better Desi was doing now and how they had met this wonderful doctor and man named Stephen Nance. She also pondered the journey toward forgiveness that she was on. She was grateful. Very grateful indeed. Her mind then shifted to all that could possibly come next.

CHAPTER 50

On the right day, Alki Beach, on the West Seattle shoreline, is an ideal place to take the family to relax and find time to ponder life. This is especially true in late August while the sun hangs still on the late afternoon horizon. Stephen had laid claim to a quiet and secluded sandy area about 25 feet from the shoreline. It was there that he spread out a large blanket. He lay on his left side propped up on his elbow, feeling exceptionally at peace. A couple of feet away, his wife was napping with her head resting on his folded UCLA sweatshirt. Her silky, long black hair reflected the sun and blew in the warm breeze. Between them, wrapped in a blue blanket, was their one-year-old son, Robbie, cooing into the vast sky above with the tattered teddy bear grasped in his arms. Kneeling in the water was Stephen's new eldest daughter, and cancer survivor, Desi. She had an amazing way of keeping herself entertained. Her young but defined character was very charismatic, wise and social. Stephen admired her simple ability to be happy. Even when she had to endure all her medical treatments and the side affects that go along with it, she had remained in good spirits. He recalled one day when she was having difficulties with her treatment and struggling to get the slightest comfort or sleep, she asked him the most surprising and powerful question. It was six simple words that caught him off guard, but at the same time solidified his belief that she was one of the most special children he had ever met. She simply asked. "Are you doing alright Dr. Nance?" How extraordinary it was for a child going through so much herself to be concerned about his well-being. Today that special little girl, with the same silky black hair as her mother's, playing at the water's edge while talking happily to herself, was now his daughter.

So much had transpired in the last two years since being mesmerized by this special little girl's blue eyes that early morning of her first day in the hospital.

Through many conversations, Stephen and Sophia had realized just how many times their paths had crossed in their lifetimes. Five times, to be exact, the Lord had brought them together for a brief moment, only to separate and go in their own direction once more. Now Sophia was his wife, their daughter –Desi –was healthy, and their son rested between them.

Stephen took everything in as he looked over at this wife. He admired her perseverance and deeply loved her eloquence and grace. His mind and heart filled with happiness and pride as he thought about The Robert Nance Memorial Medical Center they were having built in Sophia's village in Vietnam with Graham's financial contribution. Her dream to go to America, become a nurse and return to help her community may have been dashed, but through it all, she was now able to help the local people even more than anyone could have ever expected. He then shifted his gaze over toward Desi, the little girl who intrigued and inspired him so deeply. He watched her play without a care in the world at the water's edge. At that moment Robbie began to cry. Stephen saw Desi look back quickly, jump up and run toward them. As she got closer he saw her concerned expression, as if she was on a mission. She knelt down and grabbed the small teddy bear that had fallen out of Robbie's hands. As she lifted the stuffed toy up, the button that created the teddy bear's eye snagged on the blanket. She pulled the bear briskly to release it, and as she did, the button ripped off, leaving a straight line of thread that had held that button on for decades. Desi gently placed the toy back in Robbie's arms. Instantly his crying turned to coos again. Desi looked directly at Stephen. Her blue eyes fixed on his.

Stephen turned his head lightly and smirked, "Are you OK, Desi?"

Desi smiled with the warmest of expressions replying, "Yes, Daddy. *Destiny is perfect now.*" With that she turned and ran back to the water to play.

Stephen watched their little girl prance back to the shoreline. He then looked down at Robbie who was now holding the teddy bear with its face pointing up toward him. He looked closer at the bear that now had one button for an eye and a horizontal line of thread for the other. A smile spread across his face. Yes, the teddy bear was winking at him. He took a quick look around, again noting his wife napping peacefully, Desi playing happily in the water and Robbie smiling back up at him. Satisfaction and a sense of deep love came over him as he slowly shook his head in agreement. "*Yes, Dad. Destiny is perfect now. Thank you.*"

EPILOGUE

Abby had finally agreed that it was time for her and Graham to have their first ever date. Graham, the consummate gentleman, was simply *there* for her family, for decades, from miles away. He had always been an unselfish support for the Nance family. He was there for Robert when he needed a moment to talk to another Vietnam veteran about the war. He was there for her as emotional support after Robert's passing. He was there for Stephen to explain to him more about his father. And amazingly he was there for Sophia and her child when they needed him the most. He was there for everyone, even the villagers in Vietnam where he almost lost his life so many years ago, with an attitude of graciousness and unselfishness. Graham was a sincere man who had never had his own family. So he found it natural to bond with the family of the man who had saved his life on that horrific, rainy day, while pinned down by the Vietcong's all-out assault in that rice field in Vietnam so many years ago. It was even more natural for him to take a young woman from Vietnam under his caring wing, like a daughter, and help her get the desperate assistance she needed to save her daughter's life. It was a basic, innate, paternal instinct brought to life when he met Sophia on the plane on her way to nursing school in Los Angeles.

Now Abby was going to go see this wonderful man. She pulled into the parking lot of the small executive airport. The facility handled private aircrafts, corporate jets and a limited number of smaller commercial airliners. As she brought her car to a stop near the fence, overlooking the one-runway airport, a Boeing 737 was slowly moving in front of her from the right, making its way down the taxi way for an eventual take off. To her left were a small terminal and a control tower with a radar quickly rotating on its roof. It was one of those pleasant, sunny California mornings with puffy white clouds occasionally casting shadows across the entire area. Abby had arrived early, so she had time to pause, taking a moment to relax and reflect on life's events and the weekend ahead.

She looked over at the passenger seat. Before exiting her cul-de-sac back in Palo Alto, she had stopped by her mailbox, collecting the parcels that had built up from the last three days, and placed them on the seat next to her. She now shuffled through the numerous letters and resolved that none were so important that they couldn't wait until after she returned from her trip to visit Graham. She then picked up the package that had also been in the mailbox. She smiled when she saw it was from her precious granddaughter, Desi. She slowly removed the tape and peeled back the paper before sliding the shoebox out of one end. As Abby pulled back the lid of the box, she saw a pink card on top of white wrapping paper. She removed it and gently opened the envelope, displaying a card with a teddy bear reaching out for a hug and saying the words "*I Love You.*" Abby smiled again, this time even wider, and looked up and to the left. She could see the airliner parked at the far end of the airport going through its preflight checklist. Abby then looked down again and opened the card. She began to read the poignant words written by this special child with the beautiful, translucent, blue eyes and a heart of gold. As she read the words she could actually hear Desi's little voice in her head.

The little voice said, "*Gramma. I love you so much. God has been so good to me. I am all healthy, I now have a baby brother, a new daddy, my mommy is so happy, and I have you too...*"

At that moment the little girl's words in the letter seemed to naturally shift from Desi's voice to that of Robert's loving tone. "*I was given so much in life. Yet sometimes one needs to go through being sick to realize what you truly have. We may not be able to see each other all the time, but my heart is always with you.*"

Abby looked up again as the tears started rolling down her cheeks. She could hear the airliner go to full throttle as the engines began to slowly move the heavy aircraft down the runway.

She continued reading. This time it was a blend of Desi's and Robert's voices. *"Sometimes the thing we love the most we must let go of. You need this now. This gift is for you. I love you very much. I always will. Love you, Destiny."*

Abby took the box and pulled back the paper, revealing the very teddy bear that she had received as a gift from Robert on their first date on the boardwalk in Santa Cruz. The missing button, leaving a line of thread, created the familiar wink that Robert had always shared with her. Abby squeezed it tightly against her chest as tears freely flowed. She then looked out the front window and saw the airliner lift off just to her left. She followed it skyward until it passed through a break in the clouds, causing the sun to hit the fuselage, casting a bright ray of sunshine upon her and the stuffed toy. A moment later it was gone. As the plane disappeared, so did Robert. Just like that, he was gone. But before he left he had given her *the gift*. His blessing to move on, to find her destiny, and to love again. As Abby sat there in silence, hugging the small teddy bear and savoring the moment, she realized she was feeling *absolute peace*.

Abby placed the bear upright on the dashboard and collected her belongings in the seat next to her, placing them in her handbag. She grabbed the small overnight suitcase from the floor in front of the passenger seat, opened the door, got out, closed it and began to walk to the terminal, soaking in the pleasant, warm morning air with each stride.

On the dashboard, the small bear, which had been to both sides of the world, sat and watched her enter the building. It was worn, torn, battered and weathered but had its ever-present smile. Smiling perhaps by the way things had turned out. Yes, it had done well. Everyone's life was in place now. The gift to them all, from a simple purchase so many years ago, had served well as a constant presence prompting, guiding and consoling its owners through a purposeful journey toward each of their destinies.

****

Surely we have all had a teddy bear in our lifetime. We have felt the comfort and love it brought to us. Where does the magical, loving power of a teddy bear come from? Is it from the inanimate object itself? Or is it the need we each feel for love within ourselves? Or could it be that God uses the stuffed toy as an instrument to reveal his own abundant love he has for each and every one of us? Yes, the teddy bear had done well. Initially, a gift given out of young love so many years ago before being passed down to their son. Then it was given to a newborn and sent ten thousand miles away, before becoming the comfort for her special child who was eventually diagnosed with cancer, only to return home as a gift to its original recipient. Where the loving power comes from is a free interpretation for each individual to decipher. The truth, though, is that the small, tattered inanimate object was now on the dashboard of a car, with a smile on its face from all that had transpired. Let us all believe that love always brings a smile, and perhaps a wink, from wherever God chooses it to originate.

If we follow love, we can't miss our own destiny . . . .

CLOSING THOUGHTS: HUMANITY, HEALING AND HOPE

I had vowed to myself that prior to this novel being published, I would visit Vietnam out of honor and respect. I would do so as a tribute to its people since I borrowed their country for the writing of this story. Surely, if I was going to write about their history, I must experience a small part of that which I wrote so deeply about.

I landed in Ho Chi Minh City (formally Saigon) on the afternoon of January 2, 2020 with a sense of anxiety, for I felt as though I was entirely out of my element. I was at the mercy of others' good will, or lack thereof. With my insides a bit in knots, I found a taxi and began my journey toward the hotel where I would be spending the next four days. I had no idea what I would see, experience or feel but said a small prayer that the experience would be the Will of God, for truly he had inspired me to be here, so far from the comforts of home.

You see, I was only 10 years old in 1969 at the height of the Vietnam War. I watched and heard about it every day on our old, beige Zenith television set. Walter Cronkite would give us the daily updates and body counts. Body counts had become the system of determining success or failure in a war that had become so unpopular at home and worldwide. Body counts would not be a fair assessment or the true determination of success or failure because within those numbers were the innocent, the civilians, and the children who simply got in the way of the battle going on around them. War is never fair. Never clear-cut. Never precise. It leaves collateral carnage. It is heartbreaking. Truly heartbreaking.

My ultimate goal for this trip was to visit the Vietnam War Remnants Museum. When I arrived at the museum on the third day, my stomach again found itself stressed and in pain. I knew this feeling well. I had felt it before when I went to Thailand after the 2004 Tsunami to help on an individual humanitarian effort. I felt that the Lord was preparing my heart to open up so he could freely imprint his message on my soul. In Thailand years ago, as I walked the hollowed grounds of Khoa Lak, through the rubble of hotels and bungalows along the water's edge, my stomach was tied in knots. It was as if I were grieving for all those that I had never met, but who had perished as the land succumbed to the ocean's wrath. Now in Vietnam, as I viewed, read and embraced the horrors of the war, my soul again ached in agony. The spirits of those living and dying in the nightmares of the photos that I was looking at loaded their pain upon my soul. I could not escape it nor did I try. I realize that all our souls are connected. As a Christian, I also know that the Lord works in the spiritual realm. This all being said, I embraced all that I was feeling, for that is why I came here in the first place – to experience what this country and these people went through. So I grieved for those innocent of the war and our brave soldiers who were only following the orders of a governmental administration that had truly lost its vision, its goal and its true course - an administration only trying to save face, while searching for an exit strategy to a war that could not be won.

So I came to this country with the interesting name and fulfilled my vow to connect with the country and people that I shared about in my novel. I felt them. I connected with them in a deep way whether I had planned for it or not. That was up to God. He knew best what I should feel and experience at a personal, emotional and spiritual level. Again, the word that comes to mind is heartbreaking. Truly heartbreaking.

I have learned in life that once we see tragedy, we must see healing. That Earth has a way of taking care of itself if we simply let it. We see it every day. Out of the ashes comes rebirth, whether from a volcano, earthquake, tsunami or even war. After a decade I went back to Thailand and the areas that had been devastated by the tsunami were now beautiful and flourishing with tourists from every corner of the world. It was back to normal as a tropical paradise. Unless you had seen it after the tsunami or you had the privilege to talk to a person that had gone through it, you would not have known that it had ever happened. Earth took care of itself. It is good at that if we let it. Ho Chi Minh City

(Saigon), once devasted by war, is now quite advanced with a luxurious downtown, thriving business district and lavish skyscrapers. There are still wounds from the war, some visible while some are not. After all, it was only 50 years ago. The adults that I encountered on my visit were young, like I was, during the war. They were only small children, scared to death, often in tears, who had seen and experienced things no child should ever have to endure. While at the museum, I talked to a man missing both arms and one leg, his visible wounds from the past. He was selling books about the war in order to make a living off the sympathies of the visiting tourists. Right or wrong, who am I to judge? I am simply a visitor in his country. He lived through the nightmare that I only watched on that beige Zenith television set so many years ago, in the safe confines of my home 10,000 miles away. I think he deserves some grace and respect. I will give him that. Heartbreaking. Truly heartbreaking.

I am glad I went and am proud of myself for keeping the vow that I had made. I am glad that I genuinely felt grief from the close connection that I felt with the spirits of the Vietnam War. Perhaps those were the same spirits that inspired me to write this story. Perhaps God wanted those spirits to be heard, and simply used me as an instrument to bring it to fruition. If so, I feel blessed to help heal them in some small way. I know this novel was put on my heart by God. I am not a professional writer, but even I must say the story is powerful and beautiful and needed to be shared. For God wants us to care about our fellow man. I have seen in life that in time a foe can become a friend, that forgiveness initiates healing, respect encourages hope, and in the end love prevails. I truly think humanity needs our sincere and genuine love. Thank you Vietnam. Thank you, Lord, for putting this beautiful story on my heart. I am surely a better man for it.

- Chet North

Hello Vietnam
Tell me all about this name, that is difficult to say
It was given me the day I was born
Want to know about the stories of the empire of old

My eyes say more of me than what you dare to say

All I know of you is all the sights of war
A film by Coppola, the helicopter's roar

One day I'll touch your soil
One day I'll finally know your soul
One day I'll come to you
To say hello... Vietnam

Tell me all about my color, my hair and my little feet
That have carried me every mile of the way
Want to see your houses, your streets, show me all I do not know
Wooden sampans, floating markets, light of gold

All I know of you is all the sights of war
A film by Coppola, the helicopter's roar

One day I'll touch your soil
One day I'll finally know your soul
One day I'll come to you
To say hello... Vietnam

And Buddhas made of stone watch over me
My dreams they lead me through the fields of rice
In prayer, in the light... I see my kin.
I touch my tree, my roots, my begin

One day I'll touch your soil
One day I'll finally know your soul
One day I'll come to you
To say hello... Vietnam

One day I'll walk your soil

One day I'll finally know my soul
One day I'll come to you
To say hello... Vietnam
To say hello... Vietnam
To say xin chào... Vietnam

Singer – Quynh Anh

ACKNOWLEDGEMENTS - CHET

I would first like to thank God for putting this storyline on my mind, heart and soul in 2002, and then giving me the inspiration to put it into words.

Thank you to my countless friends who listened to my thoughts, analogies and philosophies about life and love.

Thank you to my father who is now a great friend, yet some of this book surely represents my desire to have had him more a part of my life as a child. It is truly incredible what can come out of trying times if you keep the proper attitude.

I would also like to thank my mother whom, when I was young, would always quote the phrase, "Whatever the mind can conceive, and believe, can achieve." Those words inspired me for a lifetime.

Thank you, Brian Bliss, one of the Kansas City Wizards coaches who came up to me on a team flight, handed me a Nicholas Sparks book and said, "My mom gave me this. It has your name all over it."

Thank you, Taylor Graham, an ex-player for the Kansas City Wizards who shared the basic geography of California with me. Yes, one character in the book is Graham Taylor. Thank you Taylor, for believing in my initial dream to write this book.

And finally, thank you to Doug Brown, my high school literature teacher and assistant football coach. He inspired me in many ways, and I am grateful that I had the opportunity to share these with him recently. He believed in me when I sent him the first couple chapters of this story, of which he critiqued, gave me advice about and looked forward to seeing the full story. He inspired me in probably the most profound, life changing way back at Orcas High School when I asked him a question about the book we were reading, *The Old Man and The Sea*. His simple response unknowingly altered the course of my life.

I was small, about 5 feet 10 inches tall and only weighed 125 pounds but still played every sport. Yes, even football. He said, "The old man rowing the boat and fighting the storm is small and frail. A lot like you and I are, Chet." At that moment I decided I would change that. I was not going to go through life small and frail. I lived in the gym, lifting with my great friend Roger Scharnhorst, the star of every sport, and whose family I was living with, as my family had moved off the island. Within two years, I was 180 pounds and on the Varsity Rowing Team at Western Washington University. During the next four years I became a National Rowing Champion and an all-star in City League Hockey as a goalie. Eventually I became an Athletic Trainer for Seattle University, the University of Washington, the Seattle Seahawks, and have now been in Major League Soccer in Kansas City for the last 24 seasons. I have been all over the world with my career, met the soccer greats like David Beckham and even went to the White House in 2013 after Sporting KC won the MLS Championship and we were invited to meet President Obama. I became a pilot and went to Thailand after the Tsunami of 2004, supporting the children at a school who were emotionally devastated and grieving. And today I coach my beautiful young sons, Noah and Kaiden's, soccer team. I know that none of these things would have happened if a wonderful man had not spoken those poignant words so innocently and honestly so many years ago. I can't exactly tell you why, but it touched my soul in a way that made me realize that I had to take control of my life or I would be just like that old man, struggling as he rowed through the storm. Life would toss me about and control me and I decided I wasn't going to let that happen. At that very moment I took control of my destiny. Thank you from the bottom of my heart, Doug. Our paths crossed, and your subtle words had a lasting impact on my life.

Thank you to all the Vietnam veterans who may feel they were not properly welcomed back home and honored after the war. We all owe you more love, appreciation and gratitude than you could imagine for your service to The United States of America.

Thank you to those who have had their dreams dashed by circumstances that you felt were unfair, or who were betrayed by the selfishness and immaturity of others and are trying to forgive and move forward with your lives. And to those who desire to, once again, become vulnerable, and experience the true meaning and depth that sincere love can bring. All of you directly and indirectly inspired this wonderful novel. For you all, it is now time to let the past be the past and step through the door of the first day of the rest of your life.

ACKNOWLEDGEMENTS - MELISSA

First and foremost, I want to thank God for giving me the opportunity and the creative inspiration to help with this novel.

Thank you, Rodney Morris, for your loving support and for always believing in me, even in times when I don't completely believe in myself.

Thank you, Max, for being patient the many times I was working diligently on this book during your childhood.

Special thanks to my mom and dad, Sharon and James Kropf, for instilling in me confidence, the initiative to try new things, and the desire to challenge my own capabilities in order to grow as a person.

I want to thank our veterans for dedicating their lives to our freedom and safety.

I also want to thank our healthcare providers and researchers for their commitment and persistence in helping those who face not only cancer, but also many other physical and emotional challenges.

Thank you to all who read this novel. I hope you enjoy it and find something in it that gives you hope as you journey through your specific challenges in life.

We would both like to give a special thanks to Austin Nordstrom for his wonderful work creating the book cover. His skills, photography, creativity and patience are so appreciated.

ACKNOWLEDGEMENTS FROM CHET TO MELISSA

Melissa, we met in late 2015, becoming true friends from the start. We usually met at a coffee shop or sports bar – something casual to simply get to know each other better. One early evening, after work, at Johnny's Tavern in Olathe, Kansas, I began to share with you the novel that I was working on. I had actually written the entire storyline in six months, penciling my words and thoughts in notebooks while traveling for my job in professional sports, exercising at the health club or quietly sitting at home. As Sean Connery so brilliantly said in the movie *Finding Forrester* when instructing his young protégé to type faster when writing, "Hit the keys. First you write with your heart and then your head." It is so true. The words that flowed so freely in those early months were just concepts coming out of my mind and placed on paper. It was like pouring all your paint onto the canvas, but not yet choosing your paintbrush. It was time those brief descriptions be elaborated upon. As my high school literature teacher told me, " I need to know smells, tastes, textures and the surroundings in depth." Thus, one paragraph turned into a page or two. And then, as I wrote, I would think of other scenes that I believed would enhance the book as a whole. So I continued to write, read, copy and paste. It seemed that I would never finish this novel. That didn't really matter to me. I liked writing the story and sharing it with others. At this moment I was sharing it with you, Melissa, in Olathe, KS. I started from the beginning and went chapter by chapter, as you so intently listened. You would sincerely smile when this big, professional man in front of you naturally teared up with emotions and would have to stop to catch himself during certain poignant parts. We probably lost track of time as I told you the highlights of my story. I am sure some patrons around us that night must have thought this nice couple were breaking up because I would talk, and then both of us would be overcome by emotions. When I was finally done you simply said you loved it because it brought into focus love, faith, surviving cancer, veterans of war and the finding of one's destiny. Then you said that you had always wanted to write a novel. The moment you said this I simply replied, "Help me finish mine."

I really needed someone to corral my thoughts and help me bring this story to a final conclusion. Otherwise I would have just kept adding to it. I remember your astonishment and excitement over this special opportunity. As for me, I felt it was a win-win situation for both of us. You would get to take part in writing a book that really touched your soul and I had a person to make me bring this novel to fruition. I had typed a few chapters and the rest were in my notebooks written in pen or pencil. You were great with the computer so away we went, transferring the story into a more professional form. There were parts here and there that I thought you should write from a woman's perspective involving a love scene and a mother/daughter relationship. I simply didn't believe many men were going to rush out and purchase this book. It was targeted for a female audience, as most romance novels are, so some parts were best written by a woman. What I appreciate the most about you, Melissa, is that as you wrote particular sections of the book you never varied from the premise of the story that I firmly believed in. You sincerely realized that I had been on this journey for well over a decade, respected where in my soul the story truly transpired from, and appreciated that I had brought you into this journey with me. You understood that in the end the true concept of the book had to be adhered to so that the questions deep within my heart would be fulfilled. For the question, from so many years ago, had to be answered by the one who conceived it. Melissa, you were a blessing from above at the perfect place and time. I truly believe this. As with the question as to why paths cross and others don't, well, ours came together to finish this book. It was simply DESTINY. Thank you, Melissa, for such support, belief, respect, creativity and true friendship. We will always be connected by this journey we took together writing this novel.

ACKNOWLEDGEMENTS FROM MELISSA TO CHET

The story of our coming together to work on this novel is truly an example of paths entwining in remarkable ways. God definitely puts people in our lives at just the right time and in ways we could never think of on our own. Having a love for writing, but being content writing articles, I never dreamt I would write a novel. When others would ask if it was something I would like to do someday, my response was always that "I never saw myself coming up with a story elaborate enough to be a full book." Then I became friends with you, Chet. And you had just the story. I fell in love with the characters, the storyline and the concept almost immediately. What I loved most was how it encompassed Faith, overcoming struggles, and how relationships and people intertwine despite time and distance. And although my goal was to stay true to the story you had in mind, I truly appreciated how we worked together and you were open to my own creative liberties as we evolved the characters and plot. Sometimes I still chuckle to myself when thinking how most people would not believe this big, strong man involved in the world of sports came up with a romantic, sentimental story surrounded around a teddy bear. You really have a big, gentle heart. Thank you, Chet, for the special opportunity of joining you in this journey. It has truly been an honor and created a friendship for which I appreciate and will never forget.

CPSIA information can be obtained
at www.ICGtesting.com
Printed in the USA
BVHW052255300123
657453BV00010B/102